Edward and the Edwardians

William Nicholson.

H.R.H. The Prince of Wales.

EDWARD

and the

Edwardians

by PHILIPPE JULLIAN

Translated from the French by

PETER DAWNAY

NEW YORK / THE VIKING PRESS

TRANSLATOR'S NOTE

A number of the excerpts from English-language sources, translated by Philippe Jullian for his original French edition, are from now widely scattered letters and documents. It has been necessary in some cases to retranslate them from the French, and the wording used here may not correspond precisely with the original.

The illustrations are taken from prints by William Nicholson.

ACKNOWLEDGMENTS

In France, my thanks are chiefly due to M. André Maurois, of the Académie Française, for kindly allowing me to quote him in numerous instances and for giving me invaluable guidance on the source material, to M. Jacques Chastenet of the Académie Française, for his advice on the politics of the Third Republic, to Mme. Maurice Bérard for allowing me to go through the papers of her grandmother, Countess Edmond de Pourtalès, to Mme. Simone, for some of the stories about the King at the theatre, the Marquis de Ganay, and the Marquis de Castellane, to M. G. L. Pringue for supplying me with several anecdotes, to the Marquis d'Arcangues, who was kind enough to recall for my benefit his memories of the King at Biarritz, and to Don Antonio de Gandarillas for his memories of the great figures of fashion in Paris and London.

In England it is to Sir Harold Nicolson, for allowing me to delve into his works and for telling me a number of hitherto unpublished anecdotes, that I am most indebted. Also to William Plomer for allowing me to quote from the story of Anthony Butts, which I have taken from *Curious Relations*, and for drawing my attention to the more absurd pieces of Edwardiana, and to Mr. George Painter, of the British Museum, the author of *Marcel Proust*, for giving me information on the King's Parisian life. I should also like to thank Lady Juliet Duff, the Honorable Mrs. Cubitt, and Mrs. Trefusis for telling me about the King, whom they knew in their childhood, and Mr. Robin MacDouall, the Secretary of the Travellers' Club, for his patient research into Edwardian memoirs and Mr. Simon Fleet for his collection of anecdotes.

For information on the King's relations with American Society, I am greatly indebted to Mr. Stuart Preston.

Finally, my thanks are due to the librarians of the British Council in Paris, whose patience enormously helped me in my research.

Contents

1	The Education of a Prince	3
2	Marriage	22
3	A Man of the World	36
4	Edward as Prince of Wales	60
5	Edward as a European	77
6	The World of Proust	93
7	The 'Eighties	113
8	*Fin de Siècle*	135
9	The Widow at Windsor	153
10	The King	178
11	The Court	198
12	The Edwardians	217
13	The France of Monsieur Loubet	239
14	Politics	253
15	The Final Year	275
	Bibliography	301
	Index	305

Illustrations

H.R.H. the Prince of Wales   *Frontispiece*

Prince Bismarck   79

Sarah Bernhardt   95

W. E. Gladstone   115

Lord Kitchener   137

H.M. the Queen   155

The Archbishop of Canterbury   181

H.M. Queen Alexandra   201

Cecil Rhodes   219

Rt. Hon. Joseph Chamberlain   255

Kaiser Wilhelm II   277

Genealogical Tables

The Royal Family of England   296

The Battenbergs   298

The Royal Families of Greece and Denmark   299

Edward and the Edwardians

CHAPTER ONE

The Education of a Prince

ON NOVEMBER 9, 1841, Queen Victoria gave birth to a strapping child who was later to be baptized as Albert Edward: Albert after his beloved father, Edward in memory of those Saxon and Plantagenet kings from whom the House of Hanover, not without ingenuity, traced its descent. The Queen, the youthful gaiety of her girlhood now fading, was already assuming, if only half-consciously, the role of mother-goddess that she was to play to the very end of her reign. As yet the cultivated mystique of monarchy was not practised with the aplomb that was to come, and some time was still to elapse before Victorians would view this birth through the eyes of a Pre-Raphaelite painting a triptych of the Nativity.

The central panel of such a work, skillful in execution but naïve in sentiment, would have shown the young Queen seated on a throne, a diminutive figure wrapped in ermine, her large eyes a pale blue identical to that of the sash of the Garter coursing diagonally across her bosom. Her gaze would have been directed not to the infant held out before her for the people to see but to her husband standing behind her, a handsome and reassuring figure, ever aloof and dignified in a country in which he is loved by very few other than his wife, and understood only by professors and engineers. The three magi come to pay homage to the infant at his birth would also have featured in the picture. The most distinguished of them would have been the hero of the past, a daunting figure with all the orders of Europe glittering on his scarlet tunic,

3

the Duke of Wellington. Beside him, the Prime Minister, Sir Robert Peel, a rich businessman sombrely clad, bowing stiffly to the Queen, who cares little for him. The third, a charming old gentleman still employing the manners of the preceding century, Lord Melbourne, kisses Victoria's hand, the hand of his last love. As an old friend, he would have been frank: it would be better for the prince to be known as Edward, a name familiar to the English. But the parents would have looked askance: to the family the child would always be Bertie—the diminutive of Albert. The wise men would have come bearing gifts: the first, glory; the second, the grudging respect of wealth for a monarchy to which it owed little; the third, an epicurean wisdom little appreciated in the serious nineteenth century.

Of the two wings on either side of the central panel, one would have depicted Heaven and the other Hell. In the right-hand one, in tones of forget-me-not blue and dark green, would have been seen the heraldic device of the father's family, those Saxe-Coburgs who thirty years before, despite some fine alliances (the Duchess of Kent, the Grand Duchess Constantine, and the Duchess of Württemberg were Coburgs), were still mouldering in obscurity, but whose blood was now to be mingled with that of the greatest dynasties. But it was a blood of dubious quality: the prince's mother and grandmother had been of little consequence. The important member of the family was Leopold, the first King of the Belgians, the uncle both of Prince Albert and of the Queen (the Duchess of Kent was his sister). Cunning, deep thought, and a series of romantic misfortunes retrieved by amazing strokes of luck had earned him the reputation of a sage and the rewards of a seducer. The son-in-law first of the Prince Regent and then of Louis Philippe, he had known both Talleyrand and Metternich; as adviser to the young couple, he had an answer to everything, believing himself to be as much an expert on England as he was on Europe. The Queen wrote to him at least once a week.

Beside this large, cold, tight-lipped man stands Baron Stockmar, the leader of the German party at the English court. A Machiavellian idealist, a Lutheran Jesuit, he might well have chosen as his motto *To the greater glory of the Coburgs*. In the eyes of the

Queen no legion of angels ever shone so brightly as the honest and ever-present, knowledgeable and tactless members of the German party, and there were none whose example and precept the Prince could better follow.

On the other wing, representing Hell, would have been depicted devils, German too, most of them; they belonged to the mother's family, the Hanoverians. At the slightest misdemeanour on the part of the future Prince of Wales, the English were to be reminded of that phrase in the Bible: "The fathers have eaten sour grapes, and the children's teeth are set on edge." For they had eaten all sorts of grapes, those terrible children of the mad George III and of the good Queen Charlotte. The eldest, the Prince Regent (from whom our hero was to inherit both his taste for high living and his feeling for diplomacy), after a clandestine marriage to a Catholic and a scandalous marriage to a German, spent his life in an undignified scramble from one avaricious mistress to another. Three other brothers got themselves involved in both morganatic marriages and debt. The Queen's father, the Duke of Kent, had been an honest junior officer, but of the King of Hanover himself, the ex-Duke of Cumberland, it was said that he had had a child by his sister and had murdered his valet for equivocal reasons. His sisters had either lived with their equerries or married princelings. The English were not greatly attached to the royal family; for them it was no more than a constitutional convenience and a fountainhead of honours. Queen Victoria was to change all that. She retained from her childhood not only a horror of scandal but a dread that her descendants might inherit the characteristics of their ill-starred forebears.

On the number of her descendants she had no need for anxiety: she was to have nine children, and from the day after her wedding she expressed her happiness with such fervour that Stockmar was encouraged to write, "The Prince gives satisfaction." But it was in the eldest child, the Princess Royal, the future Empress of Germany, that all Prince Albert's qualities reappeared. After the Prince of Wales came Alice, the prettiest of the daughters, later to become Grand Duchess of Hesse-Darmstadt; then Alfred, Duke of Edinburgh, an intriguer; Helena, usually known as Princess

Christian following her marriage to a Schleswig-Holstein; Louise, Duchess of Argyll; and then two more sons: Arthur, Duke of Connaught, a popular soldier and courtier, who doubled for the Prince on official duties; and the Duke of Albany, who died young. Finally came her favourite, Beatrice, who was to marry Prince Henry of Battenberg.

The frame of the triptych would have been richly gilded; for the country was rich: it provided its Queen with a hundred thousand pounds a year. Its style would have been at once pure and elaborate—a Gothic piece recalling the greatness and the piety of her ancestors. In an England studded with chimney-stacks and gasometers, in which railway lines were driven through parklands, a medieval mantle was cast over industrial development by nostalgia for the past. Regency colonnades were now symbolic of a decadence on which the young Queen and her subjects had turned their backs. The Palace of Westminster, recently completed, was the finest expression of the grave and enterprising generation that was to come to power on the dissolution of Melbourne's final administration.

The Prince's youth was to be divided between the romantic Gothic of Windsor Castle and the puritan Gothic of Balmoral; he himself was to prefer the rococo of the Second Empire. The Queen disliked London; Buckingham Palace reminded her of her uncles; St. James's Palace was too small except for levées; Kensington was rather bourgeois and evoked the humiliations of her childhood. And, besides, Albert preferred Windsor.

The royal family, which by the end of the century was to have spread its influence to every court in Europe, was at the time of the Prince's birth, however, of a very reduced status and its position in Europe was not highly regarded. Elderly princesses nursing ancient scandals were immured in Kensington Palace; the Queen's mother was kept secluded, never forgiven for having been surprised with her equerry; even that hardened old trooper the King of Hanover could afford to insult Prince Albert and get away with it. And the Austrian Court refused to recognize Albert as a Royal Highness. Then there was, of course, the cadet branch, the Cambridges, a good-natured family crippled with debt. With them the

Prince of Wales was to find the gaiety and ease that were lacking at Windsor. The Cambridges numbered three: the Duke, who was head of the British Army for thirty years and who was destined to become the archetypal Colonel Blimp; his sister Augusta, Duchess of Mecklenburg-Strelitz, who died in 1916, aged ninety-four, possessed of the secrets of every court; and the fat Duchess of Teck, whose daughter was to become Queen Mary.

Thus the Coburgs made a better showing in the Almanach de Gotha than the royal family, despite its connections with the Hohenzollerns and the Württembergs. Their sons were good-looking, and, on the principle that a good match was worth a mass, they brought off the finest alliances: Uncle Leopold with Louise d'Orléans, and Augustus with Clémentine, her sister. Their son was to be Ferdinand of Bulgaria. In the succeeding generation another Ferdinand would marry Doña Maria da Gloria, the last of the legitimate Braganzas.

In the middle third of the nineteenth century, the shocks of 1830 and 1848 once over, the Catholic dynasties lost ground, and the less illustrious Protestants became preponderant. In France, the Bourbons were driven out, to be followed by the Orléans. In Spain, Carlist insurrections rocked the throne. In Portugal, the Braganzas were divided into equal halves and shortly afterwards decimated by mysterious deaths. In Italy, Bourbon and Este disappeared. In Germany, the Wittelsbachs were to be invested with madness. The Habsburgs were to retain their prestige, but a series of crises was to test their strength. On the other hand, the Hohenzollerns were to prosper even in Rumania. We shall see the children of the King of Denmark on the thrones of Greece and Norway. The house of Hesse was to take root in Russia. The morganatic lines of Teck (Württemberg) and of Battenberg (Hesse) were to see an extraordinary rise in their fortunes.

Prince Albert encouraged marriages with houses that brought in new blood. "We need people with darker hair, we are too fair," he said. Their Protestant majesties were endowed, like the Swiss, with qualities that were in keeping with the nineteenth century, while the devout and gallant Catholic monarchs were in effect a hangover from the eighteenth century. But although Queen Victoria found her German relations exemplary and reassuring, she never lost an opportunity to remind the world of her equally venerable Stuart blood, and adopted the tartan of this family that had been supplanted by her own.

The Hanoverian court, with its alternately bourgeois and scandalous mode of life, sorely needed prestige. Since the eviction of the Stuarts the great nobles had ignored the Crown. Their political position had been so strong, their fortunes so considerable, that they had had nothing to gain in the antechambers of Windsor. Besides, they had their own beautiful houses and castles. "I am leaving your palace to return to my house," said Queen Victoria once after a reception given by the Duke of Sutherland. The etiquette and ritual of official Court life were insupportable to men as untrammelled and well-heeled as the great Whigs; the less wealthy Tories hated the House of Hanover. The Prince Regent alone succeeded in gathering around him a circle of brilliant people amidst the Chinese follies of the Brighton Pavilion and the Roman splendours of Carlton House Terrace. The Prince of Wales will often remind us of his dandified uncle: a Florizel where attractive women were concerned, even if the Prince Regent had had more taste and less discretion; he had belonged to a generation of realists who did not resort to cant and hypocrisy. *Vanity Fair*, which stigmatized the customs of the Regency with a bourgeois bitterness that stemmed from the jealousy incited by aristocratic display, had just appeared. Puritanism was triumphant and the gay world condemned to the everlasting fire.

The politicians were intent on gaining control over the sovereign. Peel sought to inflict ladies-in-waiting of his own party on the Queen. The Queen refused to submit. Public opinion did not support her. This same public opinion had risen against her shortly before as the result of an unfortunate incident. The rumour had gained currency that one of the ladies-in-waiting, Lady Flora Hastings, had become pregnant after travelling in a carriage with the Duchess of Kent's equerry. The slanderous whispers grew to such a pitch that the young woman demanded to be examined by doctors and was declared innocent; the Queen had to apologize for having suspected Lady Flora. Society as a whole took the victim's side, and the Duchess of Montrose went so far as to hiss the Queen at the races.

To members of Society, Prince Albert appeared pedantic and pretentious, and he lacked all interest in sport. To the Cavendishes and Russells the Coburgs did not amount to much, and their castles, compared with Chatsworth and Woburn, were mere rabbit-warrens; such families refused to bow and scrape, as the Queen expected them to, before her husband. And it was not surprising that Victoria, who as a young girl had loved parties, should rarely have asked her nobles to receptions, which both she and they found tedious. She surrounded herself with the most serious members of the aristocracy, an aristocracy far from lacking in virtuous young ladies interested in outdoor pursuits and in officers with the manners of bishops. The Court derived little prestige from its strait-laced atmosphere, and it was not until the 'sixties that this severity became exemplary. Prince Albert, who was given the title of Consort only in 1857, had an excessive taste for perfection; he came close to it himself in more ways than one, but he expected it of others. Wishing his son to be endowed with every virtue, he tyrannized over him from his earliest years in order to inculcate in him his own severe moral standards. The Prince of Wales never spoke of his father except with respect, but he spoke of him rarely. On his succession he never spoke of him at all and dispatched all his busts, with which the palace was littered, to the attic. An element of the subconscious also came between the young man and his father: the Queen was openly in love, and this provoked her sons to jealousy. Preoccupied with her husband, and later with his memory, the Queen, who worked twelve hours a day, had very little time to give to her children. As she confided to a friend, "My children have been brought up among people of consequence and they are almost strangers to me; I have nothing to say to them." Her confinements did not trouble her, and she would receive her ministers a few hours afterwards.

At Edward's birth, she wrote to Uncle Leopold:

> Our little boy is a very fine baby, he has large dark blue eyes, a well-defined but rather large nose and a small mouth. I hope and pray that he will turn out to be like his dear papa.

But very soon Greville, the diarist, was noting:

> The Prince of Wales is less wide-awake and more timid than the Princess Royal; the Queen says that he is stupid. The hereditary and unfailing antipathy of our sovereigns to their heirs apparent seems thus early to be taking root, and the Queen does not much like the child.

The Princes and Princesses were entrusted to governesses of irreproachable character, and then to tutors persuaded of the fact that Prince Albert was the incarnation of perfection on earth. The instructions given to these people, which they followed blindly, took no account of the children's age, health, or character. German pedantry and German discipline ruined the Prince's childhood from the moment that he was able to read, with the result that this intellectual force-feeding filled him with a horror for the things of the mind; he never opened a book and entered museums only in order to inaugurate them. Military science and political economy bored him, and he could see nothing amusing in Germany.

In 1841 Prince Albert was still young, but his responsibilities, his routine of grinding hard work, and his wife's amorous ardour were to age him rapidly. When he went to Paris in 1855, the French Empress found to her astonishment that he was already bald, heavy, and pallid, for he had been very good-looking in the conventional manner for which Winterhalter's brush was made. The Prince's life was not a happy one. A stranger in the country of his adoption, and misunderstood to the point of being accused of treason by the press on the eve of the Crimean War, he fought ceaselessly against the government to protect the prerogatives of the Crown and took an interest in everything from international exhibitions to such matters as drainage and the drawing up of artillery regulations. Such zeal is not popular with the English. He employed his time with such exactitude that one of the ladies-in-waiting was to say that he always made a joke at the same moment during every lunch. This inhuman regime could be traced to the advice so often repeated by Baron Stockmar: "Never relax."

"No relaxation," such was the first rule of that political theoretician, the little Saxon doctor whose influence was so strong in England and who had done so much to set up the kingdom of Belgium. Leopold I wrote to the Queen:

> What luck to have Stockmar with you, he will make your son worthy of your throne and of the virtues of his father, and will counteract the disturbing tendencies of the family.

Stockmar advises, Stockmar approves, Stockmar insists, Stockmar is anxious, these phrases constantly recur in the correspondence between Windsor and Laecken.

Stockmar had a room in each palace; he was exempted from wearing knee-breeches at dinner on account of his rheumatism. It was Stockmar who chose the English, Scottish, and German nurses, and the governess, Lady Lyttelton. The child took some time to learn to speak and seemed to show a preference for German. Stockmar supervised everything, even providing models of handwriting. Nothing escaped his control; he excused no caprice and permitted no indulgence. The future king was to be the Baron's *chef d'œuvre*. He was to counteract in him every influence that was foreign, that is to say English. If the child had to play, then it would be with his brothers and sisters. Some of the most distinguished boys from Eton were brought to play with him at Windsor, where Prince Albert organized instructive distractions for them which he supervised himself.

"We lacked spirit," wrote one of them, Lord Redesdale; "I can still see the Prince's unhappy face when he was brought to the school to hear recitations from Demosthenes or Cicero; it was heart-rending."

As he grew up the child was dominated by his elder sister, a small and very composed individual, in whom could be detected all the Coburg qualities. "I am not Vicky," she once said to a visitor, "but the Princess Royal of Great Britain and Ireland."

Visiting sovereigns afforded some distraction; presents and even decorations would be exchanged. The high point of the Prince's childhood was the inauguration, in 1851, of the Crystal Palace, in which was held the Great Exhibition, the Prince Consort's masterpiece. This apotheosis of industry and of the arts was hailed as the dawn of a new era devoted to prosperity and science. Beneath the glass vaults the Queen and her family inspected the marvels that had been brought from every quarter of the world, and listened to an oratorio sung by fifteen thousand choristers. Official journeys, excursions by yacht around the Isle of Wight or by horse across the Balmoral estate broke the monotony of his lessons, but Bertie remained surrounded by important people, by relations and tutors. He wore, according to circumstances, a sailor suit, a kilt, or a guardsman's tunic, and thus acquired early in life his taste for dressing up. *Punch* mocked at his severe and undemocratic education.

His various tutors were chosen from amongst the most irreproachable of army officers and clergymen. They sent daily bulletins to the Queen:

> 28th January. The sums left undone last night were finished, but the Prince became excited and disobedient during the walk, encouraging his brother to insubordination; he broke off some branches in the park.
>
> 8th March. A very bad day: the Prince behaved as if he were mad, made faces and spat. Doctor Beecher complained of having heard some naughty words.

Any illusions the Queen and her husband may have had about their heir were soon dispelled; lazy and dissipated he may have been, but it was their duty to make him perfect.

In 1854 the Crimean War caught the child's interest. It astonished him that the Russians should have resisted his mother's troops for so long. There is an engraving that shows Lord Cardigan telling him about the charge of the Light Brigade. Whatever his parents may have thought of their son, they were not going to miss an opportunity of presenting the world with the melting image of a rather plump boy with blond hair and a sweet expression.

For the French, England's allies in the Crimea, Bertie conceived a tremendous enthusiasm. His parents did not altogether share this sentiment. "The time has come to curb the vanity of this immoral nation," Prince Albert had said. With his strong Orléans connections, he regarded Napoleon III as an adventurer. The family discussed a possible visit. The Queen was not in favour; the ministers insisted; but by an indiscretion, the first of his career, the Prince precipitated the decision. While having tea with his Cambridge cousins he blurted, "Papa is going to Paris."

But it was the Emperor and Empress who came first to London. In 1855 the Queen, her husband, and the Prince of Wales returned the visit. Everything went off wonderfully. The sovereigns were enchanted with each other. The French public found that Victoria was badly dressed, and the English visitors that the Imperial Court was not to their liking. Such prejudices satisfied, everyone was happy, particularly the little Prince, who could never have had enough.

Wearing his Highland clothes, he was a great success. He was taken to kneel before the tomb of Napoleon and to see the *grandes eaux** at Versailles. Naturally gay and sociable, he was captivated by the breath of victory in the panache that so delighted France and irritated Europe. Panache! The future Edward VII would not forget this lesson; at home it was lacking, and there was something common about that. But there were sentiments of a more intimate kind that appealed to the boy. He breathed in the Tuileries for the first time that *odore di femmina* in whose wake he was to follow for the rest of his life. The scented and attractive women not only kissed him (was he not a child?) but also curtsied to him, and as they bent forward their décolletage discovered beauties that were veiled at Windsor. "I don't want to go, let me stay with you," said the little Prince to the Empress as the moment came to say good-bye.

"But the Queen would be sad if she had to go home without you."

"Oh! but she has lots of other children at home!"

After these excitements he returned to the unvarying routine of lessons, healthy walks, and supervised games at Osborne and Balmoral. Let us pause for a moment in these homes that the royal couple had created, and in which the Prince of Wales watched as the sands of so many monotonous days ran out. Osborne, in

* The display made by the fountains when they are all turned on at full force.

the Isle of Wight, is a vast white Italianate villa, with belvederes, pergolas, and terraces. Marble statues that were too white sprang from lawns that were too green, and whichever way one looked were to be seen countless rhododendrons. Paths flanked by hortensias ran down to the sea. White yachts cruised in the Solent and circled round the royal yacht, *Victoria and Albert.* Summer-houses of a more or less rustic nature were put up in the park as the children got married. The interior was more Viennese than English: gilded white furniture, cerise hangings, flowerpots overflowing with begonias, and walls festooned with Winterhalters. It served more than anything else as a family home. But to the Ministers who had to make a three-hour journey from London, often involving a rough crossing, in order to consult the Queen, its position was hardly convenient.

When the Court moved to Balmoral, in the very north of Scotland, as it did for several months of the year, their tempers were even more sorely tried. Lord Palmerston, who liked his comforts, never felt particularly disposed towards making concessions after twenty-four hours in a train. The site was discovered by husband and wife during an excursion into the highlands. With forests in the foreground and gaunt mountains on the horizon, it seemed ideal. Yes, it was amongst these honest and pious Scotsmen, far from the cities, and in this pure and rarefied air, that the children should be brought up. Balmoral Castle had a square tower in grey granite, whose appearance was forbidding enough, and the house itself was turreted and gabled, with narrow windows and an occasional bow-window. Every room was papered with the Stuart tartan, and the hall, which was decorated with trophies of the chase, looked like a stage-set for *Macbeth.* The family dined to the sound of bagpipes and went to bed very early. When the Queen became a widow Balmoral became more of a convent than a hunting-lodge.

The royal family, wearing kilts, would shoot stags, fish for trout, and set off for long mountain walks, with their ghillies following behind, from which they often returned soaked to the skin. The function fulfilled by the more worldly Winterhalter at Osborne was carried out at Balmoral by Landseer. The Queen found the moist-eyed dogs watching over aged shepherds, stags troating on the edge of lochs, and the grouse composing a still-life among the heather, deeply moving. It was at this time that the Kerry dynasty was founded, black shaggy dogs, that trotted behind her on their little paws.

Every summer the young Prince was sent on an excursion into the damp countries beloved of the Romantics, sometimes on foot to make a tour of the Lake District, or else, accompanied by tutors and young men who were particularly highly thought of, to Switzerland or to Germany—but all he ever brought back was a healthy complexion. "What," gasped Prince Albert, "didn't you make a note of any great thoughts from the tops of mountains, or paint a water-colour at the edge of a lake, did not the castles inspire you to write even the shortest poem?"

The young Prince visited the ageing Chancellor Metternich, who, though he had survived the upheaval of 1848, was now enfeebled and pessimistic; the aristocracy was losing its grip on politics. The Chancellor wrote to his friend Guizot, "Everyone liked the Prince of Wales, but he appeared sad and ill-at-ease." Prince Albert, thanking his brother for having received the young man at Coburg, delivered himself of a judgement which could have been applied fifty years later, without the need to change a single word.

> Bertie returned home very well and happy. He has a curious nature. If he has no very great interest in things, he has more than enough in people. It is a trait which is very common in the royal family and which accounts for much of its popularity, but it is not without a distressing tendency for what is called here *small talk*.

In 1858, at the age of seventeen, the Princess Royal married Prince Frederick William of Prussia. A young person of exemplary character, she was, despite her excellent intentions, destined to exacerbate the Germans' inferiority complex toward the English, and to irritate her own countrymen by making them aware of her importance. Her husband, with his Wagnerian good looks, was first and foremost a soldier; dazzled by his wife's intelligence, he allowed himself to be influenced by her ideas, both good and

bad. Spiritual heir to Prince Albert, she alone of the Queen's
children felt herself free to offer advice to her mother. Their
correspondence was carried on twice weekly for more than forty
years. The Empress Frederick, as she was to be called after the
few months of her reign in 1888, had all the qualities of a governess: an authoritarian, she pretended modesty; indifferent to
honours, she wished to have a moral influence on those around
her; her pedantic side led her into correspondence with philos-
ophers, but she was also a sentimentalist moved by betrothals and
weddings. Irrepressibly tactless, she vaunted the comforts of
England in Germany, and in England the morality of the Germans. In the palace in Berlin hot baths brought in from a
neighbouring hotel were limited to one per week, and when, after
she had expressed her astonishment that there were no egg-cups
on the breakfast table, the butler told her that they used liqueur
glasses, she felt like a missionary in an outlandish country. Re-
finements of this sort were soon to have an irritating effect on
Bismarck's coarser character. The Princess Royal was more of an
agent provocateur than an ambassador for her country. But as
far as her brother was concerned, she enjoyed all her life that
prestige that the studious hold in the eyes of the frivolous.

Thinking to escape from the tutelage of his masters, the Prince
announced that he wished to become a soldier. He was housed in a
little villa in Richmond with a small staff under the command of
a Colonel Bruce. He had instructors in strategy and ballistics, but
great care was taken to keep him away from the guards officers,
who were notoriously debauched. On each of his birthdays he received a letter full of advice. When he was fifteen he was sent a
little money with which to buy cravats and was told "never to
wear anything unusual or vulgar, so as to avoid having anything
in common with vain and useless people who dress in a loud manner." At sixteen, the year of his confirmation, the advice was
of a more religious nature. Edward remained all his life very attached to the forms of the official religion. At seventeen he was
reminded that he must never in his position indulge in practical
jokes (in fact these were to become his favourite form of relaxation), but to keep the tone of his conversation elevated and to

resort to topics other than his health and the weather (those two sheet-anchors of royalty). At eighteen, as he entered upon the age of virility, he was given a document signed by his father and mother which began as follows: "Life is composed of duties, and in due, punctual and cheerful performance of them, the true Christian and the true gentleman is recognized . . ." There were four pages written in this tone. On reading it the young man burst into tears.

"There is no question of a season in London for Bertie, who is still neither fish nor fowl," wrote the Prince Consort. He was sent to Rome, with Colonel Bruce, "an educated man and a fine Christian," still in charge. What dangers were there not lurking in Italy to ensnare the young man! Supposing his search for instruction were to lead him to discover sensuality? How they must have wished that the Forum and Florence had been in Norway or Switzerland! And it was the examples set at the highest levels that had to be avoided. Victor Emmanuel, in Turin, was famous for his below-stairs gallantries, and the old Queen of Spain was living with a young lover in Rome. All over Italy there were rich milords indulging in pleasures that were now dangerous in England. We can hardly doubt that the young Prince's one thought was of losing his overprotected innocence, but it is scarcely likely that he succeeded, since his time-table was filled with walks of an instructive nature, literary lunches (Robert Browning and Ruskin were invited), and evenings spent reading.

Because her Catholic subjects in Ireland were proving particularly difficult, the Queen was anxious to improve her relations with the Pope. The Prince had an audience with Pius IX, but to the fury of the cardinals Bruce remained present throughout the interview, coughing if the Prince strayed from the narrowest formulas of politeness. When they visited Queen Christina, he never for a moment took his eyes off his pupil, so alarmed was he by her excessive cordiality. The turmoil of the Risorgimento cut short their stay. The Prince and his suite came home by sea, stopping en route in Spain and Lisbon: the sight of the disorder which reigned in these sensual countries should, it was thought, inspire him with horror! The slenderness of the journal with

which the Prince returned from his travels upset the Prince Consort. Perhaps if he were to spend some time at a university it
would knock a little sense into him.

The choice fell on Oxford, but in order that he should remain
under Bruce's tutelage he was not placed in a college; a house
was taken for him to which dons and the more serious-minded
students were invited to lunch. Although he could not share in
the noisy life of the rich undergraduates, the hunting, the wild
drinking parties, the dinners whose echoes scandalized the dons,
he was not allowed contact either with the two movements which
were emerging from the university at the time and which were
to have an enormous influence on intellectual life: the Catholic
revival and the aesthetic movement, whose following consisted of
the Pre-Raphaelites' youthful clan. Thus he found himself cut off
from both what was amusing and what was important.

One unhoped-for distraction broke this routine, and gave the
young Prince a taste of liberty and the assurance that people liked
him. The Prince Consort wanted the royal family to travel and in
doing so to act as commercial travellers for English prestige in
the world. England's ties, which wisely were not too closely de-
fined, with enormous countries which she no longer dared call
colonies, needed from time to time to be strengthened with the
help of popular enthusiasm. The Queen busied herself at the
centre of the hive while her family went out across the oceans to
spread her glory and to distribute her smiles and her decorations.
Thus, when the Canadians asked her to come and visit them, she
sent them her son. Needless to say, Colonel Bruce and a numerous
suite, presided over by the Duke of St. Albans, followed Edward
and wrote his speeches for him, whispering to him before each
reception the life stories of the people who were to be presented
to him. In short, nothing was to be left to chance, in the conviction that the unexpected could only turn out for the worst.

From Newfoundland on the young Prince made the best possible impression. His openness and his frank and simple manners
delighted the Canadians. He watched the acrobat Blondin cross
Niagara Falls on a tightrope and met a young Indian chief called
Burning Snow whose ambition was to go to Oxford. He opened

railway-lines and new towns. As he had a marked taste for flattery, he revelled in the even warmer reception that awaited him in the United States.

President Buchanan had asked the Queen if the Prince could come and spend a few days in Washington. Americans are always excited by the presence of English royalty; they love to show their former masters, in the nicest possible way, what they have become. And apart from this sentiment they are always curious about people who have a distinguished ancestry, and they have a passion for anything new and possibly strange. The visit came to compete with Barnum's celebrated circus, and in New York society there was an outbreak of snob-fever that was only surpassed forty years later when Edward VII's name alone could create the same effect.

The ordinary people gave him a delirious welcome, but Society was ecstatic; the President accompanied the Prince across the prairies to see enormous shanty-towns called Chicago and Detroit. The hubbub and bustle of America delighted him and in time to come the only guests that he was ever to forgive for a lapse of etiquette would be Americans. The blond, fresh-faced youth was literally assaulted by the most attractive ladies of New York during a ball at which there were so many gate-crashers that the floor caved in. The next morning one shrewd operator sold souvenir-hunters the bones of a duck eaten by the Prince. More than a hundred birds provided the raw material for this commerce.

The open spaces of the New World, and his success, which, though facile, gave him assurance in the one art which he was ever to practise, that of pleasing, filled the Prince with an even greater distaste for the discipline to which he had to submit as soon as he returned to Oxford. Not only was all feminine company forbidden him (the Queen hauled over the coals any lady-in-waiting who took it upon herself to go and see him), but he was only just given permission to join the smartest of the clubs, the Bullingdon. It was a sporting club, and in the group photograph the Prince, surrounded by rowing and cricketing bloods, looks like a small boy who has just been punished, with no chin, downy cheeks, and drooping shoulders. These undergraduates were very rich;

they owned their own horses and carriages and laid out fortunes in bets. It was here that the Prince came to know Harry Chaplin, who was to become his most faithful friend, a chivalrous individual extravagantly nicknamed "the magnifico." He had his own pack of foxhounds; for one evening alone he ordered twelve cases of eighteenth-century cognac. His monocle, his intimate friends, and even his paunch were the glass of fashion. With women he was timid, kindly to men who knew their place, and ruthless with those who did not. It never occurred to Chaplin that he was up at Oxford to sit for examinations. On the racecourse he cut into his vast fortune, but at twenty-six he won the Derby and a hundred thousand pounds in bets, which enabled him to become a Member of Parliament.

After Oxford, the Prince was sent to Edinburgh to gain a grounding in science, and finally to Cambridge—so as not to cause any jealousy between the rival universities. A mansion close to Cambridge was taken for him, from which he would slip away to join his friends. On one occasion he managed to reach London but only to find an equerry and one of the Court carriages waiting for him at the station. The young Prince was clearly escaping the influence of his mentor, Colonel Bruce; perhaps he had already begun to taste those pleasures which should have served as the reward of a sensible marriage. The news reached Windsor, at any rate, that a young girl in Cambridge was in a delicate situation. Memories were immediately evoked of how much such adventures had cost the Crown during the time of George III's sons, memories of morganatic unions, illegitimate children, blackmail, and scandal.

His mentor's report arrived at a bad time, for Windsor was weathering a crisis of quite another order. The American Civil War had just begun and a ship carrying several Southern envoys was stopped in English waters by a Federal man-o'-war. Palmerston, who supported the South, was indignant; the country backed him up, and in a very short time people were talking of war. At this point the Prince Consort had to go to Cambridge to box his son's ears. Already weighed down with worry, he arrived there on November 10, 1861, caught a chill, and returned in very poor shape. In his absence Palmerston had turned the Queen against the North. With his remaining strength the Prince managed to stop a telegram whose arrogant wording would in all probability have led to a war with the Northern States; he insisted that only formal excuses should be asked for. It was indeed this action that prevented war. But the cold with which he had returned from Cambridge degenerated into a violent fever. By the thirteenth he was already in a coma; the Queen sat by him, holding his hand tightly, already in despair. "It's me, your little wife," she said to him at intervals in German. She could not help remembering that only a few months before he had said to her, "I am not as attached to life as you are. If ever I have a serious illness, I shall let myself go quickly."

The Prince of Wales was summoned to Windsor; his father did not recognize him. On the night of December 14 a terrible cry is said to have echoed through the vaulted chambers of the enormous castle. The Queen had placed her hand over Albert's heart and had found that it had stopped beating.

CHAPTER TWO

Marriage

FOR FORTY YEARS the Queen remained alone with the memory of her husband, and despite some sentimental effusions which are more characteristic of the time in which she lived than of her own nature, she never forgot that her son's irresponsibility had been one of the causes of her widowhood. Somebody has to be made responsible for every catastrophe. Having given the Prince Consort so little satisfaction, the young man was now sacrificed to his memory; he was never to gain the Queen's confidence. Her affection he had never had.

The Queen sank into so deep a despair that it was thought she might not survive or might even go mad. Abdication was spoken of, and the character of the Prince of Wales became of crucial importance; his bearing and demeanour in the course of long ceremonies in which he replied in his mother's name to the condolences of sovereigns and ministers were closely observed. He exhibited a dignity that was astonishing in so young a man (when he was twenty-four years old, he looked eighteen), and a grief that was sincere. Throughout his life Edward was adept at expressing the sentiments most suitable to the occasion. As he was not a cynic, it can be presumed that these sentiments were spontaneous.

It was not long, however, before the Queen was asking to see state papers again and signifying to her advisers that she intended to continue alone the work of the dear departed; no doubt she would have preferred to share his fate, but duty retained her on the throne. Her common sense saved her from madness. Reading the condolences of a bishop who wrote that now Christ would be her husband, she muttered, "Ridiculous." The position of the Prince of Wales diminished in importance. In a group photograph taken with the bust of the Prince Consort in the centre, he still has the air of a gauche young man, the one note of white in that sea of black, his mother and sisters foundering in the crape folds of their skirts.

The Prince of Wales would have to live in London. Marlborough House, which had been empty since the death of William IV's widow, would be restored, and thus he would enter a world whose outlook was very far from that which hitherto he had known. Lord Palmerston and Lord Granville were the rulers of England. They were aristocrats who had been greatly admired by Lord Melbourne, but they lacked the charm and polish of that minister; such social problems as the famine in Ireland, child labour, and alcoholism troubled them little, and Palmerston regarded foreigners with arrogance. Much of the responsibility for the hatred which was felt for England in the second half of the nineteenth century must be laid at their door. They conducted the affairs of state in much the same way that they ran their own lives, for they were lavish spenders. The public concurred in their efforts to make public life glamorous. A few wise men, like the Prince Consort, had deplored them. It was this that gave to the middle years of the century the name of the "fighting fifties." Lord Palmerston and Lord Granville were to retain power until almost the end of the decade. They had more respect for institutions than for persons and paid very little attention to the young Prince.

In the legacy left by this generation were their magnificent clubs and their proud, colonnaded mansions, filled with the busts of politicians dressed as Roman senators. In these great halls everything was inspired by the concept of Empire, from the silver glinting on the mahogany tables of the dining-rooms to the cutglass chandeliers sparkling in the candlelight. The Members of Parliament, of both parties, would lounge on the enormous black leather sofas, and Ministers would take their ease with bishops and ambassadors over a bottle of brandy. The great feuds that

had burst suddenly into the open during the debates at Westminster would flare up anew or obtain their quietus. Most of the
Members were landed proprietors or great figures at the Bar;
industrialists and bankers were only just beginning to gain a foothold; generals and admirals would snore away their retirement,
the most elegant of them schooled by Count d'Orsay and Lady
Blessington.

A great deal of time was spent in the country (if one was not
rich, in the country houses of others), and an enormous number
of letters were written, but from this closed world nothing indiscreet ever escaped. The fear of the press already existed, and
journalists, even more than the Church, were responsible for the
hypocrisy of society. As one can see in Disraeli's *Lothair*, appearances had to be respected. The prolific Trollope paints an even
better picture of the closely knit society of this time with its
pyramidal structure. It is quite true that he was concerned only
with the top of the pyramid: the base and sordid he left to
Dickens. In this world everybody knew one another; three-quarters
of the year was spent hunting and shooting in the country, but in
the spring the aristocracy took up residence in their houses in
Mayfair; and they were more at home talking about horses than
about the fairer sex. The metaphysical and the spiritual did not
concern them, and such problems were not discussed outside the
cloisters of Oxford; any mention of reform was thought to be
in bad taste.

Their ladies were supposed to be above scandal. Lady Waldegrave, however, slightly exceeded the bounds. Although married
to her fourth husband, she kept the name of her first and the
fortunes of her second and third. Thus happily widowed, this
daughter of a Jewish cantor was able, bedecked like a Titian
portrait, to receive a horde of royalty and politicians, of beautiful
women and elegant wits, at Strawberry Hill. The Duchess of
Manchester had a beauty of that rather ponderous type that
Ingres would have delighted to paint. German in origin, she had
been for fifty years the first lady of London. Her liaison with
Lord Hartington was common knowledge; in the end she was to
marry him, once she had been widowed and he had become the

Duke of Devonshire. "My dear Duchess" (the form of address used by her most intimate correspondents) had political aspirations; because she attracted confidences she was extremely well informed. Lord Clarendon wrote to her every day to put her in touch with what was going on; his letters were often indiscreet and studded with pieces of French that were not at all Victorian. Of the King of the Belgians he wrote: "Leopold has a new wig, which, this time, looks like nothing so much as a nightcap, which is to say that he still has pretensions."

The future Edward VII was to suffer from her gossip for as long as she lived. The majestic Duchess could hardly take him seriously when the Foreign Minister was in the habit of sending her letters containing lines such as these:

> An old friend of Prince Talleyrand once said of a young man, already ruined by gambling and women, as he was ordering a magnificent dinner: *"Il est bien, ce petit: gourmand, joueur, libertin; il est très bien, ce petit."* People will soon be saying the same thing of our future sovereign.

Could it be wondered at that a minister with so low an opinion of the Prince refused to show him the state papers. Besides, the Queen had forbidden him to do so. But the Prince of Wales had to have something to do. Despite his self-confidence, people felt that he needed a court. The Queen's mourning seemed interminable: "I cannot tolerate ladies-in-waiting who have not suffered a great sorrow," she said to one of her rare visitors. Foreign monarchs passing through London had to put up at hotels. Public opinion was upset when it was rumored that the Queen was prepared to disburse from her enormous income from the Civil List only in order to raise monuments consecrated to the memory of Prince Albert.

The Prince had hardly settled into his new house in London when letters edged with black began to arrive from Balmoral or Osborne, letters that he was unable even in his sixtieth year to open without apprehension. Phrases such as "I am distressed to hear" or "You must never forget" abounded, and the more important words were underlined with a firm hand. The Queen seemed to know everything that was going on, and sometimes, as though to prove her right, scandals broke the surface of society, for all its civilized ambience. Lord Hastings ran off with his friend Harry Chaplin's fiancée and then got through an enormous fortune on the turf. Lord Willoughby de Eresby relieved his mistress of £30,000 and then went off with his chambermaid. Lord Wicklow was found dead in a house of ill repute. There was nothing left for these debauchees, once they were ruined, but to end their days in a family *pension* in Boulogne or Menton. The public's insatiable curosity about upper-class secrets forced Society to adopt so moralizing an attitude that both victims and wrong-doers ended in disgrace. When a certain young lady wanted to divorce Lord Henry Somerset, the son of the Duke of Beaufort, after she had surprised him in the arms of a footman, every door became closed to her. No well-brought-up lady should have known that such things existed.

The enormous and gloomy capital, however, catered for every taste. Here, vice—one cannot say pleasure—was facile and brutal and had nothing of the gaiety of the Second Empire in France. Only one courtesan attained the renown of her French counter-parts, and less on account of her amorous exploits than as a con-sequence of her prowess on a horse; her name was Katharine Walters, but to the young guards officers she was known as "Skittles," since she threatened one day to knock them all over like ninepins if they went on drinking. She dressed very well and spoke very badly. Skittles managed to seduce Lord Hartington from "My dear Duchess"; he spent considerable sums of money on her and introduced her to the Prince of Wales. Towards the end of the 'sixties she moved over to Paris, where her horses and coaches caused a sensation.

It was with a sense of horror that Dostoevsky christened Lon-don "Baal." In *Winter Notes on Summer Impressions* he describes the gin-sodden crowd wandering in the evening in the Haymarket, the pimps offering young girls to old men, sixteen-year-old pros-titutes clad in ragged lace, guardsmen in tightly fitting red tunics, and prosperous provincials, harassed by pick-pockets, staggering from music-hall to gin-palace. The tall gold lettering on the black walls glistened in the gaslight. Behind the proud façades of Regent Street and the Strand lay an absolute maze of mean alleys, of courtyards and stables where children's markets and thieves' kitchens abounded. Even Dickens himself never got to the bottom of this subject. Towards the end of the 'sixties, as people lost their tolerance and adopted moralizing attitudes, a more efficient police force began to put some order into the scene, although it avoided interfering with the pleasures of influential people. A whole district like St. John's Wood with its villas and spacious gardens was reserved for kept women. Discreet houses near the edge of Regent's Park provided everything one could wish for. The Prince's first friends guided him through this maze; they consisted of Lord Hardwicke, nicknamed "Glossy-Top," the faithful Harry Chaplin, and Christopher Sykes, as well as officers in the guards. They all belonged to boisterous and exclusive, if ephemeral, cliques and enjoyed low company; putting sport before all else, they felt at their ease amongst grooms and pugilists. They would go down in gangs to the docks to watch cock-fighting and ratting, a sport practised in the stables which consists of placing a fox-terrier in a small space with a number of rats. Lord Hastings would preside over these entertainments and bring with him cases of champagne. It was he who let two hundred rats loose in Cremorne Gardens and revelled in the entertainment as the rodents, terrified by the lights, took refuge in the dancers' crinolines.

Gustave Doré drew a number of sketches of the London of this time: barges loaded with straw sailing up the Thames amongst the steamers, the black docks bristling with cranes and derricks; the streets, in which ragged little girls danced to the tunes of barrel-organs; policemen's torches illuminating the bodies huddled on the ground where they had sought refuge for the night; all this in a heavy sulphurous haze pierced only by the gaslight. The same atmosphere is to be found in Paul Féval's *Mystères de Londres* and it inspired Stevenson's *Dr. Jekyll and Mr. Hyde*.

Doré also painted the indescribable confusion of buses, carts, and cabs as they whirled down the Strand and along the roads through the Park, where impeccable Amazons, followed by flunkeys, rode past under the critical eyes of gentlemen in white waistcoats and side whiskers. And ladies in bustles playing croquet in the long twilights of summer, on lawns beside the Thames, far from the madding crowd as it returned from the racecourse, the mail coaches heralded by the sound of the horn, the black minstrels, the bookmakers, and the ruined dandies in their charabancs.

In such a city it did not take the youthful Edward long to earn the nickname that Disraeli gave him, "Prince Hal"; it was the same as that given by Shakespeare to Henry V. The Prince Consort had foreseen all this, and the Queen was quick to see that in marriage lay the only hope of curbing her son's ebullient nature. The Prince was not hostile to the project, but he insisted on a girl of good looks. Several German princesses, virtuous but not very agreeable to look at, had to be struck off the list; there was only one that had both the virtues for which the family sought and the beauty that the Prince demanded. Before he died, Prince Albert's approval had been obtained.

A great deal of trouble had been taken to find her. In Berlin, particularly, Vicky, the future Empress Frederick, busied herself in scrutinizing these Gothic flowers at close quarters. Walpurga of Hohenthal, the Prussian Princess's lady-in-waiting, helped her. She was a Wagnerian beauty, dedicated to the sublime. Together they toured the German courts. Some of the princesses were Catholic, others were infirm or else provincial or notoriously irresponsible. The photograph of a Dutch princess was sent over, but the Prince turned her down in horror; it was closely followed by that of a princess of Wied, who was to become Carmen Sylva, the Queen of Rumania; but she had too intellectual a face! Taking time off from these duties, Walpurga married Sir Augustus Paget, the English Minister at Copenhagen. There she found a cousin of the last king in the direct line, Prince Christian of Schleswig-Holstein-Sonderburg-Glücksburg. Although he was the eventual heir to the throne, he was living in poverty and encumbered with children. Walpurga went to Windsor, where she praised the charm and beauty of one of Prince Christian's daughters, Alexandra, then aged seventeen years. Following the example of the Prince Consort on another occasion, the family called for photographs. The Princess Frederick also wanted to inspect the marvel and asked her cousin Augusta, the Grand Duchess of Mecklenburg-Strelitz, to arrange a meeting. Queen Victoria heard nothing but unending praise for the young girl. A German whose father would be unlikely to involve the crown in some international incident would of course have been preferred. Caroline of Anspach and Charlotte of Mecklenburg were the type of thing she had in mind, for they had been such good queens.

The net was spread in the greatest possible secrecy, but somehow the Duke of Coburg got to hear about it; with that need to assert himself that goes with princelings in inverse proportion to the size of their states, he wrote directly to his nephew, to put him on his guard against the matrimonial trap. This indiscretion cost him a severe reprimand from his brother, Albert:

> We have taken great care not to talk to Bertie about Princess Alexandra, but only of other projects. We therefore find it extremely singular that you should have warned him behind our back, whilst from every side he has heard her beauty spoken of, and the photographs which he has seen of her, at the Duchess of Cambridge's, have confirmed these rumours. We had explained to him the difficulties that this marriage will not fail to create, and he has understood them as much as a young man of his age and his intelligence could understand them. I hope that he will get married quickly; that is in his own interests, moral, worldly and political. There is absolutely *no other princess*, except Louis's sister and that would give us another link with Darmstadt.

A meeting was arranged; the Prince travelled over from Cambridge and the Princess from Copenhagen, on the same day, as though by accident, to visit the Cathedral of Speyer. From the very first moment he saw her, the Prince was enchanted. Alexandra was small and slim; her eyes were grey, her hair was golden, the oval of her face was perfect, and its expression contained a youthful gaiety. The elegant simplicity of her travelling clothes was also very pleasing. The next day they had tea together at Heidelberg and the success of the first meeting was confirmed. At that point the Prince Consort died; the Queen shut herself up for several months, and her first journey out of England was undertaken to meet the girl who was to become her daughter-in-law, with her family. Uncle

Leopold entertained the two families at Laecken; Walpurga (Wally to other members of royalty) and her husband, Sir Augustus, had written more than a hundred letters in order to bring this meeting about, and needless to say they too were there. The numerous and slightly intimidated Danish family waited in the drawing-room. The Queen was in tears in the boudoir, unable to bring herself to join them. "You, my dear Wally, you adore your husband and you know what I have lost, so you will understand my feelings." She came away from the meeting reassured: her future daughter-in-law was, in fact, charming. The next day the young couple went for a walk in the park after lunch; in a grotto, the Prince of Wales declared his love. When King Leopold gave the news to the Queen, she did not ask to see the engaged couple; their happiness was too much for her.

The temptations of London are something to be avoided during an engagement. The matter was too important to allow of even the smallest detail being neglected. The Queen was determined to arrange everything herself, so she packed her son off to the Middle East. Hardly had he gone when Alexandra was summoned. At Windsor, now dark and silent, the young girl conversed each day with her future mother-in-law. Although she was not intelligent, her warm-heartedness made up for her lack of experience. Alexandra was moved by the Queen's sorrow and was able to tell her this quite simply. She made an excellent impression. The "dear sweet Alix" would not interfere in politics, would forget her own country and adopt the manners of the English, would have many children, and on everything would consult the Queen; "We are not marrying the family," the Queen reiterated, as though she was afraid that the starving Danes would start sponging on the crown, or that her kingdom might become involved in some international quarrel. Victoria had but one reservation: "Our dear Alix's distinction is not exactly royal; it is rather that of a woman of the world."

The fiancé, during all this time, was on a tour round the Mediterranean. Colonel Bruce was still with him and once more promised the Queen to inculcate in his pupil a taste for suitable pastimes. The travellers spent five months away, first visiting

Vienna, and then travelling on to Venice, in the strictest incognito, in order not to be recognized by the Italian patriots, who might have captured them in order to gain an advantage over Austria. In Corfu, which was then an English protectorate, they met Laurence Oliphant, a brilliant if rather vague wit, and for once the Prince must have enjoyed the company of an intellectual at his table. In Cairo, a clergyman joined the expedition; he was to act as a guide to the Holy Land and help them to avoid the temptations offered by the luxury-loving Khedive. They quickly left for an expedition up the Nile to escape the festivities of Cairo, and one Sunday Dr. Stanley held a service in the Temple at Karnak.

In Jerusalem the royal suite was received by cohorts of Turkish functionaries, by Catholic and Orthodox monks, and by both Jews and Arabs. The journey continued, as far as Constantinople, with the rigour inspired by those "tours" which the young Thomas Cook was pressing on his clients. Finally they returned through Greece, where the occupant of the throne had just been expelled; his crown was being offered to Lord Derby. The final week of the tour was spent at Fontainebleau, with Napoleon and Eugénie.

In this agreeable court the Prince was able to relax, and his suite did not dare to interfere. He was making friends with the members of a society whose company would afford him more pleasure than any other and whose manners he was to import into England. The ladies whom he had kissed as a small boy were ready to refuse nothing to the young man. The panache and the beauty of Madame de Pourtalès, Madame de Mouchy, née Murat, and the Baronne Alphonse de Rothschild captured him forever. The men were worldly, interested only in the stock market, politics, and gallantry. Everything was freely discussed, particularly the gossip of the *demi-monde*. To the young man Napoleon III appeared the model sovereign; he was a ladies' man, married to a beautiful woman; he discussed the fate of the world amidst clouds of cigar smoke, preferring always to charm rather than to intimidate.

But the Prince had to return to London. He arrived as his mother was asking the Commons to increase his income from the

Civil List and to assure the future of his intended spouse. Every time that one of the Queen's children married, these questions of money stirred up public opinion and provoked the insolence of Parliament, obliging the Chancellor of the Exchequer to engage in delicate bargaining and in a continual coming-and-going between Windsor and Westminster. The Prince's income was already £60,000; he obtained £40,000 more from the Budget, and a further £10,000 for the Princess. The restoration of Marlborough House and the construction of Sandringham were pressed on; the members of the young Prince's household were chosen; Francis Knollys and his sister Charlotte were to become the Prince and Princess of Wales's silent and faithful shadows for sixty years. Edward and Alexandra inspired immense devotion, and the tact of their entourage not only protected them from the prying eyes of the public but prevented them from making many mistakes.

To the people of London, who adored the gilded carriages, the Court uniforms, and the gleaming cuirasses of the household cavalry, the wedding was the long-awaited opportunity to come out of mourning. To the official world, it was an opportunity to hold a public ceremony that would be worthy of them. The Queen would not hear of a ceremony at Westminster Abbey as it would have obliged her to show herself in public; the marriage would have to take place at Windsor, in St. George's Chapel, which could hold but few guests, the less important having to remain outside. "Couldn't we even have a seat at the back, considering all the expense we were put to when the Prince came to Blenheim?" sighed the Duchess of Marlborough. "I have heard that Dizzy and his wife have been invited."

"That's too much. You can count on me to cut them," promised the Duchess of Manchester, and "my dear Duchess" kept her word until the day Disraeli became Prime Minister. *Punch* published the banns as though it were the wedding of a squireen in his manor, adding: "No invitations will be sent!"

But when *Victoria and Albert* moored in the Thames and the fiancée landed on the steps of the Tower, her beauty aroused an enthusiasm which made up for the meagreness of her escort and the poor turnout of her coaches; the verses of the Poet Laureate, Tennyson, were on everyone's lips:

> *Sea King's daughter as happy as fair,*
> *Blissful bride of a blissful heir,*
> *Bride of the heir of the King of the sea.*

Alexandra had scarcely arrived at Windsor when she found herself posing for a photographer in one of those funereal groups, beloved by the Queen, in which the Prince Consort's bust was the dominating feature.

It was very cold on that tenth of March, 1863; the courtyard of the castle was drenched by showers; in the draughty corridors the very tapestries shivered. The guests who came down by train from London were not in the best of humors. The fortunate possessors of tickets piled into the Royal Chapel. "Those Disraelis really look like mountebanks," they whispered. The fat Duchess of Cambridge, very décolleté, sprawled on the front pew, hiding the other royal princesses; the bridesmaids perished with cold as they stood about in their tulle. In a sort of box, above the altar, could be seen a single blue Garter ribbon slashing across acres of black velvet; the Queen was watching the ceremony with red-rimmed eyes. She sobbed when the choir, with Jenny Lind taking the solo part, sang an oratorio by her husband. Wearing the blue velvet robe of the Garter, held in place by long gold tassels, the Prince of Wales entered, accompanied by his uncle Cambridge and his brother-in-law of Prussia; he bowed with an earnest air before his mother and waited at the foot of the altar. The Archbishop of Canterbury and two assistant bishops, erect beneath their golden copes, also waited. The Queen drummed on her prie-dieu with a black fan, and the ladies kept turning their heads towards the door. Pages were sent out on reconnaissance, but the Princess had not arrived; the congregation began to murmur. Finally she appeared, so ravishing that the ill humor immediately turned to admiration.

The same performance was to recur at every official ceremony for the next sixty years. Alexandra had not the slightest sense of time, but her smile made up for everything. Lord Granville wrote to "my dear Duchess" that the dress was much too fussy and had been spoilt by the addition of orange leaves. The ceremony wound on with the solemnity desired by the Queen, and as soon as it was over she immediately retired to her apartments. There was some relaxation over lunch, which was served to the non-royal guests standing up. The wedding cake was a Gothic monument in nougat, decorated with allegories in sugar and embellished with coats of arms made from preserved fruit. In the Highnesses' dining-room a small boy caused a scene which attracted some attention; he was the Queen's eldest grandchild, William of Prussia. He succeed in slipping under the table and biting the leg of his uncle Connaught, who was wearing a Scottish uniform. To the cheering of the assembled Etonians the young couple set off to spend a one-week honeymoon at Osborne; they then returned to London, took part in official receptions, and began to receive at Marlborough House with "a dignity without aloofness, like your dear papa," as the Queen advised. Even their least indulgent critics recognized that the young couple seemed to be perfectly happy.

Before long a political crisis revealed to the public the strength of their common outlook; they took, during the so-called Duchies' War, an attitude which displeased the Queen, and stuck to it with great courage. It is impossible to go into detail over this affair, of which Lord Palmerston said: "Only three people have ever understood the Schleswig-Holstein question: the Prince Consort, who is dead, a German professor who has gone mad, and myself —and I have completely forgotten about it." These Duchies were a personal apanage of the Princess's father, although they were not exactly Danish; a German cousin had laid claim to them. On the pretext of re-establishing order, Bismarck occupied them, for the reason that they gave Prussia access to the North Sea. The Danes took to arms and were rapidly crushed. Bismarck had dragged Austria into this sordid affair but Russia could not support the Austro-Prussian alliance, on account of the fact that Dagmar, Alexandra's sister, had just married the Tsarevich.

"We are not marrying the family," repeated Queen Victoria, who could not hide her pro-Prussian sympathies; her beloved son-

in-law was in command of a corps in the army. Palmerston counselled moderation to his sovereign; public opinion was on the
side of the oppressed, and Lord Napier, the Ambassador at St.
Petersburg, had to submit to Prince Gorchakov's saying to him,
"Well, Excellency, I discount the possibility that England could
ever make war on a matter of honour." It was not until the Congress of Berlin, in 1878, that Disraeli re-established England's diplomatic prestige. Bismarck's brutality infuriated the Prince but, as
the Queen wrote to her brother-in-law: "My dear Angel Albert always regarded a strong Prussia as a necessity. It is therefore for
me a sacred duty to contribute to it."

The Prince of Wales attempted, through the Prince de la Tour
d'Auvergne, to win over Napoleon III to the Danish cause. But his
ambassador was indiscreet. In consequence the young couple were
severely reprimanded when they went down to Windsor, and the
Princess was reduced to tears. On July 18, 1864, a peace was
signed that ratified the annexation of the Duchies by Prussia. The
crisis had widened the breach between the Prince of Wales and
his mother. Less than ever was she ready to allow him to read the
state papers; she looked upon her son as a grasshopper and her
daughter-in-law as a child. It was with a rather morose satisfaction
that she wrote to Lord Granville, after the Commons had reproached her for her isolation: "Oh! what horror to be suspected,
saddened, without guide or support! How alone the poor Queen
feels!" But she added: "I am resolved that no one shall lead or
guide me, and that there shall be no regency."

CHAPTER THREE

A Man of the World

FROM THE TIME of their return to London the young couple immediately found themselves involved in a round of receptions and visits to different parts of the country, which was to last for more than thirty-five years without either of them showing the slightest sign of fatigue or even of boredom. The Queen, who was not at all fond of her son, respected in him the future King. She counted on the Princess of Wales to keep up that famous "dignity without aloofness" which had been the order at her own functions. To the frivolous, the memory of these official jollifications was one of profound boredom, but the more earnest spoke of them as if they had been a mystical experience. The Prince banished boredom from his receptions. But, although they may have been lacking in formality, he rarely forgot his dignity. He led the life of one of those great nobles whose enormous fortunes made them the equal of royalty, though their position was certainly more enjoyable. Lord Derby had, for example, an income of £150,000 a year; the Duke of Bedford, £100,000; the Dukes of Westminster and of Sutherland and the Marquess of Bute were even richer. In the respectful atmosphere of England they enjoyed their luxury with a tranquillity of spirit that was lacking to Russian princes and Continental bankers. The Prince was a little less rich than some of his friends, although his rank and his tastes made him a greater spender. The Duchy of Cornwall and various properties assured him of £62,000 a year. At the time of the Prince's marriage,

Gladstone succeeded in obtaining from Parliament an income for the Princess, which gave the young couple a little more than £150,000. Two enormous establishments, where they were continually entertaining, absorbed a large part of this sum. Their life was a continual coming-and-going between Marlborough House, their house in London, and Sandringham, their house in the country.

Marlborough House stands about halfway along the Mall, across a narrow street from St. James's Palace. It was built by Wren in the early eighteenth century for the Field Marshal and his scheming wife. It is not so much a palace as a very large house, the starkness of whose unrelieved walls of darkened brick is emphasized by the cornices and cornerstones. At the time when the building was restored, the façade on the garden side was spoilt by the addition of a conservatory with glass domes, and that giving on the courtyard by a portico with stucco pillars. There are two main staircases, decorated with battle scenes. The reception rooms, with their painted ceilings and their Lawrences and Winterhalters hung on acres of damask, were arranged in an imposing if somewhat bleak manner, for the tall windows are too narrow. In one salon could be admired the Gobelins that were the gift of Napoleon III, and everywhere there were busts and statues in white marble. There was an Indian room decorated with presents from maharajas; the cloth of gold which had adorned the Prince's elephant in Delhi now covered the grand piano. On the dining-room table stood silver centre-pieces of allegorical design presented in the course of official journeys. The private apartments, which face on to a large garden, were gayer, and were painted nut-brown and rose. The Princess, who loved an atmosphere of intimacy, made the rooms seem smaller by the liberal use of screens and curtains, and by filling them with pouffes, little sofas, and settees. Palm trees in china pots provided recesses which were soon filled with knick-knacks. The heavy royal furniture was submerged by the new fashion of cosy comfort.

High walls and an unobtrusive gate shield Marlborough House from the view of the curious. On fine days the family would have tea in the garden in a tent, and cushions would be placed on the lawn for the guests, as in one of James Tissot's paintings. It was a more convenient house to live in than Buckingham Palace and an even smarter address than "the Queen's Palace in Pimlico," as they said in Mayfair, where everything that happened on the other side of Piccadilly was thought to belong to another world.

The visitor to Marlborough House would be received at the door by a Scotsman in a kilt, at whose signal a pair of footmen in powdered wigs and red coats would come forward to relieve the visitor of his hat and coat; then a porter in a short jacket and leather epaulettes would ask his name. If he was expected, or if he was an intimate friend, a page (in a deep blue jacket and black trousers) would conduct him to the drawing-room, where the Prince would be waiting.

Every day he received a large number of people. He rose early: if the weather permitted he would go for a walk in St. James's Park, accompanied during the 'seventies by his poodle Bobèche, and later on by the basset hounds Babil and Bijou, given to him by the Countess of Paris. He would return at nine o'clock for a second breakfast, do some work, and visit the stables, which held sixty horses. At midday the brougham would come to the door; upholstered in deep blue, it contained an ash tray and a desk. Having paid a few calls, the Prince would return for lunch, but never before half past two. He would often have tea with his family; the hour at which he ate dinner would depend on the number of guests.

At Marlborough House the Prince and Princess of Wales were not far from Devonshire House in Piccadilly, and Lansdowne House off Berkeley Square; their closest neighbour, in Carlton House Terrace, was Lady Waldegrave, whom they used to visit to pass the time of day. Two steps away at Clarence House were the Edinburghs, whom they visited often, although the Duke was surly and his Russian wife insisted on speaking French and creating the atmosphere—illuminated icons and bearded singers—of an Orthodox monastery. The Prince was also surrounded by clubs: White's, Boodle's, and Brooks's in St. James's Street, the Carlton and the Travellers in Pall Mall. He had been an honorary member of all these establishments from the time he came down from Oxford, and he frequented them often, with a simplicity that astonished strangers. He even forbade the members to rise when he entered. But he was less frequently to be seen in those other pompous and less elegant institutions such as The Reform or The Athenaeum. One day he decided to start a club for himself and his friends, after an incident at White's in which a waiter had had the effrontery to mention to him that he was smoking outside the smoking-room. The Marlborough Club was directly opposite Marlborough House. There, Edward would meet his more serious-minded friends, such as Lord Redesdale or Lord Esher, and his racing companions such as Christopher Sykes and Harry Chaplin; he also caused to be received there the diplomats whose company he enjoyed, and Members of Parliament were drawn there as well. Not infrequently he went there several times a day; late in the morning for a game of bowls on a lawn behind the house or to meet a friend for lunch without being annoyed by his family, or for a game of cards after dinner or to smoke a last cigar and listen to Society and political gossip after a late-evening soirée. It was an oligarchy in which worldly matters and the affairs of state were closely connected. To find three or four cousins in the same Cabinet, or several ministers at the feet of the same duchess, was not uncommon.

At Sandringham, the Prince led the life of a gentleman farmer, in accordance with his father's wishes. Situated in the county of Norfolk and exposed to the northeast wind, it is three hours from London, and surrounded by country houses belonging to the most respectable families; it was also far from the temptations of the turf. This enormous property offered him certain moral safeguards and provided him with substantial revenues. The Prince, who had inherited the Consort's taste for building and his love of nature, supervised the planting of rare species of shrubs, had a lake dug for skating, and made a new riverbed for boating. A croquet lawn, and a little later a lawn-tennis court, were put down, and finally some fields were sacrificed for a golf course. Woods and game-reserves surrounded the park.

The house is neo-Tudor in style and built of bright red bricks; it reminds one vaguely of a railway station or of a hotel. Pinnacles, dormer windows, balustrades, and weather vanes decorate the roofs, and the rooms are lit by large bay windows. If the oak-panelled hall, which is two storeys high, is very feudal, with its banners, its suits of armour, and trophies of the chase, the drawing-rooms are much more reminiscent of the Plaine Monceau in Paris than of Norfolk, with their Louis XV mouldings and upholstery, and their curtains draped like dresses from Worth. Here again, in all their profusion, were to be found the palm trees and azaleas, the knick-knacks and photographs, and, as the family grew in size, a mounting morass of portraits in armorial frames, of little boxes and little animals, of semi-precious stones, of cushions embroidered by nieces, of lampshades given by ladies-in-waiting, and of souvenirs brought back from Cannes or from Benares. The dining-room was hung with Goya tapestries presented by Alfonso XII. The smoking-room furniture was in dark blue leather, but it was generally to the conservatory that the gentlemen retired to smoke. Hunting trophies, from Bengal tigers to stuffed grouse, filled the corridors that led to the comfortably appointed bedrooms. Running water did not make its appearance until the eve of the new century. The family dogs were everywhere (the Princess adored chows and, later on, pekinese) and other dogs, in bronze, mounted guard in front of the fireplaces. Pavilions of a more or less rustic nature were scattered about the park for the use of the family. The stables drew forth the admiration of connoisseurs. Guests would find the piggeries less amusing, but they were expected to go into ecstasies when confronted with specimens of the enormous breed known as Improved Norfolks. The prize which one of these pigs won at the Copenhagen Exhibition was one of the last joys of Edward VII's life. The Princess enjoyed driving a pair of horses harnessed to a light pony carriage more than anything else, and would go trotting at full speed along the roads of that flat county.

The Prince and Princess adored Sandringham because they found themselves free there to lead the sort of life which they liked and to entertain their friends. Many an aspirant, from the 'seventies on, sought to gain admission to the simplicity-amid-magnificence of the Prince's life there; royalty, ambassadors, and often even ministers dreamt of being invited. The prestige which the young couple restored to the monarchy involved them in an expenditure for which they were reproached by the jealous-hearted. They shared the same sense of humour and their enjoyment of it spread to those around them, for they lived less among courtiers than in a circle of chosen friends. The spirit that reigned at Sandringham was more light-hearted than sophisticated. They went in for those practical jokes that the English of today find rather distasteful. The corridors re-echoed with wild laughter when some unsuspecting guest found a live lobster in his bed, or when a Danish nephew disguised himself as a ghost to frighten a lady-in-waiting. On rainy days tricycle races and crazy gymkhanas were organized in the ballroom, or they would play bowls in the room that, when he became King, the Prince was to turn into a library. The great sport consisted in sliding down from the top of the stairs on a silver tray used as a toboggan. The very correct Christopher Sykes was the favourite victim: "As your Highness pleases," he would say, after the most cruel jokes had been practised on him. This passivity only whetted the Prince's appetite, for he found it extraordinarily funny to pour the contents of a bottle of cognac down the collar of Sykes' shirt, but this passed between men, after the ladies had withdrawn.

The Prince certainly had in mind his experience of Compiègne when he had guests to stay, mingling people of a serious nature with men of the world and diplomats. In 1873, a bishop, slightly astonished at finding himself there, wrote to his wife: "I arrived as they were having tea in the hall and, although still covered with the dust of the journey, I had to pay my respects to the Princess. The company is very agreeable and very polished, but what a strange mixture: two Jews: Sir Anthony de Rothschild and his daughter; one ex-Jew: Disraeli; a Catholic: Colonel Higgins; an Italian Duchess of English descent and her daughter, who inclines towards Protestantism, and a number of young peers."

In 1883 Lord Sandwich found a company as varied and even more impressive: the Duke and Duchess of Edinburgh, the Landgrave of Hesse, Viscount and Viscountess Greffulhe, the Comte de

Saint-Priest, Baron Holzhauser, and Christopher Sykes. But, as opposed to Compiègne, one never saw a writer at Sandringham, and very rarely an artist other than Lord Leighton, a member of the Royal Academy.

Thus the Prince wrapped his solid German virtues in his English *savoir-vivre*. When still young he had made himself supreme in all matters of taste and was classed among the heavy swells, who were distinguished from the ordinary swells by their influence on fashion: the first led, the others followed. Lord Raglan and Lord Cardigan had altered the shape of the coat, and Lord Hardwicke was the first to have his top hat brushed till it shone like glass; these hats quickly became *de rigueur*. But the Prince of Wales, wiser than his great-uncle George IV, did not indulge in the sort of extravagances inspired by Brummell and would not have allowed any of his friends the insolence of this celebrated dandy. Four valets occupied themselves exclusively with his wardrobe; two accompanied him as he travelled about, in order to pack and unpack his trunks, and the other two remained at home in order to press and rearrange his clothes in the cupboards of pitch-pine which covered the walls of his enormous dressing-room. Side by side under gauze dust-sheets hung official tailcoats, casual jackets for tea-time, dinner jackets which were put on after dinner when the ladies had retired so that the smell of tobacco would not impregnate the coat in which one had dined, knee breeches worn at Court soirées or big balls, and the pink tail coat worn at hunting dinners. The morning coats, the walking suits, and the travelling country suits represented every shade of meaning in the word *incognito*. The Prince of Wales rendered a great service to the Scottish tweed makers by launching out into simplified tartans and suits of one colour which became known on the Continent by his name. The white flannels for regattas would hang next to the thick hand-woven tweeds for shooting. There were kilts for the afternoon (Hunting Stuart tartan) and kilts for the evening (Royal Stuart) which were worn with a waistcoat of black velvet and a frill of lace. One compartment was devoted to suits of mufti, the slang term of army officers for civilian clothes, another to suits suitable for racing, with a clear distinction between those for country races and those for smarter occasions. For dining at sea, the Prince adopted a sort of dinner jacket called the *Serapis*, named after the Khedive's yacht: the jacket was of a deep blue, with lapels of black silk and gold buttons. The Prince's greatest invention— more surely than the contested one of the crease in the trousers— was the hat known as the Homburg; it had a soft felt crown with a stiff brim and was the forerunner of the Anthony Eden. He had three tailors, of which the most famous was Poole, whom he discovered when admiring the cut of the coat worn by an actor playing the part of Robert Macaire. A whole room was devoted to English uniforms, which were later joined, despite the Queen's hatred of seeing her son in someone else's colours, by the uniforms he wore as an honorary colonel or admiral, when so appointed by foreign sovereigns.

Every morning the Prince would give orders to his valet as to the clothes he would be wearing during the day: sometimes he would change his suit twelve times in as many hours. He knew, to within one button of his spats, what the right thing to wear was. He would say to his Swiss valet before leaving for Scotland on his yacht, "A suit of a slightly more Scottish nature tomorrow," and the next day he would disembark in a kilt. Was young Paul Valéry thinking of the Prince of Wales when he said to Gide, "If I wanted to be rich it would be in order to be able to be properly dressed every day in whatever company or circumstances I found myself"? A diplomat in mourning once asked the Prince if it would be possible for him to go to the races. "Not to Ascot, where one must wear a top hat, but Newmarket is all right because you can wear a soft hat there." The merest degree of mourning that the deaths of foreign princes imposed on the Prince so often acquired in his eyes a symbolic value. One evening in Paris he was on his way to the *Variétés* with a few friends, when he learned that a grand duke had just died. Consternation reigned among the guests; the evening was completely aborted. "Gentlemen," said the Prince, "you will wear black cuff links and go to the theatre." Decorations, and their exact position on the breast, assumed in his life an importance which, when he became King, often embarrassed his entourage. Were he to see the Lion of Brunswick giving precedence to the Elephant of Denmark, the easy-going offender would find himself the subject of several very unpleasant remarks.

Sovereigns, who detect the impatience of their heirs, generally make the mistake of keeping them out of the affairs of state. The result is that these gather around themselves youthful malcontents and establish a group that accuses the Court of feebleness or even of tyranny, and the Ministers of irresponsibility or slothfulness. For most of the 'eighties, the Archduke Rudolf of Austria-Hungary preached a nationalism that was very displeasing to the Emperor, while in St. Petersburg the Grand Duke Nicholas expressed intense disapproval of Alexander II's liberalism. The English public was not slow to recognize that the Prince had gathered around him a group of people who, by their manners rather than by their ideas, were in reaction to the Court. Although the influence of the Marlborough House clan in politics was nothing if not discreet, its importance in the history of manners was considerable. It quickly set up a tacit opposition to most Victorian principles, and though it respected social conventions it had little time for morality. It took its tone from its young and attractive men and women, who came from families that were all related, who all shared the same background, and who were devoted to fashion and sport; for thirty years they constituted virtually the real English Court. The Prince, as we have seen, was well able to mix people in the right proportions, the serious-minded liking nothing more than to mingle with fashion, and the men of the world than to rub shoulders with power. The fear which his mother inspired in him, a shrewd appreciation of the insignificant role which the Constitution accorded him, and a strong sense of what was right, restrained Edward from involving his Court with any political party; but he took more liberty with foreign policy, and on several occasions the influence of Marlborough House gave the Foreign Office cause for alarm.

His circle was made up of people from a wider variety of backgrounds than was the case with those who had access to his mother's Court. The Prince's curiosity, his fondness for pretty faces and large fortunes, was bound to shock high Society, although this was where he recruited his friends and the majority of his mistresses. In the first rank of his intimates were the beautiful Duchess of Manchester and the future Duke of Devonshire. Large, indolent, his beard uncombed, his clothes in disorder, the latter possessed so many estates that he was once heard asking as he passed one of his country houses: "Who does that belong to?" The last of the grand Whiggery, he spoke with the same accent as his grandmother Georgina, Fox's friend, pronouncing golden as "gooulden" and chariot as "charrot." Every year at Christmas he entertained the Prince and Princess of Wales at Chatsworth. He lent them, during the season, his villa at Chiswick, on the outskirts of London, where parties were held in gardens decorated with statues and pavilions. Lord Hartington allied indolence to integrity; the glory of England and the wealth of the Cavendishes seemed to him to be equally unshakeable. When he became a minister he treated the country's affairs as if they were his own, and took even the filing clerks into his confidence; his secretaries would find racing tips among his dispatches. Followed by his dog, he would walk over to the Palace to give advice. If he had to speak in Parliament, he would often interrupt himself to yawn, so much was he bored by the debates. Such was the man, totally without ambition, whom "my dear Duchess" had decided to make Prime Minister. "My dear, you and I both married angels," she was to say twenty years later to Margot Asquith, who was herself to be the architect of her husband's career. Whatever the circumstances, the Duchess was as phlegmatic as her lover. The latter, having been taken with the famous Skittles, became for several years unfamiliar with the way to Manchester House. One fine day he returned at tea-time. "One lump as always, Lord Hartington?" said the Duchess simply, and the liaison resumed its course. One of the reasons for his return was that since he was the most eligible bachelor in the kingdom, the Queen wished to marry him off to a poor cousin, a daughter of the ex-King of Hanover. "My dear Duchess," for all that she hid her ambition beneath her worldly banter, was always up to something. Disraeli, after having sat beside her at dinner, wrote: "The Duchess Louise practically set the nearby Thames on fire; her face was still animated by the races and she had been poured into a dress that seemed unending; her hair was studded with diamonds à la Marie Antoinette, and there were other diamonds here and there on her dress."

As a political hostess "my dear Duchess" ran Lady Waldegrave a dead heat.

These mistresses of the political world played, if rather more ostentatiously, a role in English life similar to that played by the academic ladies of Paris at the time of Alphonse Daudet.* But the times at which the men went down to Westminster and to their clubs did not make a salon life possible. The fashionable round consisted of either hasty lunch parties held before the House of Commons sat (if the debates were to be important, all the guests would sit in the galleries) or solemn dinner parties. The Ministers were treated with a consideration that was tempered by family relationships. Every lady would have her protégés, and push her nephews or her lovers, extracting from them, if they obtained positions of power, a bishopric for a brother or a Garter for a husband. This had become so much an accepted part of the pattern of life, and it was done with such discretion and good taste, that there were never any of those scandals that have discredited Continental political life from time to time. Another great hostess was the Marchioness of Londonderry, who entertained the most conservative elements of society in her Park Lane mansion and who would silence with one look anyone who did not precisely share her opinions on the Irish question. Other important hostesses were the Duchess of Buccleuch, who reigned at Montague House, and Lady Tweedmouth, who ruled over the Liberals. But the two most magnificent houses, each with its clientèle of M.P.s, wits, and beauties, were Grosvenor House, where the Duke of Westminster entertained in drawing-rooms hung with Rubenses and Rembrandts, and Stafford House, which belonged to the Duke of Sutherland. This Duke, being a Liberal, once gave a reception in honour of Garibaldi; to the Queen's fury, the Prince went to it.

The nucleus of the Marlborough House clan was drawn from

* Daudet in his novels describes a number of ladies with high academic pretentions who kept salons.

English aristocratic backgrounds and from the Prince's Oxford and club friends. The families who supplied the young household with its aides-de-camp, secretaries, and ladies-in-waiting, the Knollyses and the Stonors, were also a part of it. These intimate friends were allowed to drop in on the Princess for tea or to chat with the Prince in his smoking-room without any warning. Society was not as frivolous as it was to become under Edward VII. The peers were still not very numerous (creations greatly increased after 1880) and were conscious of their political responsibilities; the prestige of the hostesses had a basis more solid than that of mere smartness. Politics and horse-racing alone animated conversation.

The Princess brought a lighter note into all this. As she was very deaf, her conversation consisted of a series of smiles with, from time to time, a wild laugh. She enjoyed dancing, and after dinner an aide-de-camp would be employed to turn the handle of a mechanical piano: she, who walked so slowly, would dance with partner after partner to the music of a Strauss waltz or a Lancers quadrille, holding the train of her dress with one hand and dangling a fan that spun at the end of a silk cord among lace tassels. Alexandra set the fashion for dresses with very tight-fitting bodices which came down low on the hips; with their skirts widening out like lampshades, they were far more graceful than the corsets of the Second Empire. Worth christened them *les robes princesses.* She also launched the fashion for coats with tight-fitting sleeves buttoned like a hussar's jacket. Equally precise was her hairstyle: a mass of poodle-like curls rising like a tower above the forehead and setting off the oval of the face. Ladies who wished to keep abreast of the fashions set by Alexandra realized now that smartness was not compatible with voluptuousness and cast upon their clothes the severe eyes of dandies. James Tissot, Degas' friend, introduced the Princess's elegance into his designs, an elegance that was better adapted to the turf, or the deck of a yacht, than to the boudoir. To the Prince, nobody dressed better than his wife; he gave her the most beautiful jewels and the finest horses, he laughed at her childishness and never got angry with her except for her continual lateness. His affection for her soon

became paternal, but their neighbour, Lady Waldegrave, was en-
raged by his egotism even as early as 1867. The Princess was then
suffering from a severe rheumatism that resulted in the "Alexandra
limp," later to become fashionable: "The Prince is the most
selfish of brutes. He only thinks of amusing himself and pays not
the slightest attention to her."

"Right to the end," wrote Marie of Rumania, "Aunt Alix
seemed like a flower. She gave the same pleasure that one derives
from a beautiful rose or an impeccable carnation. She was a hot-
house bloom grown by a gardener who knows all the tricks of the
trade."

The Prince organized his pleasures with great care; the life he
lived at Marlborough House provided him with a regular share of
those things that were to keep him occupied while he waited for
power: women and cards. Both the one and the other were to cause
him a certain amount of trouble. Towards the end of his life the
game of bridge enabled him to satisfy his taste for both flirtation
and making money, but at the height of the Victorian era it was no
more permissible to play in front of ladies than it was to smoke
in the drawing-room. When, at Sandringham or at Marlborough
House, the ladies had retired, a footman would bring in a green
cloth and some dice, and baccarat and trente-et-quarante would be
played until dawn. Never, not even during the most exciting
games, would the Prince forget his rank. When, after a bad run,
a young guest took the liberty of saying "So, Wales, you're not
doing so well?" he ordered the footman to summon the gentleman's coach. On occasion, rivalry over the ladies could make the
young guards officers forget how to behave; one evening at Marlborough House, two of them came to blows over the pleasure of
dancing with Mrs. Cornwallis-West, the celebrated Irish beauty
whose daughter we shall meet later; she added to the confusion by
fainting.

A big masked ball, which he gave in 1873, put the seal on
the Prince of Wales's sway over fashion. Imitating the way things
had once been done at the Tuileries, he gave instructions as to the
costumes which his guests should wear, and decreed the order in
which they should appear. The *playing cards* were to come in by

suits, followed by the *Venetians*, with "my dear Duchess" as "The Daughter of Titian"—"a few years and a few diamonds too many to be convincing," said a French guest—and then by the *Tales of Perrault*, in costumes inspired by Gustave Doré. The *Cavaliers and Roundheads* were next, and he teased those of his friends who were habitually very décolletées by making them dress as the latter; he himself was a somewhat stout, and rather too gay, Charles II. The Princess of Wales, as a Venetian, wore "a skirt of ruby-coloured velvet, a pinafore of blue satin embroidered with gold and covered with precious stones and tiny diamonds, with a headdress of ruby-coloured velvet, decorated with jewels." Marlborough House had been transformed by the painter Leighton in the Veronese manner. The ball was an immense success, and people spoke of nothing else: there had never been anything quite like it.

But there was another element, a Jewish one that quickly acquired considerable importance at Marlborough House, to the displeasure of the Queen, and the consternation of the public, although the fashionable took it in their stride. The liberal and prosperous English are not anti-Semitic, but at a time when the Rothschilds were masters of the City and Disraeli the master of the Tories, they could have wished that the Court at least might have resisted this invasion. A rapid and reliable intelligence system was the basis of the Rothschilds' fortunes. Disraeli supplied his old friend Lionel with very useful information. Thus the results of the Congress of Berlin were known in Lombard Street before they were heard anywhere else. The Prince, although he was never shown the state papers, was in a position, through his foreign connections, to be as useful as a Prime Minister, and he had many faithful friends amongst the bankers. Lionel's three sons were his contemporaries: there was Alfred, who had a house in Piccadilly next to the Duke of Wellington's, Leopold, the builder of Waddesdon; and Nathaniel, the master of Tring. The Prince had met their French cousins at the Tuileries, where a great deal of attention was paid to them. He found in the Rothschilds' houses that heavy luxury of the Second Empire, that refined cuisine, that international tone, that seemed a little common to the better-born of his future subjects. Deprived of money during his youth, the

Prince loved spending it, and loved even more having it spent in his honour. Did he express a wish to hear Sarah Bernhardt or Adelina Patti? One of the brothers made it his pleasure to invite the celebrity to London at a fabulous fee. It was at these dinners that ladies of fashion, for the first time, accepted actresses at the same table as themselves. The rumour that the Rothschilds were paying the young Prince's debts became so insistent that the Government had to issue a communiqué to the press: the £10,-000 which the Prince spent per annum in excess of his revenue, it said, came from the rents of the Duchy of Cornwall which had accumulated during his minority.

There is no proof that these generous friends were directly responsible for extricating the Prince from his embarrassment, but they were better placed than anyone to give him stock-exchange tips; the sums confided to them increased and multiplied like the descendants of the sage. In return the Prince pleaded the cause of his friends in Russia and Berlin, where their race was less loved than in London or Vienna, and he attenuated the resistance which they encountered at Windsor. The Queen, after having refused in 1870 to grant a peerage to one of her non-Christian subjects, eventually accepted Ferdinand de Rothschild's hospitality and had placed on her table a very large gold cup which she had graciously accepted as a souvenir of this visit. Not only did the Prince act as a witness in the synagogue at Leopold's marriage to Mademoiselle Perugia, but he encouraged his friends to marry Rothschilds. Lord Rosebery followed this advice and benefited from it, for he became Prime Minister and won the Derby. At Waddesdon Manor the atmosphere, in which the Prince blossomed like a hothouse flower, is still preserved. The Boulle furniture and the portraits by Gainsborough, the Savonneries and Sèvres, the Venetian crystals and Viennese upholstery, showed off the whiteness of the slightly fleshy ladies' skin to advantage, heightening the beauty of their dark eyes, while their broad hips were accentuated by the line of the bustle.

The Rothschilds, discreet and generous when away from their banking parlours, lived the lives of *grands seigneurs* devoted to racing and laying out gardens. Like them, the Prince was an

Anglicized European; a world exhibition was, for him as for his father, the supreme expression of a nation. It was an opinion shared by the ranks of international high finance. The Rothschilds had always been a contributory factor in the preservation of peace; they had too much to lose from war; they lent to governments that were pacific and assisted France, when she had been crushed by Prussia, to rise again. It was under their influence that the Prince took up a strong position against the policy of isolationism practised by his mother's Ministers. In addition to the Rothschilds, and soon to be allied with them, were the Sassoons, the descendants of a grand rabbi of Baghdad whose offspring had set up counting-houses from Hong Kong to Alexandria. There were also the Bischoffsheims and the Erlangers, whose family portraits were painted by Bonnat and Millais; the *wagons-lits* between Cannes and Vienna, between London and Hamburg, were filled by them as they travelled to and fro, now on their way to Chantilly, now to Ascot.

The third element that was welcomed at Marlborough House was American and essentially feminine. The really big American fortunes were still being built in the 'seventies; and to be "presentable" they needed another twenty years. But there were in Europe many Americans who were rich and distinguished enough to be welcome everywhere. The Prince was unlikely to forget the beauties he had met in New York, who were so much gayer than their English counterparts. An unbridled, if methodical, worldly ambition inevitably drew these Danaes towards the already paunchy and balding Jupiter, and he showered upon them a rain of invitations.

A certain Miss Chamberlayne, from Cleveland, Ohio, a devastating blonde who was touring Europe with her parents, caught the Prince in her toils although she never gave in to him. He followed her as far as Cannes and compromised himself on her behalf much more than he would ever have done for women whom he could have had without trouble. This adventure irritated the Queen and pained Alexandra, who christened Miss Chamberlayne Miss Chamberpot. Among the intimates of Marlborough House were a large and lively lady called Mrs. Arthur Paget, who was married to one of the Prince's aides-de-camp, and the daughters of Leonard Jerome, a New York financier, of whom the most beautiful married Lord Randolph Churchill. Henry James often drew his inspiration from these families that came to Europe to marry their daughters to Roman princes or English peers. Daisy Miller, the parents in *What Maisie Knew*, and the vapid heroine of *A London Life* were all fascinated by Marlborough House, although their wiser sisters contented themselves with a villa in Florence or with doing good works in Boston. It was absolutely vital to have been presented at the Court of St. James's, and to have, standing on a table in one's Newport drawing-room, an actual photograph of Edward, complete with his aristocratic nose, the slightly large and tender eyes, and an impeccable tie half hidden by his beard.

Another American who was often invited to Marlborough House was Madame Waddington, the wife of the French Ambassador. Her prattle both amused the Prince and was an odd contrast to the excessively Anglo-Saxon attitudes of her husband. It was she who brought the French Embassy back into fashion. Ambassadors of a rather too Republican stamp, who had replaced the dukes sent over by MacMahon, had brought it rather low.

The diplomatic corps constituted the fourth element of the Marlborough House clan. Care was taken to send to London not only wise and experienced ambassadors in order to please the Queen, but also young and well-born diplomats who were rich and liked dancing and who knew their horses, in order to please the Prince. The Russians and the Austrians were particularly appreciated. But the enjoyment of this honour was not without its perils. Thus it happened that Monsieur Larivière, who was attached to the French Embassy, lost, at the Prince's gaming-table, a sum so considerable that he had to renounce his career and leave for the Argentine; but once he was there his fashionable reputation enabled him to marry a great heiress. A charming Portuguese diplomat, the Marquess of Soveral, quickly gained the favour of Marlborough House and became, to the day he died, one of Edward's greatest friends. This little man, so dark and sleek that he was called the "blue monkey," believed himself to be irresistible. He was a marvellous conversationalist with the ladies, and he alone could get away with risqué stories at the Prince's table, stories which he told with such mimicry that even the most strait-laced gentlemen had to laugh. Discreet, although he was extremely well-informed, and always in good humour though he never sank to buffoonery, the Marquess of Soveral quickly attained an importance in London which was out of all proportion to the country which he represented. He detested Germany and worked on the Prince's prejudices where that country was concerned. There was also Count Mensdorff, for many years the representative of Austria, an agreeable and amusing Viennese who was descended from an aunt of the Queen; he was as welcome at Windsor as he was at Marlborough House.

Admiration for the Prince and Princess of Wales, the certainty that Marlborough House was the sacred temple of elegance and that there could be no amusement outside its circle, united the varied elements that followed the Prince on his visits to the country, where they would foregather repeatedly at the houses of the friends on whom fell the costly honour of entertaining him. On the twelfth of August one had to be in Scotland for the start of the grouse shooting. The Prince and Princess had a gloomy little castle there called Abergeldie, near Balmoral. In July, one had to be at Cowes for the Regatta, in September at a watering-place in Germany, in February at Cannes for the sunshine and the casino. One was expected to go often to Paris, and from time to time to Egypt or to Turkey on board a yacht. The secretaries arranged the visits, booked the special trains, and worked out the cost in advance. The ladies-in-waiting represented an area of serenity between the turmoil of domestics, busy with innumerable pieces of luggage, and their Highnesses: the equerries smoothed the way, foresaw what could go wrong, and prevented the mishaps that would have irritated the Prince: at the least snag he was to be seen playing nervously with the gold chain which he wore on his wrist; if things did not go right he would drum on the table, on his hat, and on his programme. Finally he would start shouting in a terrifying German accent.

"But," said Lord Fisher, "one put up with pleasure with his

terrible tantrums for the charming smile which he granted you once they had passed."

The Princess's lateness was the most frequent cause of these outbursts. She once disorganized the entire German railway system because she kept waiting a special train which was to take her from Copenhagen to Stuttgart. A lady-in-waiting, usually Miss Charlotte Knollys, would follow her, encumbered with handbags and dogs, only the white pekinese having the right to be in the Princess's arms. In her infantile simplicity Alexandra adopted the attitude that was, in fact, wisest when confronted with her husband's escapades. Women, she thought, were an obsession, like hunting or tobacco. She was always friendly towards the favourite of the time; possibly she loved her dear Bertie to the point of total self-effacement: possibly, as she was entirely absorbed with her own children, she only wished to see him happy and to avoid the rages that terrified the whole house. This indulgent attitude was to have its advantages when the Prince became involved in the scandals caused by his too facile pleasures.

The first of these misfortunes became known to the public in February of 1870. The circumstances of the scandal, banal in themselves, came to assume enormous importance, for in England the law is above the Crown. A Member of Parliament, Sir Charles Mordaunt, wanted a divorce; the press was immediately full of Lady Mordaunt's confessions, which seemed to emanate from one of Ouida's romantic novels; she was a very young woman who, in the horror of seeing her son go blind, repented for having so often deceived her husband: "It is the will of heaven," she said, with complete indifference to the consequences that she was bringing upon herself by mingling providence with her affairs, "that I should be punished for my sins through the person of my son." She cited several of her friends who were intimates of Marlborough House, and there were others still, as the papers discreetly hinted. The Prince was known to be one of her friends. Lady Mordaunt's father declared that she was mad in order to prevent a divorce. But the Baronet's lawyers, who had been through her desk, produced love letters of a most compromising nature and a few notes written by the Prince; these in themselves were quite innocent:

Dear Lady Mordaunt,

I am sorry that you have not been well and could not see me today. I am hunting tomorrow and Saturday, may I come and see you on Sunday at 5 o'clock? In the hope of finding you in excellent health, believe me yours sincerely,

Edward.

Readers of *The Times* took a poor view of the Prince's spending the Lord's day with a pretty woman. Why did Lady Mordaunt always receive him alone? Why did he go to see her in a cab instead of in his brougham? Sir Charles's barrister asked all these questions of the Prince, who had to appear in the witness box like any other citizen. Finally he asked him, "Did any indecent familiarity or any indecent act take place between your Royal Highness and Lady Mordaunt?" The Prince replied very calmly, "No, there was none." People in the courtroom applauded, but the public was far from being convinced. It was thought that the Prince had been too superficially cross-examined. Hostile murmurs greeted him on his first public appearance after the case.

Alexandra was perfect, but Lady Frederick Cavendish noted after a dinner: "The Princess was ravishing but looked very sad when she was not on her guard." Marlborough House acquired a bad reputation after this episode. The judge had spoken of a meet of hounds and of a race meeting as though they were evil. The Queen wrote to Delaney, the editor of *The Times*:

Underline often in your articles the immense danger represented by the regrettable lightheartedness and frivolity of the attitudes and ideas and way of life of the upper classes.

Seven years later another scandal broke out which proved the Queen right. Although a purely worldly affair, it had considerable political repercussions. In 1876 the Prince of Wales went on a trip to India. In order to make the long voyage more enjoyable and to be able to relax between his official duties, he invited, despite his mother's opposition, several of his intimate friends; they included the Duke of Sutherland, Lord Charles Beresford, and Lord Aylesford, one of the best horsemen in England, who was nicknamed "Sporting Joe." The Prince, who had just ended a liaison with Lady Aylesford, found it agreeable to take the husband with him, or, at any rate, wise to make him leave London. Thus, all at once, the young lady found herself completely on her own and lost no time in finding a new lover. But her choice, the elder son of the Duke of Marlborough, could hardly have been worse. The latter compromised her to such an extent that friends felt bound to tell her husband. Lord Aylesford asked for the Prince's permission to break off the journey in order to go home and put his marriage in order. He was to find that in his wife's ex-lover he had an ardent supporter. Hardly had the Prince in his turn returned to London than he adopted a very severe attitude towards the seducer. The latter's brother, Lord Randolph, who like all Churchills believed that he could get away with anything, cried from the rooftops that the Prince was in a very poor position to play the moralist and defended his brother's conduct. He obtained—from Lady Aylesford herself, according to some, by burglary, according to others—letters written by the Prince with all the imprudence of passion. He showed them around his clubs and declared that he would publish them if the Prince did not immediately cease his attacks on his brother.

"Blackmail!" they cried at Marlborough House. The Prince, maddened with rage, sent his seconds to Lord Randolph. This was a completely Continental reaction: in England duels had been brought to an end by ridicule fifty years before. Lord Randolph replied that he would not draw his sword against his future sovereign, but would fight with such of his friends as he chose to designate. The Queen, outraged by such insolence, demanded that things should go no further. She gave her approval when her son announced that he would never enter a house in which the Churchills were received. The young couple, recently the most brilliant in London, took refuge in Ireland; Lord Randolph's political career was interrupted and during his exile he became infected with that bitterness of spirit which was to make him, as we shall see, as dangerous for his adversaries as for his friends.

Thus the Prince was damaging the Crown's prestige by his adventures at a time when the Queen was living in a retreat so absolute that her subjects were even contemplating a change of régime. During the 'seventies moral conventions became so tyrannical that many men in the public eye were forced to lead sordid double lives and to see their careers wrecked when they were discovered: such was the case with Parnell, the great Irish orator, and with another politician, a habitué of Marlborough House, Sir Charles Dilke. Many rich Englishmen brought up illegitimate children in the suburbs of London or in the Channel ports in France. The Prince of Wales, despite the facilities that were nearer to hand, had recourse to this expedient also.

A certain Duchess of Caracciolo, who resembled the Princess of Wales, intrigued the inhabitants of Dieppe throughout the 'eighties. Her fine house was nicknamed *La Villa Mystère*. She was visited only by men, but they were of the most elegant kind. From time to time a yacht would bring an illustrious visitor, there would be policemen all over the town, and the duchess would give a grand dinner party.

Her daughter, Olga Alberta, was very expensively dressed. The Prince, who was godfather to this child, went to a lot of trouble over her and did his best to mitigate the difficulties of her life, for which he believed himself to be responsible; Jacques-Emile Blanche, however, a habitué of Dieppe, attributed her paternity to Prince Poniatowski. Henry James, fascinated by the elegant melancholy that surrounded the Villa Mystère, said to Blanche, "Your Dieppe is a miniature Florence, and your enchantress Olga has learned there far more than my Maisie ever did."

A certain number of these supposed children of Edward VII must still be alive, but their paternities would be difficult to prove, even if the English Crown had not firmly discouraged such attempts. But while many might turn in order to present a profile that bore a strong resemblance to that engraved on the golden guinea, there are few so convincing as the colonel who, during a game of charades, deliberately dressed up as a widow: with his large eyes and his receding chin he was the exact image of Queen Victoria. This old gentleman's mother was one of the frequenters of Marlborough House. When he became King, Edward was excessively generous and kind to the children of his friends.

At table, as in bed, Edward demanded the best that was available. If he was known to visit a restaurant frequently it would not be long before it acquired its three stars. It was at Sacher's in Vienna and later at Paillard's in Paris that he first noticed the young Swiss César Ritz, who was always able to provide exactly what the Prince required. He would arrange that only women of beauty were seated at the neighbouring tables, that a gypsy orchestra would be playing, and that cigarettes by Laurens from Egypt would be available: "You know better than I do myself what I like. Order a dinner that I will enjoy," said the Prince when, to his joy, he found Ritz at the Hôtel de Paris in Monte Carlo. Insisting on perfection, Ritz would supervise everything. Nothing could be allowed to jar on the Prince from the moment he set foot in the hotel. If, by some chance, there were some elderly ladies with their knitting and crocheting encumbering the hall, Ritz would lead them to believe that only *demi-mondaines* allowed themselves to be seen there, and would park the least decorative of his clients in the winter garden.

The Prince visited Cannes regularly between 1875 and 1895: the Côte d'Azur, its trim slopes studded with palm trees and bronze lamp standards, was a paradise for royalty. There, over flower-decked balustrades, they could watch the flotillas of yachts below. Royal Highnesses, and even Imperial or Most Serene Highnesses, flocked there. Every grand duke had a villa there, and the Queen of England spent holidays at Cimiez; the Empress Eugénie was building a villa at Cap Martin, and the Empress of Austria was also to be seen there from time to time. The beautiful Princess Alice, née Heine, would entertain Highnesses, bankers, and musicians at Monte Carlo. Félix Faure would come there to rub shoulders with royalty, and the republican prefects made elaborate bows. To be incognito was preferred, but the word had a variety of meanings. As used by the Grand Duchess Anastasia of Mecklenburg, it enabled her to enjoy adventures worthy of Messalina and to provide Jean Lorrain with material for his novels. But Victoria, on the other hand, called herself the Countess of Lancaster and would arrive with a suite of sixty people. The Old Guard—Mesdames de Galliffet, de Sagan, and de Pourtalès—would spend February in the latter's villa, where a certain number of Orléans, Oldenburgs, and Rothschilds were always to be found. Lord

Salisbury built himself a Scottish castle near Cannes. "My dear Duchess" contracted an unfortunate passion for roulette. In this period of moral rectitude only Infantas could get away with having gigolos and only grand dukes could be seen with those ladies who are known as half-castes in other parts of the world.

On the Prince's arrival a crowd of friends—or of people who wished to pass for such—would surround him at the station and invite him to dinner parties, picnics, and masked balls. The yacht *Britannia* would be waiting in the harbour and the Prince, taking the helm himself, would discuss the prospects for the regatta with Gordon Bennett. Abel Hermant published a series of dialogue novels in *La Vie Parisienne*, which are a brilliant study of this world. In it can be discerned the beginnings of café society—that moving camp of luxury-loving displaced persons—although it was really, to some extent, no more than a colony of Marlborough House.

CHAPTER FOUR

Edward as Prince of Wales

FROM TIME TO TIME, in the course of their history, the English have wondered whether the monarchy really does have a value: the ostentation of Charles I shocked the Puritans, and the Catholic sympathies of James II alarmed the patriotic; George III's madness and his sons' follies were unpopular with honest folk. Although Victoria had saved the House of Hanover in her youth, when she became a widow she gave the public cause to reconsider the principles of monarchy for reasons that were the very opposite of those which, in other crises, had shaken the loyalty of the English. The Queen, who with admirable conscientiousness worked twelve hours a day, refused with an almost neurotic obstinacy to fulfil her duty of appearing in public. She wrote to Lord Russell, who had begged her to attend the opening of Parliament:

> The Queen *must* say that she resents very bitterly the lack of heart of those who require her to be present at this cermony. Why is the public impatient to see an unhappy widow, nervous and stricken, labouring under her veils, all alone and in her robes of State, as if she was some strange beast and in that place where she never appeared except supported by her husband, in order to be watched without the slightest delicacy of sentiment?

In fact it was a little indelicate of the English to be so surprised at the extent to which the boring Prince Consort could be regretted, and to resent the economies which her absolute retreat permitted the Queen. What did she do with the £385,000 of the Civil

List and more particularly with the £60,000 reserved for her personal use? She never opened the doors of her palace, and sovereigns passing through London put up at hotels (which was the cause of Claridge's rise to fame). An eccentric industrialist had left her half a million pounds, the revenues of the Crown properties had accumulated but, even so, she demanded a dowry of £30,000 from Parliament when her daughter Louise married the Duke of Argyll, and an allowance of £15,000 for the Duke of Connaught when he obtained his majority.

"What does she do with it?" asked a republican pamphlet which was eagerly bought by the public. "One cannot conceive of a meaner cause for the decline of the monarchy," sighed Gladstone. From 1868 onwards the word "republic" was in the air, and meetings became more frequent, first in London and then in the industrial centres. A young manufacturer from Birmingham, called Chamberlain, who was later to become a pillar of the Conservative Party, distinguished himself by his violence in its advocacy, as did also Sir Charles Dilke, who was considered the leading politician of the younger generation. This republican movement was essentially middle-class in nature; the mass of the working classes could only turn to gin in order to forget its misery; the farmers were prosperous and followed the lead of the aristocracy. The discontent came from the shopkeepers and bourgeoisie and it had no more respect for the Queen than has a *Punch* cartoonist for a foreign sovereign. As under Charles I, Puritanism accounted for much of it. Although on this occasion there could be no comparison of the Court with Babylon, Marlborough House gave quite enough offence. The slogans of '48 were whispered by Polish, French, and Garibaldian refugees to a receptive audience. Karl Marx and Victor Hugo had little to say for the Government, for all that it had treated them generously. The pamphleteers had no respect for the Queen's private life, and strange rumours percolated through from Balmoral. She would for days on end remain secluded from her daughters and even her ladies-in-waiting, communicating with the outside world by short notes. Anyone who caught sight of the wicker basket on the back of a Shetland pony in which she took the air, wrapped in a tartan skirt, would have to take cover behind a bush. She would be accompanied by one single servant, John Brown, the ghillie whose coarse accent and rough manners had previously found favour with Prince Albert, at the time that the happy couple were enjoying their excursions on the moors. Ever since the Prince's death, the Queen felt that she was in the most intimate communion with Albert whenever this sturdy red-bearded man was near her. With the simplicity of a pure soul Victoria expressed this sentiment in her *Leaves from the Journal of Our Life in the Highlands*. When her family read it, they were somewhat upset, and unsentimental members of the public were provoked into making acid comments denuded of "all delicacy." One pamphlet made allusion to a secret marriage and called the Queen Mrs. Brown. One can understand the effect of this on those around her. It was true that Brown, who used the familiar "you" with Victoria, used to get quite angry with her if she was slow in getting into the carriage, and that he encroached with impunity on the functions of the Royal Household. Members of the Government went out of their way to please him, and the Princesses had to smile at him. To a general who asked him for news of the Queen he replied, "She's very well. Only yesterday she said to me: 'Here comes that old idiot of a general who has to shove his nose into everything.' "

The Prince of Wales grew exasperated at the rumours caused by the favours shown to Brown and by the ridicule which attached to the Crown as a result. One day he gave orders for a wooden pavilion a few miles from Balmoral to be knocked down since, so he said, it got in the way of his shooting parties; but it was a favourite resting place of the Queen's during her expeditions with John Brown. She had it immediately rebuilt and would not speak to her son for several weeks. It is extremely improbable that this pavilion sheltered scenes worthy of *Lady Chatterley's Lover*. Victoria, who had once had violent physical needs, substituted for them attachments that were exclusively sentimental, as did all the spinsters and widows who lived during her reign. A weakness that had nothing to do with love made it necessary for them to seek solitude. What it was can be guessed from the reply which the ghillie gave to a lady-in-waiting who asked him whether he had remembered to take the Queen's tea: "Tea. Ugh! She doesn't like it, we are taking whisky and biscuits." A strong arm on which to lean, once a few glasses had helped her to forget the sadness of widowhood and the cares of public life, and a refreshing frankness like one of those blasts of fresh air which she loved to let in when the atmosphere of the Court became too stifling: Victoria asked no more of John Brown. Lacking all pity for adulterers and smokers, the Queen had indulgence for drunkards only, and in this was the exact opposite to her son, who saw in alcoholism one of the most deplorable forms of bad manners. When Edward became King he was horror-struck by the quantity of whisky which the Scottish staff consumed. On each anniversary of the Consort's death, the Queen would distribute so many bottles that after the service the park would be full of maudlin drunks and unconscious figures. "That drunken ghillie" Edward was reported to have said of John Brown later on as he ordered that all the memorials of him which the Queen, a widow by vocation, had had erected, be destroyed. When her retainer died she even wished to dedicate a book to him. Horrified at the thought of the amount of ridicule this would arouse, the Prince rushed to the Archbishop of Canterbury to beg him to prevent its publication. Persuading Victoria that this work would add nothing to her glory was one of the hardest tasks of that prelate's life.

We have only to look at the portraits of the Queen during her fifties to see that the idea of a liaison between her and John Brown is absurd. As a young girl she had been not unattractive, and she became an admirable old lady, but the photographs taken of her during the 'seventies of the century, with her daughters or her dogs, show a hard, fleshy face that was ravaged with bitterness, and that certainly never glowed with pleasure. Her lack of illusions about her own appearance were undoubtedly one of the reasons for her retreat.

Although not directly connected to it, a profound feeling of discontent lent support to the republican movement. For nearly a century England had had trouble in Ireland. From the time of the famine of 1847, which had reduced that country's population by a third, emigration had continued to impoverish her. Many

Irishmen drifted hopelessly over to England in a miserable condition; they gave Karl Marx the idea for the *Lumpenproletariat*.
Gladstone alone wished to grant Ireland a sort of autonomy, with
Home Rule. As for the Prince of Wales, he thought that if he went
over there a few times he could solve the problem with his usual
charm and panache. The Queen had never really cared for these
malcontents from the time that the municipality of Dublin had
returned the Prince Consort's statue. When it was reported to her
that Lady Waldegrave had suggested that the Prince of Wales
should establish his residence there, or at least a sort of Balmoral,
with the title of Viceroy, she shrugged her shoulders. Crisis rapidly
succeeded crisis, and when the Government no longer knew which
way to turn, Edward was sent to Ireland. His first visit was in
1868; he went from country house to country house as the guest
of the English landlords, who, to avoid the insults of the peasants,
never showed their faces outside their demesnes. He returned there
in August 1871 and wrote to his mother:

> In the street the cheers and boos are mixed, particularly in the quar-
> ters where it is said that the Fenians have their followers. I prudently
> avoid any topic of conversation which could lead to misunder-
> standing.

One can imagine that horses, the only passion shared by both
the English and the Irish, were the main topic. Free fights broke
out in front of the house in which he was staying; insulting placards
were displayed where he could see them from the window of the
train in which he travelled; a few rotten eggs were thrown at him
at the stations. "But on the whole," declared the Government,
"everything went off marvellously." The Prince never for a moment
lost his good humour, and captivated all those who came in contact with him.

Thus the Queen's isolation, the Mordaunt affair, the business of
John Brown, the Irish question, and the acrimony engendered by
the democratic movement contributed, more than the words of
orators or the ideas of politicians, to the spread of anti-monarchic
sentiment. Although the mass of the population remained indif-

ferent, the press was on the whole faintly hostile, and it saddened the Queen to read the daily papers: there was no gratitude for all her hard work. She even spoke of abdicating. Possibly this explains her economies. It was during these unhappy years that Disraeli's influence began to take hold. He made the Queen's task easy for her, appeared to yield to her on everything and to do nothing without her advice; eventually he convinced her that she was a "faery" queen. An adroit impresario, he transformed the cantankerous widow into a glorious and happy being. The Prince had met this overdressed old man at the Rothschilds', and he had heard him say, with his cynical wink and his bad breath, things that were far too poetic for a politician. The heir to the throne took care to flatter him by making the rounds of the drawing-rooms with Mrs. Disraeli—a beplumed old scarecrow—on his arm, for Disraeli was his best advocate with the Queen.

The revolution of September 4, 1870, in France, and the advent of the Third Republic strengthened the republican movement in England. Victoria, it was well known, had been very friendly with Louis Napoleon and Eugénie; but then the excesses committed by the Commune demonstrated the dangers of violent revolution and revealed the advantages of a less abrupt change of régime.

In November 1871 a quite unforeseen event totally undermined the republican party. The Prince of Wales fell ill at Sandringham. When she learnt that he was suffering from typhoid fever, the Queen went immediately to him; she sat by his bedside and watched over him night and day. Fascinated by the death that appeared inevitable, she noted its approach in her diary:

Poor dear Alix was in the most terrible despair. I comforted her to the best of my ability but I was unable to prevent myself from saying amid my tears to Alice [the Grand Duchess of Hesse-Darmstadt]: "There's no more hope!" I went to the bed to stroke his poor hand. "Who are you?" he said. "It's Mother," I replied. The dear child, I stayed holding his hand. "It's kind of you to have come," he said at last. The way he gasped between each word was terrifying.

There are several pages written in this style. On November 14 hope returned. Two days later the Prince was saved. The explosion of joy with which the final bulletin on his health was received astonished the royal family as much as it did the Government. His convalescence was as rapid as the return of loyalty. The republicans organized a few meetings, but no one went to them and the party melted like snow in the sunshine. The Duke of Cambridge expressed the relief felt by the House of Hanover: "Providence sent us this illness in order to save us."

If the Queen said, "Phew!" nobody heard her. "I do not wish to make religion a means of controlling public opinion," she replied to Gladstone, who proposed to her that she should attend a service of thanksgiving with her son at St. Paul's. The Princess of Wales, for once, intervened and with energy. The service took place, the Queen and the Princess and Prince of Wales drove across London in a landau to the acclamations of the crowd, and, needless to say, Lord Tennyson dedicated an ode to this auspicious occasion. The cheering was as much for the Princess as for the convalescent; to the English, newly returned to their former sensibility, she was something to which they could respond with far greater fervour than to a woman in black. Despite her numerous confinements she still looked like a young girl, and she was the only one of the Princesses, the daughters and daughters-in-law of the Queen, that the crowd recognized and applauded in the procession.

Alexandra had five children: the Duke of Clarence was born in 1864, two months too early, after a skating party, and the hastiness of his arrival left its mark on his appearance and his mentality; then came the Duke of York, the future George V, followed by Louise, who married the Duke of Fife; Victoria, who never married; and finally, in 1869, Maud, the future Queen of Norway. The Princess had such a passion for her children that she never allowed them, until they became adults, to escape the atmosphere of the nursery. At Marlborough House she had a service lift put in between this room and her bedroom; "Let's have Victoria" or "Let's have Maud," she would say through the speaking-tube, and the cradle would arrive from two floors below.

As indispensable as the dogs, but much better behaved, the little Princesses with their long blond hair, their pale, narrow faces, and their lace frocks with mauve silk belts would walk behind their mother. As each child was born, the Queen would send her congratulations, but their tone was always marred by her irritation at the choice of first names.

> If the dear little one grows up good and wise, I shall not worry about the Christian name, but naturally, you will add Albert to the chosen name, as it was decided long ago that all the male descendants of dear Papa would carry his name as a mark of our line. In the same way the daughters will add Victoria to their names.

Victoria was a much better grandmother than mother; she had her descendants brought down to Windsor or Osborne and would compare Helena's, Bertie's and Arthur's offspring with one another. She never passed through London without spending a little time at Marlborough House and casting an eye into the nursery. But her affection did not stunt her critical sense, as we can see from a letter she wrote to the Grand Duchess of Hesse-Darmstadt: "The Wales children seem to me pigeon-breasted and a puny breed." The Queen was not wrong: they remained, with the exception of George V, who was quite a fine and well-set-up man, rather like inbred poodles, with their narrow skulls, protruding eyes, and pale complexions.

Their father, whom the memory of his own education filled with horror, wanted his children to be happy; he would interrupt their lessons in order to play with them; when travelling abroad he would send them postcards. The Princess hardly ever left them, and they called her "Mother dear." Their psychological development was in consequence arrested at adolescence. The boys' tutor was a young and sporting ecclesiastic whom they found extremely likeable. The elder wanted to be a soldier, the younger a sailor. Everyone lived in fear of the Queen. The latter issued strictures on the following pattern to Marlborough House:

> I cannot insist too much on the *absolute* necessity that your children do not mix with the people whom you constantly entertain: they must take their meals separately or you must have your breakfast and your lunch alone with them.

The Prince, in reply to these prophylactic moral injunctions, wrote:

> The children do not mix with what you call fashionable society. And those with whom they come in contact are so tactful that their innocence will not suffer.

The prediction came true for the younger son, but not for the elder. As for the Princesses, they remained until their deaths little girls whose moral character was beyond reproach.

> The Prince of Wales's children [wrote Marie of Rumania] always talk about people as "the dear little thing" or "the poor little man." They always express themselves in a minor key, and are very mute; from conversations with them one derives a strange impression that life would have been very wonderful and everything very beautiful if it had not been so bad.

After the triumph of the service at St. Paul's, the Prince returned to the world, his head held high although he was now bald. He had thickened out, but as his stance was upright, his corpulence gave him an air of majesty. His long and rather full nose and his protruding rather than large eyes came from his mother, but the high forehead he inherited from Prince Albert; a small beard hid the receding Hanoverian chin and gave authority to his face. After having been an unremarkable youth, Edward developed as he reached maturity into a fine figure of a man, and we should not attribute solely to worldly ambition the success which he achieved with women. He knew far better than the average Englishman how to talk to them, and took an interest in the details of their *toilettes* and in their gossip. His guttural voice and the deeply rolled "r" had, they said, an amazing charm when he was alone with a woman. Possessed of prestige without power, enjoying a sumptuous way of life supported on debts, charming with women and brusque with men, a faithful friend though a fickle lover, lacking in culture but a good conversationalist—the Prince of Wales attained his thirtieth birthday a mass of contradictions born of the shortcomings of his education and the falseness of his position. He knew exactly the thing to do in every situation, and his manners were always perfect, provided that some unforeseen snag did not threaten his dignity or his pleasures. He was a well-oiled machine, perfectly adapted to ceremonies that went off without a hitch. He thrived on adulation. While abroad, or in the colonies, he never showed the slightest trace of boredom in public. Never was there an ambassador so perfectly able to combine affability, a life of luxury, and the ability to avoid drudgery.

The Queen had to admit that the Crown's prestige rose visibly in his wake. All the same it required some insistence on the part of her Ministers or of foreign sovereigns before she would allow herself to be represented by her heir. Although the violent antipathy which she had felt for him after the Prince Consort's death had been attenuated, thanks to Princess Alexandra and Disraeli, her mistrust continued. And though the memory of her uncles still counted for much in the anxiety which the Queen felt about her son's life, she was reminded by a relation who was closer still, and whose scandalous life was the talk of Germany, that the Coburg side was also not all that it might have been. The Queen's brother-in-law, the Duke, lived between his two capitals, surrounded by a court of adventurers and actresses, and he consorted flagrantly with the most garish mistresses. Fat and jovial, he bore no resemblance to his brother, but there was a noticeable similarity to his nephew.

From the time of his marriage the Prince began the round of the European courts. In 1866, with the conflict known as the Seven Weeks War between Prussia and Austria hardly over, the Prince and Princess of Wales went to St. Petersburg to attend the marriage of Princess Dagmar of Denmark, known afterwards as the Empress Marie, to the Tsarevich. The young couple went out of their way to be nice to Alexander II, whose hatred of England had not subsided since the Crimean War. The Prince expressed his regrets to the Tsar for the traditional English alliance with the Porte, for the Greeks had just chosen as their King his brother-in-law, George of Denmark. He greatly exceeded his powers in committing himself to the support of this little kingdom; Russia and England, after all, would have to reach an understanding if it was to thrive.

The following year, however, the Sultan Abdul Aziz expressed his intention of visiting England, and the Prince had to receive him. The Cabinet was determined that his visit should be a success, and not only because they wished to maintain the balance of power against Russia. The Sultan, the Grand Caliph of Islam, had considerable influence in India. The Queen grudgingly agreed to admit a Moslem to the Order of the Garter, but she insisted that the figure of St. George should be removed from the medallion worn by the Knights. She then refused to hold a single reception in any of her palaces—even if she had, it would not have compared to those held at the Tuileries. Her visitor, she decided, was to be impressed in a more practical manner: the investiture would take place on the royal yacht, during a naval review. The Sultan, whose seafaring had been confined to the Bosporus, did not take kindly to the swell in the Solent. Green in the face and lashed by the wind, his legs buckling beneath him with each wave, the potentate was seen to retire precipitately during the course of the ceremony. As they returned ashore the ladies-in-waiting's plumes and the pashas' fezes were swept by squalls of rain. Only the Queen, with her passion for the open air, enjoyed the occasion.

In 1873 the Shah of Persia, Nasr ed Din, proved to be even more demanding than the Sultan. Not only did he wish to have the Garter but he also aspired to dining with the Queen at Windsor. She had to give in, for even before people wanted its oil, Persia was in a position to prevent Russian expansion into India. At his side there came a very young man whose presence was explicable neither by his rank nor by his origin, and the despot refused to be parted from him even during the most solemn ceremonies. Unfortunately, the secretary who took it upon himself to reveal to Victoria this Ganymede's exact role has not reported her Gracious Majesty's comments. The Princess of Wales could not abide the Shah; during the first dinner attended by them both he spat his peach stones on to her train; but the Prince had to put a good face on it. He took his visitor around London and found that the prisons particularly interested him. The potentate even expressed a wish to see how people were hanged in England. When the English attempted to be excused on the grounds that there was no condemned man available at the moment, the Persian was not at all put out. "All right, then," he said, "you can hang one of the members of my suite." It was with the same good spirits that he remarked to the Prince, as they were leaving the Duke of Sutherland's house: "I suppose when you are King you will immediately cut off that Duke's head and confiscate his palace: he is really much too rich."

"There are so many rich lords in this country," replied the Prince, smiling, "that I would not know which one to start with."

But however bizarre his visitors, the Prince of Wales always retained his respect for their royal dignity. Thus when in 1881 he gave a ball for Kalakoa, the King of the Sandwich Islands, he allowed him and not the German Crown Prince, who happened to be in London at the time, to partner the Princess in a quadrille. Victoria's obstinacy frequently made her heir's part in life very difficult. In 1874 the Tsar came to London to see his daughter, the Duchess of Edinburgh. He was due to leave again two days after the date on which the Queen, in her unvarying routine, was to go to Scotland. The Prince and his sisters begged her to delay her departure, since it could not fail to offend a guest as susceptible as Alexander. But it was all to no avail; this year, as in every other year, she would go to Balmoral on May 18. Twice Disraeli had to rush down to Windsor before, as he wrote to a friend:

> The great lady has finally put off her departure. Nobody, not even the Prince of Wales, managed to persuade her. But I am certainly in disgrace. Salisbury tells me that I have avoided a war with Afghanistan and Derby has congratulated me on this unprecedented triumph.

His deference to crowned heads won for the Prince the confidence of the maharajas, whose power was unceasingly being undermined by British rule. It was not until 1875 that the Prince obtained both his mother's permission and the funds from Parliament to undertake a tour of India, which, both politically and personally, was a great success. One of the reasons for his going was to invest the princes with a new order, the Star of India, the manner of wearing which established their precedence, for they were voraciously jealous of their prerogatives, each one vying with his neighbour over the number of guns fired in his salute. On his way Edward was happy to revisit Egypt, and the Khedive ruined himself over the festivities that he laid on for the Prince. Disembarking at Bombay, which was en fête to receive him, Edward saw banners inscribed with such notices as: "Tell your mother we are happy," and "How is your Royal mother?" What he read in the papers afforded him less pleasure. The Queen had just been, thanks to Disraeli, proclaimed Empress of India. The Government had done nothing to prepare him for so auspicious an event, and had not even warned him by special cable.

For four months the Prince toured India, receiving the homage of his mother's vassals and their tributes in the form of swords encrusted with precious stones, of pearls for the Princess, and of animals to amuse the children. He hunted buffalo and went peacock and tiger shooting. On one shoot, laid on by a maharaja, there were a hundred and nineteen elephants, five hundred and fifty camels, a hundred horses, sixty teams of oxen, five hundred coolies, a hundred water-carriers, and fifty messengers.

On January 1, 1876, the Prince held a durbar for the Indian potentates, at the gates of Calcutta. The Maharajas of Kashmir, Indore, Gwalior, Jaipur, and Patiala set up camp in their gold-fringed tents, seated on their precious carpets, surrounded by enormous retinues. Based on the pattern of the durbars which the Moguls had once held, the occasion served as a model for those which thirty years later Lord Curzon was to preside over, in the new capital of Delhi. The Prince went next to Nepal, resting on the way in Simla, at the foot of the Himalayas. At Lucknow he knelt before the white marble angels that adorn the fountains where the victims of the Mutiny of 1857 are buried, and left for home on a ship whose strong-rooms were crammed with jewels and whose decks were turned into a zoo. As a memorial to this visit Sir Albert Sassoon, the banker, offered the city of Bombay a gigantic equestrian statue of the Prince. Edward found that he sympathized with, and even envied, the Maharajas; did they not surround their corpulent persons with dancing girls, cut off the heads of their subjects when they spoke out of turn, and burn their mothers on their fathers' funeral pyres? He invited them to

London and he showed much more respect for them than did the Indian Office.

From henceforth the Prince of Wales became the model on which the Indian princes based their lives; they spent fantastic sums in trying to emulate him; racing stables and suites at the Savoy became *de rigueur* for them. His opinions on everything carried the force of law: thus when he expressed his disapproval of suttee, the ritual sacrifice of widows, they finally came to recognize its barbarous nature. When the three widows of Sir Jund Bahadur, a member of the Government of Nepal, demanded with cries of "*Ram! Ram!*" that they should be burnt, their Maharaja let them know that this sort of thing could not fail to be displeasing to the Prince. Thereupon the widows wrote a long letter of excuse to Marlborough House and went off to burn themselves, without further ceremony, in the country.

It was during the Indian tour that the famous Suez Canal purchase took place. The Prince, who had connections with both the Khedive and the Rothschilds, could have played a useful part in this. Disraeli, however, managed to bring the affair to a successful conclusion with his usual gusto. His secretary, Lord Rawton, tells us that hardly had the Prime Minister obtained the Cabinet's permission to buy the Khedive's shares than he dispatched Lord Rawton with all haste to see Lionel Rothschild in New Court. As the financier sipped his muscatel, Lord Rawton asked him, "Would you be willing to lend the Government four million pounds?"

"What is your guarantee?"

"The British Nation."

"You shall have it tomorrow." Lionel Rothschild then finished his wine.

"How happy I am, Grandmama, that you should have bought Egypt," said the future William II in a letter which he wrote to Windsor commenting on the affair, thus reducing this great event to the level of a piece of simple family business.

The Prince returned to London rather like a child who has been away on a long holiday. Scarcely even thanked for his efforts, he was given fresh and wearisome duties to perform: the opening of hospitals and exhibitions, government garden parties, and embassy dinners. He read *The Times* so as to keep in touch and asked Lady Waldegrave to invite him to the dinners which she was giving to push her fourth husband, Chichester Fortescue. The Cabinet Ministers whom he met listened courteously to his opinions and, with a rather distracted air, to the impressions he had gained on his travels. Occasionally he was allowed to see the state papers, but he had to wait until his friend Lord Rosebery became Foreign Minister before the Queen would allow him a key to the dispatch boxes, the red morocco caskets, embossed with a crown, that were used to carry the latest news and the ambassadors' dispatches from Whitehall to the royal residence. Only in 1893 did Gladstone manage to obtain permission to send the Prince a copy of the Cabinet's minutes.

The official biographies, such as the one written by the conscientious Sir Sidney Lee, stress the interest which the Prince took in social reform. He was made a member of a commission on workers' dwellings, protested against the law which forbade widowers to marry their sisters-in-law, and spoke in the House of Lords to ask, on behalf of the working-classes, that museums should be opened on Sundays. No doubt this was the sort of thing that was expected of a future king, but perhaps it also came from his goodness of heart. It is well known that the thought of penury is painful to men of the world. The Prince had no liking for unhappiness; his courtiers had to be good-humoured, and the people had to have cheerful expressions and strong voices with which to acclaim him. His sisters had all the virtues of professional patronesses: they patronized associations of lacemakers, musicians, and ladies in reduced circumstances, nursing schools, educational conferences, and charity concerts. They devoted themselves with passion to jumble sales, selling cushions and water colours that their own august hands had produced. The Queen encouraged these pastimes. Like everyone who has a very keen sense of duty, the Princesses loved to be deferred to, and their charitable works certainly entitled them to the respect normally accorded to their rank.

Freemasonry occupied a fairly important place in the Prince's life. He rose quickly up the rungs of the ladder, presided at ceremonies, and introduced his sons. In England, this institution is a philanthropic association, closely allied to the Anglican Church, and it never assumes any political importance except when raising its voice to protest on behalf of populations oppressed by foreign powers.

Glancing through the thick red-bound volumes of the *Illustrated London News* or of *The Graphic*, we can see the Prince's silhouette growing thicker in the woodcut portraits, the hair receding from his forehead, his gestures becoming automatic. Whatever the circumstances, and ridiculous though they sometimes are, his behaviour is always irreproachable. We see him in the Albert Hall, a gold-embroidered panel on his coat, receiving the insignia of the Grand Master of the Scottish Lodge, surrounded by aristocratic Masons: among his decorations, the three feathers and the triangle can be seen to advantage. The following week he is at Sandringham, waiting for a train, while members of the North Norfolk Hunt gallop round the station shouting huzzahs. In the orangery at Chatsworth, lit by Japanese lanterns, he is seen in contemplation, surrounded by bishops and generals, before a giant water lily. But at Baden-Baden he watches a cotillion in attractive female company; he wears a dinner jacket and a bowler hat, a combination that we might find surprising, but it was certainly the correct dress at that place and at that time. In Scotland, brandishing a torch, he dances with the Duke of Fife, surrounded by the corpses of stags; deafened by the bagpipes, the ladies, holding up their skirts to prevent them from being stained with blood, count the victims of the massacre. Deep in meditation, the Prince, dressed in a frock coat, bows before the bust of Shakespeare. Accompanied by the Princess (wearing a short veil and carrying an umbrella), he tries out a new rifle at Aldershot. We see him as the family man offering his mother tea on one of her visits to Sandringham. We see him out shooting, at baptisms, and funerals, awarding rosettes to prize-winning bulls at agricultural shows, and medals to invalids in hospitals or to ambassadors at banquets. The expressions never vary: those taking part in the ceremonies have set faces, while the onlookers appear indulgent and friendly.

There was nothing absurd about such ritual in a society in which symbolism played so large a part. It was possible to judge a man's rank by the functions he performed and thus it was easier to estimate the progress he was making in the world. The Prince found the conventional reassuring; it was the unexpected that he could not cope with. After each ceremony he noted: "Everything went off tremendously" or "Unfortunately, a few mishaps about the arrangements." Naturally generous, he loved distributing kind words and smiles. Endowed with an excellent memory which he had trained since childhood, he could remember having met the sister-in-law of an attaché in Darmstadt in 1872, the minister of a maharaja at Trichinopoli in 1875, an American banker at a casino in Cannes, or a canon at Oxford. He could play the game of "Who was she before she was married?" which took up so much of fashionable conversation, to perfection and even extended it to the notabilities of all civilized countries (that is to say, those whose most distinguished citizens could be received at the Court of St. James's).

CHAPTER FIVE

Edward as a European

THE PRINCE AND PRINCESS of Wales, whose entourage in London was drawn from the fashionable world with the inclusion of politicians and diplomats, moved, when they travelled on the Continent, amongst royalty, though this term includes mediatized* princes as well as crowned heads. Royalty defines a social class, a way of life more than a function. Royalty is descended from about twenty families, of whom more than two-thirds are German (the turn of the century saw the decline of Latin royalty); related a hundred times over, the crown-laden branches of their family trees criss-crossing interminably, they quarter in their arms as they do so the Eagle of Prussia, the Lion of Brunswick, the Chequers of Bavaria, the Crossed Swords of Saxony, and, less frequently, the Lilies of the Bourbons and the Towers of Braganza. Beside the enormous trees planted by the Carolingians, like the Wettins (all branches of the Saxon royal family), or the Guelphs (Hanover), dating from the early days of the Holy Roman Empire, stood the more recent Hohenzollerns, and the Romanovs, the most recent of all. Collateral and morganatic branches augmented these illustrious trees, and as the need arose sustained them, like the branches of banyan trees, which take root and become trunks in their turn. There were all the different varieties of Bourbon

---

* Princes whose states had been incorporated in a larger political unit, usually by Napoleon, and who were thus deprived of effective political power.

(Sicily, Parma, and Carlist), of Habsburg (Este and Tuscany), and of Saxony with its Ernestine branch and its Albertine branch, the latter divided between Coburg, Meiningen, Weimar, and Eisenach; there were Catholic and Protestant Württembergs, and the Beauharnais, not to mention the royal house of Montenegro, the Hohenzollerns, and the Glücksburgs of the Balkans.

It was a race apart, with characteristics common to all its members: they could speak every language to perfection but with a very slight accent; they had strong voices, were upright of carriage, and had infallible memories, remembering every leaf of their family trees including both the offshoots that had bought lustre and the regrettable failures. Some carried congenital weaknesses that spread to all the main stems to which they united themselves. Thus the Hesse family brought haemophilia into the Russian and Spanish royal families. The vocabulary of this heraldic botany is German, and only such terms as *Ebenbürtig* and *Hochgeboren* are allowed: nor must a *Durchlaucht*, a *Fürst*, or a *Prinz* be confused; its Linnaeus is the Almanach de Gotha. Their Imperial, Royal, and Grand Ducal or Most Serene Highnesses carried with them an aura of self-esteem that floated behind them in the wind like the plumes of their shakos; they never forgot the rôle that would be theirs if, through the death of one or two relatives, or through marriage or the decision of a congress, they found themselves on the point of mounting a throne. It was quite natural that the morganatic granddaughter of a Württemberg should marry George V and that one of the grandsons of the Battenbergs should marry the Queen of England. Even the miserable Montenegrins achieved one daughter who became the Queen of Italy and two others who became Grand Duchesses of Russia.

The Prussian House was the last to continue to rule in the eighteenth-century manner. Although vassals of the Emperor since 1871, the German sovereigns who had not been mediatized sixty years earlier were in possession of immense fortunes; they had courts on the grand scale and exchanged ambassadors. They inclined more and more towards respectability, following the example set by Windsor and Potsdam. The men almost always wore uniform, either that of their own regiment or of a regiment belonging

Prince Bismarck.

to a cousin with whom they might be staying. In the country they would put on Tyrolean dress, but their town clothes were in such poor taste that they upset their cousin Bertie.

The ladies were also quite willing to don uniform and to review troops in frogged tunics, with bearskins on their heads, their rococo palaces acting as pastel-coloured backdrops. Their appearance, when in town, resembled nothing so much as that of governesses of good families who have suddenly found their shoulders covered in sable. They all aped the Princess of Wales, with their slender waists and ringlets. In the evening they would cover themselves with jewels, load their breasts with obscure but ravishing orders, and hold court or go to the opera. The southern Highnesses, the Bourbons and the Savoys, were the gayest (though they produced two or three saints), the Austrians the most imposing, the Russians a bit mad, and the Scandinavians the most debonair. All those of Saxe-Coburg blood were intelligent but unstable; all those of the house of Hesse were very good-looking.

Such was the prestige of the Prince and Princess of Wales at the end of the century that in appearance all the Highnesses could easily have been mistaken for Englishmen. In London, however, the heartiness and sentimentality of the Germans, the pomposity and silliness of the Viennese, and the dreaminess of the Russians were still noticeable. Royalty filled the *wagons-lits*; the *Orient Express* would transport Fürstenbergs and Hohenlohes to Vienna and Coburgs to Sofia; and the *Star of the North* would carry Württembergs and Hesses to St. Petersburg. Right up until 1914 the lines of communication ran from Cannes to Marienbad, from the Peterhof to Ludwigsburg, from Sandringham to Potsdam, for there was always some new event to bring the clan together. There were marriages, jubilees, first communions (a very solemn occasion at the Prussian court), and above all funerals, but the complications of precedence never failed to create problems.

The least of these august personages never travelled without an aide-de-camp, a secretary, and a poor cousin or illegitimate niece to act as lady-in-waiting. The Prince and Princess of Wales and the Empress Frederick always had at least twenty people with them; the Emperors of Germany and of Russia at leasty fifty, without counting staff officers and detectives. They would kiss and embrace each other on red carpets at railway stations, to the sound of national anthems; they would congratulate each other in the Kurhaus; they would attend the opera together. They wrote long screeds to each other, the latest news of Adelaide of Nassau, Mimi of Dessau, or Tilla of Lippe and her little Charlotte; they kept themselves informed about the movements of Olga and Vera of Württemberg (known as Princess Eugène), of the Infanta Pilar of Bavaria, and good old Aunt Augusta. They passed on the witticisms of the Princess Waldemar of Denmark, who was born an Orléans, and discussed what Philippa of Coburg, the King of the Belgians' daughter, had worn. It was a world that had its models of propriety, the Empress Frederick, Clementine of Coburg, and the blind King of Hanover, as well as its libertines such as Queen Isabella of Spain, Leopold II, the Grand Duke of Saxe-Coburg, and the Grand Duchess of Mecklenburg-Schwerin, Crown Princess Cécile's mother. The Greeks were the gayest and the Saxons the most discreet, but the Princesses of Weimar were frankly bluestocking, brought up as they had been in Goethe's shadow. The Miguelite Braganzas were of an inquisitorial piety, and it was said of the Savoys that they were free-thinkers. The Grand Duchess Vladimir was much the most elegant, and the most beautiful was to be Queen Marie of Rumania.

It was a provincial world which kept its eyes turned towards the capitals where the alliances were formed and whence honours stemmed. Vienna remained the most imposing, but the Habsburgs usually married amongst themselves when they were not intent on folly; the Austrian Emperor measured out his Order of the Golden Fleece sparingly and was chary of promoting people in the Almanach de Gotha. St. Petersburg was fabulously rich, but the Romanovs were unstable and menaced by nihilists. The really important source of honours was the new German Empire, and it took care to make its importance felt, though it lacked the style still to be found in Vienna. London was a pleasure ground where rich pickings in the marriage stakes were to be found. Many of these royals became completely English, like the offspring of Queen Victoria's half-sister, Feodore of Leiningen: Ernest became an admiral and his brother, Victor of Hohenlohe, known as Count Gleichen, a distinguished diplomat. Their cousin Clovis was to become Chancellor of the Reich. There were also Prince Edward of Saxe-Weimar, who married Lady Augusta Gordon Lennox, and the Mecklenburg-Strelitzes, who spent several months a year in a house near Buckingham Palace. The Prince and Princess of Wales were responsible for bringing the Prince of Teck, who married their Cambridge cousin, over from Vienna, and Prince Christian of Schleswig-Holstein managed to obtain the hand of Queen Victoria's ugliest daughter, who was thereafter known as Princess Christian. With its two unmarriageable daughters,* this was the most cheerless union that can be imagined; one never saw them at Marlborough House. Boring or amusing, pretty or ugly, rich or needy, the royals would all send each other their photographs, and every one of them was to be seen on the innumerable small tables at Sandringham.

True to its military upbringing, royalty would never gather together in any quantity without immediately adopting a martial posture in front of the Court camera. One of the most astonishing groups is that taken at Coburg on the occasion of the marriage of the hereditary Prince of Hesse with Victoria's granddaughter, Melita of Edinburgh. In the centre, massive beneath a black silk shawl, Queen Victoria sits tight-lipped: "I loathe nothing more than these royal gatherings," she once said. At her knees, seated on a bearskin, are her Prussian and Coburg granddaughters, blonde and slender; beside her, her daughter the Empress Frederick, affecting serenity, and her daughter-in-law the Duchess of Edinburgh, who makes no effort to hide her boredom. Tall, beautiful, but looking pinched, Alix of Hesse and her sister, the Grand Duchess Serge, hold each other's hands. It was on this occasion that the Tsarevich asked for the hand of Princess Alix. The German Empress ("poor Dona"), very overdressed, gazes with admiration at William II, the only man to be seated. Behind him, the Prince of Wales attempts to hide a Saxon uniform which does not become him. The Tsarevich and the Duke of York, the future

* One of them eventually married a German prince but as the Queen said: "She returned no different from when she left."

George V, both in civilian clothes, look identical with their trim beards and clear eyes. Then there were the beards worthy of the brush of Cranach, the plumes, the dolmans, the boas, and the circle of dogs. The royals came together in serried ranks. But even if one forgets their names, a crooked nose here, a glaucous eye there, or an unusually long neck enables one to tell from which line each came. Although individually they did not amount to much, they could, when acting in unison, put a spoke in the wheels of state and cause considerable annoyance to the people that really mattered, such as Queen Victoria or Bismarck. The latter, like all Germans, reproached those princesses who married abroad with a lack of patriotism. The burgeoning German Empire wounded so many vanities in overthrowing precedence that the Hohenzollerns themselves felt somewhat like parvenus when they became Imperial Highnesses: "What would the Duchess of Connaught [Prince Frederick-Charles's daughter] say," von Bülow asked the Emperor one day, "if a general came to congratulate her on being the daughter of the victor of Metz?" "Louischen would find that extremely disagreeable," replied William II.

The diplomats formed another international society. Yet another, formed by the world of finance, did not gain acceptance until the new century. The Norpois* were to be found everywhere; conversation turned exclusively on such topics as "the European concert," the "Balkan chessboard," and "the sick man." Here again Bismarck was dominant, although there was the Russian Gorchakov, who was reproached by his German colleague for being too willing to accept portraits in diamond-studded frames from foreign sovereigns.

Vienna followed the Metternich tradition before falling into Aehrenthal's perfidious grip. Until the time of such great ambassadors as Cambon, France had nothing but bourgeois representatives who were at the mercy of every government crisis. England's ambassadors, such as Odo Russell in Berlin, Lord Bertie in Paris, or Lord Dufferin in Constantinople, were first class. One or two diplomats like Count Mensdorff, who had a Coburg grandmother, and the Prince of Reuss, the German Am-

* Norpois is a conventional diplomat who appears in Proust's novels.

bassador in Russia, who was a cousin of the Empress Augusta, were of almost royal rank.

The diplomatic salons aped the Courts; the principal ones were those of the Countess Klein-Michel in St. Petersburg, Princess Radziwill in Berlin, and Pauline Metternich in Vienna. Here again everyone know each other, and all spoke French, but, although the fashions were of Paris, Parisians were detested, and the representatives of the Republic were not welcome. The English, who are impressed only by their own dukes, were visibly bored by them. But there was another group of people, from a quite different background, who became very important about this time. They did the rounds of the chancelleries and salons, and would lunch at the French restaurant in St. Petersburg and at the St. James's Street Club, where they would languidly quote the witticisms that everyone knew already, such as the one that Disraeli pinched from Prince Lobanov: "The key of India is in London, not in Kandahar." They were the political journalists, whose role remained considerable right up until 1939. The most famous of them was *The Times* correspondent in Paris, a little Bohemian Jew with side whiskers and pince-nez, called Monsieur de Blowitz. The Prince of Wales was equally acquainted with these gentlemen and would speak to them without affectation, something that earned him more good will than the other royals enjoyed. He was particularly fond of taking ambassadors aside for long conversations while equerries and attachés, trussed up in their gold lace, followed at a suitable distance, as though the fate of Europe was at stake.

The product of the Treaty of Westphalia, the Congress of Vienna, and the Treaty of Frankfurt, Europe provided a sort of tapestried backdrop, the patina of usage and the sheen of old gold upon it, before which the monarchical ritual was performed. The actors had no wish to know what lay concealed behind it, although an anarchist bomb would occasionally split the silk. It was on this stage that the Prince of Wales and his wife performed, and although this pantomime sometimes bored the Prince, if the shooting was good or if there were a casino and attractive women at hand, he would be all eagerness. He would report his observations conscientiously and keep the Foreign Office informed. But if the truth be known, these gilded occasions had no more relevance to the real facts of life that lay beyond the stage-set than do the cocktail parties of today at which the Venezuelan Ambassador and the Pakistan Cultural Attaché chat to the representatives of Ghana. Diplomats are now losing out in the business of running the affairs of state in just the same way that royalty was eighty years ago, but whereas the former are entirely dependent on the whims of their governments, their Highnesses represented a tradition of entrenched territorial possessions, and their family relationships tended to mitigate the barriers of national frontiers; their influence in keeping the peace did have its importance.

The stage décor hardly varied between the palaces of the three empires: white state rooms flanked by troopers in gold eagle-crested helmets and apartments hung with Gobelins and Winterhalters and decorated with a profusion of Sèvres and Russian malachite vases. The chamberlains, the ladies-in-waiting, and the pages were adept at attributing the greatest possible importance, with international repercussions, to their august masters' lightest words, and the ambassadors were perfectly content to believe them. Such was the atmosphere in Vienna, particularly, the capital which, from the English point of view, was the least important; its fashionable society was very agreeable to the Prince, and he got on very well with the Archduke Rudolf. He respected the Emperor, while the Princess admired the Empress; here again he came across the Rothschilds, joined large shooting parties, and took his ease in the little private rooms at Sacher's, which reminded him of those at the Café Anglais.

From the time of the Battle of Sadowa, Bismarck was royalty's *bête noire*; some, like the Hanovers or the Landgrave of Hesse, he had dispossessed; others, like the King of Denmark, he had despoiled, or, like the Grand Duke of Baden, he had deprived of real power. His principal enemy at the Court of Berlin was the Empress Frederick. She was very family-minded and had the interest of her little cousins very much at heart: after an audience with her which had been difficult to fit in, and to which he had gone feeling well disposed towards her, the Chancellor was heard to mutter: "The stupid old fool, all she wanted to talk to me about

was her Lippe and Strelitz cousins." Her ideas, which she inherited from her father, were the subject of ironic comment, and
the "Essay on the Duties of a Constitutional Sovereign," which
she wrote on her honeymoon, aroused considerable mirth in Berlin. Though she was in many ways a remarkable woman, her taste
for perfection was to provoke ridicule. Her constant smile appeared
sublime to those who saw only her virtues and her unhappiness,
but mechanical to those who saw her every day. Misunderstood,
she spent her days writing letters.

Copenhagen was for some time the centre of anti-Prussianism.
But there was another, though less international, kernel of hostility
at Rumpenheim, the Landgrave of Hesse's castle, which buzzed
like an angry beehive. The Hesses and their Württemberg and
Danish and English cousins would forgather every second year in
this simple and uncomfortable building. "The influence of Rumpenheim again!" Queen Victoria would remark indignantly whenever
one of her daughters complained about Berlin. Neu-Strelitz, where
cousin Augusta lived, was also a focus for anti-Bismarckian sentiment. These junior courts lacked the importance and the panache
to attract the Prince of Wales, but he listened eagerly to the
rumours that emanated from them, wrote constantly to his sisters,
and, like all other royalty, believed hopefully that the Emperor
Frederick would one day dismiss Bismarck. Later on, other little
courts were to have their influence on the Kaiser, greatly to the
annoyance of official German circles. William II found the atmosphere at Princess Daisy of Pless's or the Viennese life of the
Fürstenbergs at Donaueschingen more to his taste.

Greece, which was prudently anti-Prussian, served as an excellent resort for Russian and English royalty; the King and Queen
were so gay and had so much spirit! Their uncomfortable palace
was never without its quota of grand duchesses or of Victoria's
grandchildren. These august relations did much for a country that
was still of very little account and very poverty-stricken.

Queen Victoria was delighted to see Germany strong, and only
the Hohenzollerns—or so at least her daughter told her—could
keep it so. The Prince of Wales would visit Berlin only if he could
not avoid it. His dissipated life did not find favour with the mili-

tary puritanism of the Prussian Court, while the interminable ceremonies, the unending blaring of martial music, and the balls
punctuated with clicking heels, were particularly distasteful to him;
the Empress Augusta, a bluestocking who dressed like an ageing
cocotte, seemed to him ridiculous. Berlin, during the 'eighties,
was undergoing a profound change; from a residential town it was
becoming a fashionable capital; thus the Germany of Wagner was
succeeding to that of Mendelssohn. William II was intoxicated by
the prodigious energy of his youthful empire.

When on the Continental stage, the Prince of Wales would never
miss an opportunity of assisting the victims of Bismarck's machinations or of getting one up on his nephew, even if it meant becoming
involved in so small a question as that of the Luxemburg succession. In 1884 he went to see Duke Adolf of Nassau, to whom
would revert, on the death of the King of Holland, the Grand
Duchy of Luxemburg, in which the Salic law prevailed; for the
King of Holland had only a daughter. Although Lord Granville
advised the Prince not to get involved in this affair, he nonetheless
encouraged the Duke to lay claim to Luxemburg, which was
situated outside the Reich; in 1890 the King of Holland died and
the British protégé became the Grand Duke of Luxemburg, thus
rising in the royal hierarchy without owing anything to the
Emperor. Ever afterwards he was to feel immensely grateful to
the Prince of Wales. But in 1905 his son succeeded him and had
the Salic law, to which the Nassaus owed their throne, suppressed
in order to permit the succession of his eldest daughter. King
Edward was highly amused, but the Kaiser was piqued.

St. Petersburg, with its marshy foundations and unpredictable
reactions, scarcely inspired confidence in the diplomats posted
there, while those in Berlin were always ready for something unpleasant to happen. Despite the neo-classical décor and the use
of French, one suspects that the Russians were only playing at
being Europeans. The imperial family was loved in a servile fashion; the Court, magnificent as long as Princess Bariatinski was
in charge of things, was later to become a bit chaotic. Russia was
the only Empire that England had to fear; to the Queen she was
an abhorrence. The Prince, who loved doing things in the grand

style, managed on each of his visits to mitigate somewhat the unfortunate impression created by his mother's ambassadors.

Everything went so well on their first visit to Russia, in 1866
(wolf hunt, troika races, and fabulous presents), that the young
Prince declared that the misunderstandings of the Crimean War
had been scattered to the winds. In 1873 he pushed his brother,
the Duke of Edinburgh, into a marriage with the Tsar's only
daughter. The English public received the news coldly. *Punch*
depicted the Tsars as ridiculous and rapacious monsters, and the
union did nothing to ameliorate Anglo-Russian relations, particularly stretched as they were at that time over Afghanistan.
The house of Hesse, which was related to both families, had arranged the match. Queen Victoria, despite her hostility to Russia,
was flattered by it; like Maria Theresa, she would have children
in every capital. The Duke of Edinburgh had his brother's defects
but very few of his qualities. One memoir writer, anonymous and
American it is true, recounts that if the younger brother was staying in Paris at the same time as the Prince and Princess of Wales,
he would charge five louis to any Americans or Englishmen who
wished to be presented to the Prince, and fifty for a lunch party.
The Grand Duchess Marie, an emperor's daughter, would never
yield precedence to the Princess of Wales, with the result that there
were scenes and interminable quarrels. Victoria had to pack the
Edinburghs off to Malta in order to get rid of them. They were
to have three children, one of whom became Queen Marie of
Rumania. The wedding took place in January 1874, and the Tsar
took the opportunity of offering the Prince the colonelcy of a regiment: "Ridiculous!" wrote the Queen, "an Englishman has no
business to be in a foreign army, especially when we cannot
reciprocate." The Prince was upset, like a small child that has had
a toy taken away from it. But the Tsar was insistent, so that the
Queen had to give in; as she pointed out to her Government:
"These honours are really dust in our eyes, we must not relax our
guard." She listened with a merely distracted air to the good
reports with which her son returned from Russia. Disraeli encouraged her in this distrust; he acted as an antidote to Russian

flattery, and the Prince of Wales found himself having to view the situation rather differently.

Balkan risings followed by terrible repression, the assassination of a sultan, a few massacres of Christians—this was more than enough to make Russia intervene in the Near East. Disraeli's Government assured the public that the name of the Sublime Porte had been blackened without cause. Gladstone got on his high horse. Was England now to become the accomplice of Turkish assassins? The Grand Old Man excelled himself, but his eloquence had little effect on the Prince. Shuvalov, the Russian Ambassador, for all that he disapproved of Gladstone, was not taken in. "Do not trust the Prince, he is at heart a Turkophile," he wrote to Gorchakov.

On April 24, 1877, Russia declared war on Turkey. The Queen and her son both violently condemned Lord Derby's refusal to have anything to do with it. England would never allow the Russians into Constantinople, the Government should make this quite clear to Russia. In January 1878 the Government promised the Turks assistance, and the British fleet left Malta for the Dardanelles. The Prince was now an ardent warmonger and demanded to be sent to the front so that he could distinguish himself. The Princess, however, managed to calm him down. She herself was Russophile and kept her sister the Empress in touch with opinion at Windsor. But before the English could get themselves involved in a second Crimean War, the Turks had been beaten, and the Treaty of Santo Stefano was signed in March 1878. The Prince had not had time to become a hero. He had wanted this war with all the ardour of a young man (thirty-six), but the peace gave him the opportunity to prove his diplomatic skill; for the first time his advice was to be followed, and people were to be glad that it had been.

He had met Bismarck at Berlin early in 1878, and had been conquered by the Chancellor's expansive affability, despite the aura of stale tobacco smoke. Germany, the latter had confided to him, was anxious—as was Austria—over the influence that Russia was gaining in the Balkans; and England would need to have the sympathies of the Reich if she were to go to the assistance of the Turks. Once the smoke had cleared, the Prince regarded this proposal coolly, sensing a trap; nor was he wrong, for that same day Bismarck reported the entire conversation to Gorchakov. When the powers decided to summon the Congress of Berlin to settle the Eastern Question, the Prince, who fully appreciated that there was only one English statesman who was a match for Bismarck, wrote to his mother:

> I beg you to ask Lord Beaconsfield to go to Berlin. It is of vital importance for the country and for our dignity that we should be masters of the situation there.

The Queen replied:

> Berlin is much too far away; Lord Beaconsfield is seventy-two years old, and is very far from being strong. You know well that both I and the nation attach an immense price to his health.

The Prince insisted that the Prime Minister should accept this mission, a role worthy of Talleyrand or Metternich, and got his way.

His broken body reeking with perfume, and still very much alive despite the approach of death, the old actor made his farewell appearance on a stage even more important than that of Westminster; but he had to face a hostile public in which the Russians and the Germans were in the majority. The contempt which Gorchakov and Bismarck felt for this Jew contributed greatly to his success.

Throughout the Congress, Disraeli kept the Prince informed as to the course of the negotiations:

> Dining with Bismarck, I had to smoke a great deal, but that enabled me to win a few points.

The Prince insisted that the King of Greece, his brother-in-law, should have some of the Turkish spoils. Disraeli replied:

> I managed to do something for Greece yesterday, it wasn't easy. I was thinking of Marlborough House at the time.

Then he added:

> With the Sultan's consent, we will occupy Cyprus. It is the key to
> Asia and to Egypt. Malta is not close enough.

Thanks to Disraeli, Russia was kept out of the Mediterranean,
Turkey was allowed to continue to oppress a large part of the
Balkans, while holding Austria in check, and England was enabled
to consolidate her position in the East. The participants at the
Congress of Berlin—other than the English, of course—returned
from it so dissatisfied that the slightest incident could have undone
all the good work. The diplomats, however, were to succeed in
retaining the precarious balance for thirty years, until Bosnia was
annexed by Austria, in fact. A few months after the Congress, the
German Ambassador suggested an Anglo-German *entente* to
Disraeli, but the Prime Minister explained to him that the Queen
had such strong feelings about Bismarck, and that the Prince was
so Francophile, that there was no point in such negotiations. If
Disraeli had approved of this project, he would have gracefully
overcome the objections from Windsor, but they came in useful
in sustaining his policy of isolation.

In March 1881 Edward found it necessary to drop his bellicose
ardour. With only his tact to rely on, he represented England,
taking with him the insignia of the Garter destined for the new
Tsar, at Alexander II's funeral, after the Emperor had been killed
by a bomb. The Prince and the Princess of Wales arrived—the
train guarded by soldiers with fixed bayonets—in a Court terrified, suspicious, and bursting with detectives. Alexander III and
Marie had gone to ground in a minor palace and took their exercise
in a courtyard which seemed to the Prince "worthy of a London
slum." The investiture of the Garter took place in a little salon,
between two of the interminable ceremonies that went on around
the corpse day and night. The few words which the Prince spoke
were, according to the English Ambassador, "in the best taste
and pronounced gracefully," and once again the new Tsar's
brother-in-law left Russia convinced that he had charmed everybody. But very soon it became clear that Alexander III was no

more a lover of England than his father had been. An autocrat and a Panslavist, he despised democratic institutions and had aspirations of consolidating his Empire in Siberia at India's expense.

Only a few months passed before the Prince was off again, this time to Berlin, for the wedding of his nephew William. It was at this point that the uncle suddenly became acutely aware of the young man, the Queen's favourite grandchild. Up till now he had accorded him only a benevolent indifference, but the future English King found himself shocked by the future Emperor's megalomania and sense of the theatrical.

All these years of official visits and diplomatic congratulations may appear vain and empty if one sees only the elegant trappings and the ephemeral consequences, but they did enable Edward VII to mount the throne with a knowledge of Europe which that of his Ministers and even of his ambassadors was very far from approaching. His habit of personal contact with heads of state often embarrassed the chancelleries, and alarmed the public, both in England and in Germany, but it did have a beneficial effect; not that the projects worked out during these meetings had any great significance but they inspired those taking part with a horror of rupture. This royal policy, active but superficial, lent to the Crown a prestige which it had not known for centuries.

CHAPTER SIX

The World of Proust

FROM THE TIME of his first visit, when still a child, to the Tuileries, the Prince of Wales, as we have seen, had become a convinced Francophile. Napoleon and Eugénie, who were somewhat isolated among the older monarchies, paid so much attention to him, when he returned to see them, that he was completely conquered; he was to be invited often to Fontainebleau and Compiègne.

After the ex-Emperor and his wife had been driven into exile as a result of the revolution of September 4, 1870, the English royal family still treated then with real affection. Till the end of her reign the Queen insisted on giving precedence to the Empress when she dined at Windsor, saying to her in French: "Go ahead, my dear sister." The Courts of Windsor and of the Tuileries were as different from each other as an oratorio from a comic opera. The Empress, a woman of the world rather than a sovereign, was adept at putting the Prince at his ease; and Princess Matilda, Napoleon III's cousin, knew exactly how to talk to young men. With such young ladies as the Princess of Metternich, who was permitted every audacity by her birth, and Madame de Persigny, who had a disordered mind, the atmosphere was free and easy. The gallant Galliffet*—a lively wit who was adored by the women and whose ambition was disguised by his frivolity, was an object of admiration to the still timid young man.

* An aristocrat of very ancient lineage, Galliffet was a well-known general during the Second Empire and a Minister during the Third Republic.

The Prince found this brilliant company far more amusing than the starchy Orléans, whom he visited from time to time at Twickenham and whom he also met at Strawberry Hill, which belonged to Lady Waldegrave. "The Aumales invited themselves again and stayed for two hours," she was sometimes heard to complain. As one of the Orléans was to write to one of the Bonapartes: "I belong to a family in which all the men are brave and all the ladies chaste." The Count of Paris, with his blond beard and his studied manners, however, looked rather like a German. "You cannot thrust friendship down somebody's throat," the Prince once said to his mother when she reproached him for his coldness towards the Pretender. But despite this, the Prince's French friends were Orléanist, with the exception of the Pourtalès, and after 1870 this influenced his policy.

Before 1870 he asked scarcely anything but to be allowed to meet the ladies of Paris. The Marquis de Massa, who wrote the "Mirliton" revues, Gramant-Caderousse, and the younger members of the Jockey Club had something of the eccentricity of the dandies of the preceding generation who had founded the club; after the war this institution was to become the final bastion of the upper crust. Like the Baron de Gondremark in *La Vie Parisienne*, the Prince of Wales would arrive singing: "I am going to plunge in, plunge in, plunge in." He would put up at the Hotel Bristol in the Place Vendôme; sometimes his brother the Duke of Edinburgh would accompany him. Lord Lawrence, the Ambassador from 1867 to 1880, a reserved and solitary individual, must have dreaded the arrival of these pleasure-bent young men. The heir was to be seen at Anna Deslions' and La Paíva's salons, and in Hortense Schneider's box. This is how Zola describes the visit of the "*prince d'Ecosse*" to Nana at the Variétés Theatre:

A murmur ran through the crowd: "The Prince! The Prince!" All eyes were turned towards the little door of the room. Nothing as yet could be seen but Bordenave's round back and butcher's neck, as he doubled up and swelled again in a series of obsequious bows. Then the Prince appeared, large and strong, with his blond beard, his complexion the unmistakeable red of the complete *bon viveur*, his square frame standing out beneath the irreproachable cut of

Sarah Bernhardt.

his frock coat. Behind him, Count Muffat and the Marquis de Chouard. That corner of the theatre was dark, and the group became lost in the shadows. When talking to the son of a Queen, the heir to a throne, Bordenave adopted the voice of a ring-master, trembling with false emotion. He kept repeating: "His Highness overwhelms me," as he bowed over and over again. "The theatre is quite small, we do the best we can . . . now if his Highness would deign to follow me . . . if His Highness would be kind enough to enter . . ."

A woman's scream was heard, and Nana could be seen, naked to the waist, dashing for safety behind a screen, while her dresser who had been drying her was left with the towel in mid-air.

Only his Highness, the Count, and the Marquis were left in Nana's dressing-room. Bordenave had gone off with Barillot, advising him that it would be better not to knock on Madame's door without giving her advance warning.

"Gentlemen, you will excuse me?" said Nana, who was working on her arms and body with particular care for the nude scene in Act Three.

The Prince sat down on the divan with the Marquis de Chouard. Count Muffat alone remained standing.

"Then it's settled," said the Prince, quite relaxed on the divan, "that you will come to London next year, and we will give you such a good time that you will never come back to France . . . You see, my dear Count, you do not take enough care of your beautiful ladies. We are going to have them all."*

The defeat of 1870 proved the Prince's faithfulness to France. With the superficial, the strongest ties are those that concern their pleasures. It is only those whom we have failed to amuse that are ungrateful. From the outset of the war Marlborough House and Windsor adopted opposite attitudes. The Queen was proud to think of her relatives, the Prussians and the Hesses, charging at the head of their Uhlans to strike down the pride of a frivolous and atheistic nation. She was piqued when she learnt that her son had suggested to Count Apponyi a Franco-Austrian alliance to crush

* Curiously enough, at the very same time that the Prince's visit to Nana's dressing room was being described by Zola, he also figured in one of the stories that Mallarmé wrote for his own fashionable review. Two pages of this magazine were filled with a precious and untranslatable account of his visit to Dampierre followed by a drive in a phaeton with the Duchess of Luynes. It is hardly surprising that, filled as it was with this sort of in-group joke, this publication did not have a very long life.

Prussia. Angry and pained letters arrived from Berlin. Lord Granville had to deny all knowledge of the Prince's proposals, and Gladstone advised Edward to hold his tongue. But he was not discouraged; on the eve of Sedan he asked his mother to write to the Emperor and the King of Prussia, and for permission to act as mediator. After the revolution of September 4, he wrote to the Empress:

> As the Princess and I thought that a residence close to London might be agreeable to you, I am presuming to offer your Majesty our country house at Chiswick, which would be entirely at the disposal of your Majesty, and we would be very happy if you would accept it.

Victoria was annoyed by the desperate resistance put up by the French. As she said to her son, "A powerful Germany cannot cause England any anxiety, but quite the opposite." She had to insist on the Prince and Princess of Wales receiving the Crown Prince and his wife when they came to London soon after the Peace of Frankfurt.

Galliffet had been taken prisoner; he wrote to his friend and asked him to arrange for him to be exchanged for a German of equal rank, since he blushed "to be between four walls while his compatriots were being killed." The Prince alerted the Foreign Office, wrote to Berlin without result, and kept in constant touch with Galliffet through the Duchess of Manchester ("my dear Duchess" had been born in Hanover). The armistice freed that brilliant officer in time to enable him to crush the Commune. The Powers were a little put out by France's rapid recovery after Sedan and the revolution. Despite the compassion inspired by the ageing Thiers as he turned to the different capitals for help, it was thought that he recovered his self-confidence a little too rapidly. With MacMahon, and his republic of dukes, things seemed to be ready for a return to the old order. The new Ministers wished to create a proud and prosperous France, self-reliant and respected. The great families who had sulked during the Empire and under Louis Philippe now had their opportunity. The clubs became annexes of the Assembly, which was all in the best traditions of the aristocratic English style of parliamentary government.

Profiting from the absence of the Comte de Chambord, the Orléans family assumed the airs of dauphins. Lady Waldegrave, who represented their interests in London, asserted that the Duc d'Aumale would succeed Thiers as president of the Republic. She was already earmarking the Paris Embassy for her husband. The aristocracy, whose more prominent members obtained jobs as Ministers and ambassadors, had their heyday during the decade between 1875 and 1885. Old families recovered an importance that they had not known since the days of Charles X. The Faubourg St. Germain replaced the Tuileries, and their town houses, or those which they still owned, were opened for the most fabulous receptions. For the previous forty years they had had nothing to do but economize and reflect.

French Society greeted the future King of England with great respect, although its more conservative and pious members still found him slightly rakish. One day a member of the old aristocracy decided to teach him a lesson. While staying at a château he met the Marquise d'Harcourt (who died at the age of a hundred in 1955), and ardently paid court to her. He appeared to be having some success, for she said to him, "I will put a rose on the latch of my bedroom door so you will know which it is." Hardly were all the guests in bed than the seducer slipped down the corridor and, opening the door which bore the rose, found the ugliest kitchenmaid in the house in the Marquise's bed.

At the invitation of the Duc de Bisaccia, who had been an extravagant ambassador in London, the Prince did a tour of the châteaux in 1874. The Republican press was upset and the Foreign Office worried. He went first to the Duc de Bisaccia's place at Esclimont, and then to Serrant to stay with the La Tremoilles. Visits to several other famous homes followed. Finally he went to Chantilly to shoot with the Duc d'Aumale. From this time dates the friendship with which the Prince honoured the ducal families that Proust was later to celebrate as the "Guermantes." Whether they were in real life the La Rochefoucaulds, the Noailles, or even the Greffulhes makes very little difference.

The Guermantes had a style that was part upper crust, part sophisticated boulevardier—all plays on words and so unaffected that it even delighted in stupidity. This gaiety, a relic of the Second Empire, gave Oriane de Guermantes such influence over the Prince that he was soon eating out of her hand; it characterized Edward's three great women friends of this period.

The Comtesse Edmond de Pourtalès, whose beauty, as portrayed by Carolus Duran, remained unimpaired for thirty years, entertained in a vast town house at 7 Rue Tronchet, whose gilt-ceilinged salons and courtyards full of antique statues can still be seen today. Her Protestant faith, and her connections with Swiss and German relatives, gave her a European character. She was very closely attached to the Empress Eugénie and carried on a correspondence with the Empress Augusta and Princess Metternich. A great lady of fashion, she sparkled within her own circle, attracting the most brilliant company around her; when racing or at an embassy reception she was always surrounded by men of the utmost distinction. She remained outside the intrigues of the Guermantes, whether Orléanist or legitimate, and was a reliable friend to the Prince. He came across her again in Cannes, where she was at home to all royalty, in the villa Saint-Prix. After the loss of Alsace, which was her home province, the Prince, in a charming gesture, offered her a bracelet on which there were three pearls in the form of tears.

The Princesse de Sagan, the daughter of Seillière, the rich financier, lived apart from her husband as a result of an unfortunate quarrel over money. The Prince was Talleyrand's great-nephew and he was considered the most elegant of the clubmen. The artist Caran d'Ache has immortalized his beautiful white horses, his black-ribboned monocle, and his sponge-bag trousers. His wife, whose beauty was a little cold and whose elegance was a little dry, was an inseparable friend of the Marquise de Galliffet. The latter, on the other hand, was all ringlets and flounces and was exaggeratedly feminine. The Princess's town house was on the corner of the Rue de Grenelle and the Esplanade des Invalides. Here she gave the finest balls in Paris, during which she would receive the Prince of Wales at the foot of a staircase flanked with lackeys, her dress sweeping the marble flags as she made a deep curtsy. Between pyramids of flowers, the guests in the gallery

would lean forward as in a fresco by Tiepolo, so as to miss nothing of the scene, admiring, as they did so, the tact with which
their hostess had dressed so as to match the Princess of Wales:
a diamond choker and a very simply cut dress embroidered with
jet.

Madame Standish resembled the Princess of Wales even more
than did Madame de Sagan and imitated everything she did, but
with this difference: she had a terrifyingly sharp tongue. She had
married an American whose mother had been a Noailles, and
was determined that no one should forget her ancestry; people
tended to talk of "Mrs. Standish, née des Cars." Of modest wealth,
she did not entertain on a large scale, but her intimate friends composed the first international smart set. She stayed every year for
some time at Sandringham. Of these three women, Mélanie de
Pourtalès was the most beautiful and the most intelligent.

Another of the Prince's friends was the Baronne Alphonse de
Rothschild, who gave sumptuous receptions in her mansion in the
Faubourg St. Honoré. So completely had all trace of her former
beauty disappeared when Proust's Bloch met her staying with Madame de Villeparisis in about 1895, and didn't quite catch her
name, that he took her for a slightly mad old Englishwoman. When
he later realized to whom he had been introduced, he exclaimed,
"If only I had known," a remark that delighted the writer. Other
friends to whom the Prince was closely attached were the Breteuils, the Jaucourts, and the Ganays. He would go racing with
them and dine with them at restaurants, something that seemed
rather daring to the more old-fashioned members of the Faubourg. Among the Prince's less intimate friends, or those whose
friendship was more episodic, were Madame Legrand, née Fournès,
the original of Madame Leroy, to whom Proust attributed no other
virtue than chic (Madame Leroy was the despair of the Marquise
de Villeparisis as she never accepted her invitations); Madame
Howland, of whom the Duchesse de Guermantes said, "All the
men used to call on her"; and an occasional member of the upper-
bourgeoisie such as Madame Hochon or the beautiful Madame
d'Hervey de St. Denis, who had inherited a very large fortune
from her father, a certain Mr. Ward, once the favourite of the

last Prince of Parma. The Prince of Wales could also be met at
the little tea parties given by Princesse d'Arenberg and her sister,
the Marquise de l'Aigle. Gyp's first novels, *Professional Lover* and
Monsieur Fred, are possibly a little more accurate than Proust's in
depicting the atmosphere of the fashionable world in the early
years of the Third Republic.

As for the men, all those with whom the Prince made friends
can be seen in James Tissot's picture, "*Le Cercle de la Rue
Royale*," painted in 1866. They include the Marquis and the
Comte de Ganay; Prince Edmond de Polignac, who was vague
and musical; the Marquis du Lau, of whom the Prince was particularly fond and who wrote to him some very far-seeing letters
on French political divisions; Baron Hottinguer; and, standing in
the doorway, Swann, or rather Charles Haas, thanks to whom
Edward VII obtained in Proust's work a place comparable to
that of Napoleon in Balzac's *Comédie Humaine*. We catch only
a glimpse of Edward in person, but he is thought about at length.
He appears, once, crossing a salon, accompanied by the Duc de
Guermantes, who acknowledges the narrator and receives a low
bow in return. Swann appears from the very first pages as "one of
the most pampered members of high society in the Faubourg St.
Germain, a personal friend of the Count of Paris and of the Prince
of Wales." When the Verdurins were astonished to hear that he
had been invited to the Elysée, he was too well brought up to tell
them what friendship had earned him this invitation from the
President. Odette's naïve snobbery, when she wanted an invitation to the private view of an exhibition, he found touching and
"no more ridiculous than the pleasure he had once had when
lunching with the Prince of Wales." At the start of *A la Recherche
du Temps Perdu* all Swann's worldly glory is behind him; like
the setting sun it touches him with its rays in the same way that
the Hulot family still basks in the glory of the Empire. Though
we may look in vain for a single model for Oriane de Guermantes,
the Duke was almost certainly Count Greffulhe. A large man with
a red beard, he was also one of the Prince's friends; he gave
lavish shooting parties at Boisboudran and receptions in his town
house in the Rue d'Astorg and had once been the lover of all the

prettiest women in Paris. Monseigneur was not so well acquainted with the Princesse de Guermantes as he was with Oriane; he would not have dared to introduce the Baron de Hirsch to her. As a child Proust had devoured the gossip columns in *Le Gaulois*, in which he had found detailed descriptions of the parties given in the Prince of Wales's honour, and of the guests' dresses; later he was to meet some of his friends. Oriane, for instance, tells Gilberte when she asks her about her father's friends that the Marquis du Lau

> was a typical Périgord gentleman, with all the charm and fine manners of that province. Once, when the King of England was staying at Guermantes, there was a tea party after a shoot. Du Lau was in the habit of changing out of his boots and putting on thick woolly slippers at that time of day. The fact that King Edward and all the grand dukes were there didn't worry him in the slightest. He came back into the large salon at Guermantes with his woolly slippers on. The Marquis du Lau d'Allemans saw no reason why he should alter his habits for the King of England.

Ever since the Restoration, the fashionable world had been Anglomane, and the *demi-monde* had followed suit; towards 1880 the more fashionable *cocottes*, such as Laure Heyman and Liane de Pougy, began to adopt a slight accent and copied the Princess of Wales's appearance, even to her fringe and the shape of her face, that face which the young painter Helleu described as "without expression, a silver veneer, a Japanese double peony"; sports ending with the letters "ing," like skating or even *footing*, began to come in; the *demi-mondaines* of the Second Empire had not gone in for that sort of thing. Odette's conversation is studded with English words. This is Abel Hermant's account of the agitated preparations made by a leading *demi-mondaine* when giving a luncheon party for the Prince:

> "The form should be, it seems to me," said a clubman who had been consulted, "as follows: you receive the Prince alone in the salon, and since his incognito is absolute, there should be no question of lunch being announced with the words: *Son Altesse Royale est servi*. Your head butler will approach you and whisper two words

in your ear; you will hesitate for a moment and then bend towards your august visitor and ask him in a low voice for his orders, which you will transmit to the butler. If he says 'Yes' the butler will go out walking backwards, and say: *'Cinq couverts:'*—But if the Prince says 'No'? He will of course not be able to do so if the forms are so discreetly observed. Then the doors will open, and the butler and the footmen will line the way, but without too much ceremony. An under-butler will present himself. He will take his time, draw a deep breath as though about to announce: *'Son Altesse Royale est servi,'* but will simply say: 'Madame'; you will offer your arm to the august guest and everyone will go to the table without further ceremony."

We can imagine the Prince disembarking at Calais on a winter's day in the 'eighties; clad in a tweed Ulster, he would change into a sable pelisse given to him by his Russian sister-in-law when the train arrived. An equerry and two valets would be his only companions: the Ambassador would meet him at the station with his personal brougham, drive him to the Hotel Bristol, and put him in the picture on the political situation. A little later an attaché, usually Reggie Lister, would come and brief him on the latest gossip. Paris, after the 1870 Revolution, was the only capital in which the fashionable and political worlds were totally separate. The Prince's close friends would now come to greet him; he would meet them again at lunch with Madame de Pourtalès or with Alphonse de Rothschild. He would go himself to call upon Queen Isabella in the Palais de Castille in Avenue Hoche and Princess Matilda in Rue de Courcelles, and sometimes he would call on the Empress Eugénie at the Hotel Continentale. If time permitted he would go to the races in the afternoon, chat with the ladies in their fur toques around the braziers, and with one or other of these return to have tea in a little hotel in Rue Fortuny or in Rue La-Pérouse. Every evening he would go to the theatre to see his favourite actresses, the divine Sarah, Jane Hading, and Granier, and then on to the Epatant for a game of baccarat. Sometimes the evening would end very late after a visit to a new establishment in Rue Chabanais to which he would give, by dint of going there often, a world-wide fame. He also enjoyed the tours which the

Prefecture of Police arranged for Grand Dukes who wanted to see the seamy side of life and which were more or less authentic. He was also to be seen at the Chat Noir, appreciating the work of Maurice Donnay and the shadowy landscapes of Caran d'Ache. Rudolph Salis, the proprietor of this night-club, conducted him respectfully to a box one evening, relieved him of his coat, and then inquired with an air of grief as he bowed: "And your dear mama?"

If he came over in the spring he would not fail to visit the Salon, where there would be more flesh on view and greater panache than was to be found at the Royal Academy. The Duchesse de Guermantes once asked him to lunch to meet Detaille, from whom he ordered an equestrian portrait of himself and his brother the Duke of Connaught at the Aldershot Review. His admiration for the accuracy with which the painter depicted the smallest button on his uniform was similar to the enjoyment he obtained from the way in which Flameng or Gervex reproduced the silkiness of flesh. The news of the Prince's visit would scarcely be out before the Ledas of the Plaine Monceau* would be all readiness to receive their benevolent visitor from Olympus. Afterwards he would always send an equerry round to them with some small jewel which, in consequence of its origin, would glitter more brilliantly than the diamonds of less illustrious admirers, and which was always worn on its own. They would all be burning to ask him the secret of the Princess's everlasting beauty, whether she put curlers in her hair, and the address of her corset maker, but these were the only familiarities which he did not encourage.

The following decade, however, saw a very different pattern. The 'nineties had very little respect for anything, and those crowned heads whose heirs had behaved rather stupidly found themselves in trouble. In Abel Hermant's trilogy, *La Carrière*, *Le Char de l'Etat*, and *Le Sceptre*, good society is clearly losing its considerateness, and even in bad society the same thing is happening. Despite the setting, which owes more to Vienna than to London, Prince Paul —the hero of the trilogy—has much in common with the Prince

---

* The Plaine Monceau is a part of Paris near the Parc Monceau in the 9th Arrondissement.

of Wales. He dallies on the Côte d'Azur and the boulevards, a prey to avaricious little women, unknown ingénues, and dangerous adventuresses.

Hermant was a very close friend of Prince Poniatowski and was kept informed by him of the Prince's conquests and failures. Poniatowski, it was said, was the real father of the mystery girl in Dieppe, Olga Alberta. In 1891 *La Vie Parisienne* savagely attacked the most Parisian man in England. It published a skit in which the members of a club were rehearsing their annual Christmas pantomime. "We must be careful," says one of them. "I hear that Monseigneur is going to come."

"We shall have to cut out everything that might be offensive to Monseigneur," exclaim the members immediately and a couplet on the ghillie John Brown is removed, and then another on whisky, a scene on debts and gambling, and a tirade against the Baron de Hirsch; in fact everything funny is taken out of the revue.

It was at this time that Proust's Prince Von made his famous remark at Madame de Villeparisis's about the future King: "If he were a private individual, he would have been kicked out of all his clubs."

But Proust's speaker is, of course, German.

"The end of the notables," to use Daniel Halévy's phrase, began in 1876, when MacMahon replaced Jules Simon with the Duc de Broglie in the Cabinet. The elections which followed brought to power the petty bourgeoisie, to whom English chic meant nothing. The aristocrats were out; Jewish intellectuals and Protestant engineers were in; doctors and lawyers from the provinces now lorded it with their ladies. Those who were not intimidated by their sumptuous official residences displayed the manners which they had learned in the *brasseries* of the Latin Quarter; conversation gave way to an eloquence borrowed from Gambetta's phrase about Hugo: "Now we behold arising in this man the glorious dawn of righteousness." They had grand ideas but narrow minds. Most of them were patriots, but this virtue, which sometimes raised them above the level of the Palais Bourbon, only made them more dangerous. They knew nothing of other countries, and they were haunted by the idea of *revanche*. Some of them had had outstanding university careers but they lacked knowledge of the world and were quite out of touch with the old and tried methods of Court diplomacy. Several years were to pass before Hanotaux or Delcassé was to count for something in Europe.*

The Court of St. James's did not appreciate this régime. Monsieur Challemel-Lacour, who had been preceded by a Harcourt and a La Rochefoucauld, was sent to London as Ambassador by the Republic. He was described to the Prince by his friends as "a *communard*, a Red like that dreadful Clemenceau." The Prince asked his mother to decline such a choice, but the Queen, who never saw the ambassadors, accepted him. The alleged *communard* was, however, succeeded by W. Warrington, whose stay in London lasted from 1883 to 1893. He had rowed in the Cambridge Boat and was more English than the English. His wife was very much appreciated in Society. Having, as Minister for Foreign Affairs, represented France at the Congress of Berlin, he could state with a clear conscience that "France has returned from Berlin with clean hands," although of course she did obtain a few promises relative to Tunisia. The Foreign Office appreciated his good manners, which were very different from those in use in the republican French capital.

The English, ever since the time of Louis Philippe, had looked down from some height on the French official classes, and the Prince shared these prejudices. He did not enjoy meeting the aged Thiers and his wife when he encountered them at Dieppe in 1873, and although he had often been seen in the Elysée during MacMahon's time and had indeed inaugurated the 1878 Exhibition with him, things were different under Grévy: "Keep us a place in your stand," said Edward to the Prince de Sagan as he set off for the races. "I don't want the Princess to be seen with that cook." It was said that Madame Grévy had indeed exercised this profession, although it would seem that she had forgotten it, as the menus at the Elysée were celebrated for their frugality. The Marquis du Lau and General de Galliffet advised the Prince not

---

* Hanotaux and Delcassé both held the position of French Foreign Minister, the former strongly advocating a Russian alliance, which the latter also supported, if not so strongly.

to copy his friends and laugh at them. France had become republican and he would have to accept its choice and adapt himself
to its political personnel, who were likely to be in office for some
time.

The same warning came from England. Sir Charles Dilke, one
of the republicans of 1870, advised the Prince that he ought to
meet Gambetta. He fell for this audacious idea, and Gambetta
for his part was delighted to meet the future King of England.
The orator believed his popularity to be such that he could indulge
in the luxury of an entirely personal policy. Had he not gone so far
as to suggest, through an intermediary, an interview with Bismarck? The Chancellor refused, though not without compromising
the other's position in parliament. Gambetta was of a calibre far
superior to that of his colleagues. Once those who have listened
to them have gone, most of these great men leave behind them no
more than the vague prestige enjoyed by the great actresses of the
past. Their speeches become unreadable, and their ideas, thought
up on the spur of the moment for their popular appeal, appear in-
consistent. Gambetta was intoxicated by his own words and by the
adulation he received and did not hide his contempt for the
Chamber of Deputies, although he was to pay for this. One cannot
imagine a greater contrast than that between the Prince, who lacked
imagination and whose thinking was narrow but who was well
informed and sure of himself, and this demagogue who sought in
the rest of Europe support against the intrigues of his own parliament. His appearance must have given his Highness the impression
that he had wandered by chance into the Cyclops' cave. With his
long hair and his beard and general air of disreputableness, his
livid complexion, his bad teeth, and his clothes disordered by the
vehemence of his speeches in parliament, he was indeed of the
same race as Danton and Mirabeau.

The meeting took place on October 30, 1882, with Sir Charles
Dilke in attendance, at the Moulin Rouge Restaurant in the
Chaussée d'Antin. Gambetta, whose famous "Grand Ministry"
hadn't lasted for more than sixty days, now wished to retake the
offensive. Odd governments succeeded each other but he alone felt
that he could speak in the name of France. Like Richelieu, he

looked for support abroad. We have no evidence of how this first
interview went off, but it must have been a success since a few
days later the Prince dined alone with Gambetta at the Café
Anglais. Galliffet happened to be there, possibly by chance, and
the Prince invited him to his table. The general noticed that the
conversation was animated and cordial. At one point the Prince
expressed his regret that the French aristocracy no longer took a
part in government. "The nobles are not important any more; the
Republic knows only one aristocracy, that of merit," was the reply.

"You are a real republican, Monsieur Gambetta."

"And you, Monseigneur, are, of course, a royalist. I wouldn't
be surprised!"

Oriane de Guermantes would have found this meeting *très sport*,
intelligente vraiment. It was during the same visit that the actress
Judic said to the Prince, "Monseigneur ought to come and live
over here and popularize the idea of a monarchy."

"No, no! You are much too hasty with your kings," replied Edward.

With a great many *ifs*, the conversations between Gambetta
and the Prince ought have been of some consequence: if Queen
Victoria had died and if Gambetta had lived, the *Entente Cordiale*
could perhaps have been advanced by twenty years. France, still
licking the wounds of her defeat, and no more satisfied than
England with her isolation, was ready for friendship. But it was
not to be, for in the decade which followed this meeting, Anglo-
French relations were to deteriorate and almost reach the point
of war over Fashoda.

Egypt was the first cause of friction; the English blamed the
French fleet for having left them in the lurch at the siege of
Alexandria, and the French believed themselves to have been
wronged over the Suez Canal shares which the Khedive had sold
to Queen Victoria. Boulanger's chauvinism exploited this feeling.
To Galliffet, this sentimentalist, this politico, was anathema, and
he turned Marlborough House against him. He wrote:

> The first year of the Boulangerie: the hero of the day, Monseigneur,
> is no more handsome than he was a month ago, nor more intel-
> ligent, nor more useful nor more glorious.

To the English, Boulanger was grotesque. The more intelligent French saw clearly that to seek revenge prematurely would only lead to catastrophe and the Prince's friends therefore put pressure on him to intervene discreetly in French politics through the Count of Paris.

Boulanger had need of royalist support to overturn the Rouvier ministry and to take power by constitutional means. The Prince called on the Count of Paris and told him that if Boulanger came to power it would mean war. The Count of Paris hesitated, for the Duchesse d'Uzès had promised him that Boulanger would put him on the throne. But eventually he listened to the Prince, for in fact he could not stand Boulanger, and the Rouvier ministry was saved. Boulanger avenged himself by demanding the expulsion of the Orléans after the sumptuous wedding of Princess Amélie to Don Carlos of Braganza (May 15, 1886). So arbitrary an act had the worst possible effect abroad, as such pettiness was not a sign of strength.

The weight which the future King of England's opinion carried in the world was clearly shown in a little intrigue which, as events turned out, did not have any importance. Prince Poniatowski records it in his memoirs. Before becoming a great businessman, he was a brilliant lieutenant at Saumur and often met the Prince at the Epatant and at the races; he was also held in very high regard by the Orléans. One day in April 1887, the Duchesse d'Uzès summoned the young man and said to him in the presence of Arthur Meyer, "You are to go to London and see your friends at Marlborough House. No one in official circles must be allowed to think that you are going for any other reason than pleasure."

"But," replied the young man, "I am only on twenty-four hours' leave."

"Go immediately to the War Ministry, the General will arrange all that."

An hour later the lieutenant was ushered in to see Boulanger, who gave him a month's leave. "They do not understand the intentions of the French Army in London," he said. "The Prince believes only in Galliffet. But he will have to listen to another tune.

Try and find out what he thinks of me." Poniatowski was also to appease the Orléans.

The moment he arrived in London the young man went round to see Lady Sykes and Lady Randolph Churchill, who were good friends of his; in no time he was invited to Marlborough House. The Prince put a number of questions to him about the General, to which the Frenchman replied a little too enthusiastically. "Huh!" the Prince said. "Boulanger will never achieve anything"; but Poniatowski's perfect knowledge of the stud book eventually restored the Prince's good humour. The trusted messenger was to meet the Prince at numerous parties, but he found that no further interviews with him could be arranged: "The Prince of Wales has had enough," said the Duc d'Aumale. "He doesn't wish to hear any more on the subject of the General." Thereupon the Ministry fell and Boulanger played no further part in politics: "Well, didn't I tell you so!" exclaimed the Prince delightedly when he met Poniatowski the same day at the races.

During the interval between its escape from *Boulangisme* and the Panama scandal, France celebrated, under the Presidency of Sadi Carnot, the centenary of 1789 with a World Exhibition. The monarchies of Europe decided to snub these republican festivities, and their ambassadors pretended indisposition or mourning so as to avoid being present at the inauguration. The Queen of England forbade her son to go there: but this did not stop him from slipping over incognito with Lady Warwick. He even went so far as to climb to the second floor of the Eiffel Tower. France was decidedly republican, it could no longer be doubted. Anglomania survived only in the most decorative and least representative class of society. On the other hand, Russia was beginning to have charms for the French, although the slightest incident could still influence them against Germany. William II was in no sense hostile to France; he longed to make an official visit to Paris. His Ministers were irritated by this childishness, and when his ambassadors made allusion to a possible visit the French Government regretted that it would be unable to guarantee a warm welcome. The Emperor sent his mother to Paris to explore the ground on the pretext of organizing a Franco-German art exhibition. In semi-incognito, the Empress Frederick visited museums and studios, but then had the unfortunate idea of going to Versailles, where the Empire had been proclaimed, and from there to St. Cloud, which had been burnt by her husband's troops. The League of Patriots rose up. What! Had the Empress come to taunt France by this pilgrimage to the scenes of French humiliation? There were demonstrations and, once more misunderstood, the Empress left Paris hurriedly.

Then came that final decade of the nineteenth century, so fertile in scandal. And, as always, the French tried to make out that these scandals had their origins abroad. England had had nothing to do with Panama, but it was in London that the arch-crooks Cornelius Hertz, Arton, and the Baron de Hirsch took refuge. It was the latter who, in 1882, had precipitated the crash of the Union Générale, the big Catholic bank. Clemenceau, so it was said, was in the pay of the City. The patriots were galled by the comparison between the dignity of Parliament and the corruption of the Palais Bourbon. The Dreyfus affair widened still further the gap between French and English feelings. The basically religious English have nothing but contempt for the eternal political crises of the French. The army's victory over justice in the first Dreyfus trial and the anti-Semitism which then split France were hateful things in English eyes, and the Prince, who had friends in both camps, was embarrassed. If one had to choose between the Guermantes and the Rothschilds, Paris would lose much of her charm. Through the Prince of Monaco and the Court of Berlin the Prince knew that Dreyfus was innocent. Queen Victoria spoke of the captain as of a martyr. Seen from abroad, the Dreyfus affair did seem absurd, and it revealed the weakness of France. Lord Dufferin, the English Ambassador from 1892 to 1896 and a friend of both Bismarck and de Crispi, was accused of undermining the Franco-Russian alliance; the press insulted England with unbelievable violence. Glancing through the pages of *Le Rire*, we find cartoonists depicting Victoria as an enormous behind surmounted by a tiny crown, and during the Boer War, Caran d'Ache depicted its horrors in pictures worthy of Goya. Even the anarchists supported the patriots in their hatred of the solid English.

Fashoda inflamed anti-English sentiment to such an extent that the Prince had to give up his visits to France. In the spring of 1898, Kitchener, ordered by Lord Salisbury to pacify the Sudan and to avenge the death of Gordon, found the French flag floating above the camp at Fashoda, in the south of the country. For five days Commandant Marchand refused to lower his flag. Tension rapidly increased; the Foreign Office demanded Marchand's departure. At the Quai d'Orsay, Hanotaux telegraphed to him to remain where he was, but a government reshuffle put Delcassé in Hanotaux's place and he immediately ordered Marchand to give way. Delcassé was a patriotic and cultivated bourgeois, uncompromised by parliamentary scandal of any kind. He distrusted Russia for all that Hanotaux admired her, and declared that he would not leave office without having first established good relations with England. He sent his friend Cambon to London, a man with the same qualities of serious purpose and persistence as himself. Delcassé and the Prince of Wales had one thing in common: distrust of Germany.

The three years between Fashoda and Edward VII's accession to the throne, however, saw no attempt at rapprochement. French public opinion was outraged by the Boer War and the concentration camps, and the attacks on the Queen and her government were redoubled. Relations between the two countries were now thoroughly poisoned. The muddle-headed young Duc d'Orléans, forgetting the hospitality extended to his family, allowed a letter to be published over his name in which he approved of the anti-English demonstrations. The Prince had him ticked off by his sister, the Queen of Portugal. The caricatures became so wounding that in 1898 the Prince went to Denmark for his holiday instead of Cannes and refused, despite the urging of Lord Salisbury, to attend the inauguration of the Exhibition in 1900. But his former friendships and his hatred of William II were to bring him back to Paris.

CHAPTER SEVEN

The 'Eighties

THE DECADE THAT runs from 1880 to 1890 corresponds, to within two years, with the forties of the Prince's life. Although it did not bring him any political power, it confirmed his influence in Society. His elegance became an institution; his prestige virtually gave him the power of a dictator. The Prince known to history now emerges; as a result of the grand style in which he lived, his pleasures became fashions and his whims became policies. The admirable cut of his clothes made that swelling girth majestic. His beard was now pepper-and-salt and his hair had receded, but the nose remained aquiline and the fleshy face tended to turn red after a good meal or an outburst of rage. His large eyes, which were kind when he talked to the ladies, and were indulgent to his old friends and those whom he found amusing, developed a terrifying fixity if he observed the slightest breach of good manners; and they became half-closed if there was the least danger of boredom. And the Prince was easily bored, incapable as he was of concentrating for more than five minutes on any given subject; but his extraordinary memory made up for this lack of application. Though he never opened a book, he read *The Times* and the foreign newspapers every morning. Solitude frightened him; he could never be without someone with whom to chat or play cards or go for a walk. Thus Sandringham was always full of people, like the hotels the Prince was so fond of. The mechanical smile which to his future subjects appeared to be turned on and off when he was receiving and inaugurating, in reality disguised his profound bitterness. He was too intelligent to be unable to see the emptiness of his official life, but he had too much *amour propre* to give it up. The success which he achieved in India, and elsewhere abroad, was not the kind which is calculated to make one popular at home; it did him no good even with the politicians, for they found his enthusiasm indiscreet. Edward loved his mother, or at any rate respected in her the Queen. Although he was so impatient in little things, it would have been in appallingly bad taste to have shown the slightest impatience over mounting the throne.

During the 'eighties the Queen, whom Disraeli had brought out of retirement, became, through her hatred of Gladstone, a great political figure and regained her people's affection. If she had died before 1880 she would scarcely have left any more impression than Queen Mary, whose husband was also a remarkable man. From 1880 to 1890 she dominated the Empire. An embittered widow, a stranger to her people, a termagant to her Ministers, she became a myth, a small but all-powerful goddess, who never appeared without the greatest possible pomp but who was always dressed from head to foot in black, with one or two enormous diamonds. Disraeli, who had made her an Empress, told her she was the "faery" Queen; she found that natural enough. But to those whom her power exasperated, the French nationalists, the pan-Germanics and the American Irish, she seemed more like a hideous oppressor. Her common sense—warped though it sometimes was by personal antipathy but unhandicapped by imagination—and her perfect sense of dignity gave her a far better title to speak in the name of her people than either Parliament or her ambassadors had. Lytton Strachey, who regarded the Queen's life up to that point as no more than a rich source of touching and often ridiculous ancedotes, finally yields to her:

> Naturally it was in the Crown that the mysticism of the English polity was concentrated—the Crown, with its venerable antiquity, its sacred associations, its imposing spectacular array. But for nearly two centuries, common-sense had been predominant in the great building, and the little, unexplored, inexplicable corner had attracted small attention. Then, with the rise of imperialism, there

William Nicholson.

W.E.Gladstone.

was a change. For imperialism is a faith as well as a business: as it grew, the mysticism in English public life grew with it; and simultaneously a new importance began to attach to the Crown. The need for a symbol—a symbol of England's might, of England's worth, of England's extraordinary and mysterious destiny—became felt more urgently than ever before. The Crown was that symbol, and the Crown rested upon the head of Victoria. Thus it happened that while by the end of the reign the power of the sovereign had appreciably diminished, the prestige of the sovereign had enormously grown.

Next to his mother, whose place in history is like an allegory in a high-warp tapestry, the Prince's life is a tapestry woven of anecdotes and ceremonial, of an elegant if monotonous design. In its daily thread, however, can be distinguished two principal themes: in internal policy the wish to keep in touch with the *avant-garde* elements of public opinion and an anxiety not to appear retrograde; and in foreign policy, as we have seen in the preceding chapters, the desire to put an end to England's isolation.

The Prince sought to establish friendly relations with the new men of the age; but he was indifferent to their ideas, and the thinking of the intellectual élite was quite beyond him. The aestheticism fostered at Oxford by Walter Pater was carried to a wider public by Oscar Wilde. The Pre-Raphaelites' vision and their use of colour, at first thought to be revolutionary, had now become fashionable. In intellectual circles the worship of beauty was on a par with that of God, as in industry that of progress was on a par with Christianity. But the sporting aristocracy and the provincial bourgeoisie would have nothing to do with such an ideal and mocked its votaries.

The difference between the Prince's generation and that which became influential towards 1880 is clearly demonstrated by two cartoonists in *Punch*. Keene, whom Degas so much admired, depicts a country society centred on horses; the men are still dandies, the ladies porcelain dolls. The furniture is upholstered in an unpretentious style. Du Maurier, on the other hand, shows us a world whose setting reveals a hankering after Japanese or Florentine art. Elegant men pass their beautiful hands through silky side whiskers, and young men, freshly down from Oxford, their hair rather on the long side, go to concerts or look at pictures. They may laugh at the aesthetes, but these are already important enough to have made an impression on the slightly dimwitted readers of *Punch*. The ladies are dressed and coiffed like the Princess of Wales, but from the odd trinket, or the occasional attitude they strike, one suspects them of having a soul. Their ideal is the Duchess of Towers, the pure and passionate heroine of the same George du Maurier's novel *Peter Ibbetson*.

The bearded prophet Lord Tennyson was slipping into the past, while Kipling was beginning to publish his stories. Swinburne was in retreat; Thomas Hardy, writing in solitude, and Henry James, immersed in the fashionable world, were beginning the long novels that were later to bring them fame. As always in a period of literary dearth, it was the romantic novelists, such as Marie Corelli and to a greater extent Ouida, who were most talked about. The latter, despite her sentimental gush and soap-opera style, accurately depicted the circle in which the Prince moved in London and on the Riviera. Her stories are all about peeresses and guards officers, Russian princesses and millionaires, and pure souls shipwrecked by their passions. In *The Massarenes* she deals in a slightly more bitter vein with the intrigues of a shady financier. The Prince himself appears, and it becomes fairly plain that Marlborough House is a short cut from the City to Parliament.

The official Church, so far as religion went, was losing ground. Its indifference to the misery of the poorer classes and the problems of the upper classes left the lower orders to drift into the Non-conformist sects, and Society towards Rome. Catholicism, led by Newman and Manning, was making immense progress, and the Jesuits installed themselves in Farm Street, the very heart of Mayfair. Elegant monsignors worked at converting marquesses and smart young men. Edward went to church every Sunday to appease his conscience, but if the sermon exceeded a quarter of an hour he would pull out his watch ostentatiously. Once, when a pompous bishop entered a room at Windsor, one of the ladies was heard to murmur, "Here comes God's butler," a witticism which exactly described the spiritual role of the Anglican Church.

We cannot really reproach the Prince for his lack of intellectual curiosity, for his forebears and his descendants were not over-gifted in this respect, but his indifference, and it almost amounted to distrust, meant that he never got to know the most interesting set of people in the country, those from whom his future Ministers were to be drawn. About halfway through the 'eighties the liberal and aesthetic movements brought together a group of intelligent and rich young people who were related to families in the ruling classes; it consisted of women of the world who were bored with fashion and good works, and of a few writers, and it centred on a lively and curious-minded young girl who aspired to other joys than hunting and dancing, although she excelled in these pastimes. Her father, a rich Scottish industrialist, indulged her every whim. At twenty, Margot Tennant had made many enemies but among her friends were Arthur Balfour, Lord Curzon, who was later to be Viceroy of India, Lord Pembroke, and George Wyndham, the politician who called his *art nouveau* house in the country *Clouds.* At twenty-seven, still unmarried, she had created the group known by the jealous as the Souls. The Souls had no programme, and their ideas were often divergent but they were understood by them all; even in politics they remained aesthetes. They had a common hatred of anything that they thought vulgar; their language, which was highly polished, contrasted with the fashionable vernacular; they adored intellectual games, although this did not prevent them from dancing, hunting, and playing tennis. They discovered Bayreuth, and preferred Florence to Monte Carlo. To them everything, in fact, depended on the way in which you looked at it. They were aristocrats with a social conscience; they visited the poorer quarters and wrote articles on workers' dwellings. They had faith but no religion (an Oxford professor said to Margot, "My dear child, believe in God despite what the church says"), and above all they worshipped what was beautiful. Seldom was there a more platonic society, although this little group included several of the greatest beauties in England. Slender and pale in grey or lavender-coloured dresses, like Burne-Jones's nymphs, they all resembled each other. Margot, small and nervous, with her slightly large nose and prominent chin, was witty rather than charming; too intelligent to follow fashion, she invented one to suit herself.

She was to marry Asquith, the least aristocratic of the group, and for thirty years was the most sought-after and the most lively figure on the English political scene. Of all the memoirs of this period, hers alone are readable, for she had no fear of making enemies. Her writing retains its freshness today. An account she wrote of meeting the Prince at a party given by the Churchills is typical. She arrived in a very simple dress, for the Souls affected to ignore fashion; they would wear bunches of holly on their dresses or in their hair instead of jewellery.

On my arrival at the Churchills', I observed all the fine ladies wearing ball dresses off the shoulder and their tiaras. This made one very conspicuous, and I wished profoundly that I had changed into something smarter before going out.

The Prince of Wales had not arrived, and as our hostess was giving orders to the White Hungarian Band, my father and I had to walk into the room alone.

I saw several of the ladies eyeing my toilette and, having painfully sharp ears, I heard some of their remarks:

"Do look at Miss Tennant! She is in her night-gown!"

"I suppose it is meant to be 'ye olde Englishe pictury'! I wonder she has not let her hair down like the Juliets at the Oakham balls!"

Another, more charitable, said:

"I daresay no one told her that the Prince of Wales was coming. . . . Poor Child! What a shame!"

And finally a man said:

"There is nothing so odd as the passion some people have for self-advertisement; it only shows what it is to be intellectual!"

At that moment our hostess came up to us with a charming *accueil*. . . . She had a forehead like a panther's and great wild eyes that looked through you. . . . Had Lady Randolph Churchill been like her face, she could have governed the world.

My father and I were much relieved at her greeting: and while we were talking the Prince of Wales arrived. The ladies fell into position, ceased chattering and made subterranean curtsies. He came straight up to me and told me I was to sit on the other side of him at supper. I said, hanging my head with becoming modesty and in a loud voice:

"Oh no, Sir, I am not dressed at all for the part! I had better slip away. I had no notion this was going to be such a smart party. . . . I

expect some of the ladies here think I have insulted them by
coming in my night-gown!"

"You are so original! You must dance the cotillion with me."

The Souls both amused and irritated the Prince, but they had
very few affinities with him. Their influence at Marlborough House
was thus nil and the new cult of simplicity, which was empty-
ing the drawing-rooms of their ornaments and banishing upholstery,
made no impression there. To such pure spirits Edward must have
seemed rather vulgar.

Another phenomenon that developed at this time put the brilliant if slightly immoral ladies of the Marlborough House set in a
new category as far as the public was concerned. Thanks to the
improvement in photographic techniques the Prince's lady friends
became "professional beauties," an expression which indicated,
not courtesans, but women of fashion whose portraits could be
bought in the shops. The success of this commerce in images was
assured by its two profoundly English characteristics: snobbery
and aestheticism. The French might be satisfied with the anonymous
nudes which they could buy for a few louis in the Palais Royal or
the girls whom they met at the *maisons* they frequented. But the
English worshipped their inaccessible goddesses in Court robes,
dwelling in historic mansions. How admirable they still appear to
us in the russet tones of bromide paper, on those thick gilded cardboard mountings, with their cold expressions, their elbows propped
on velvet-draped tables, and a child or a dog at their feet. The
cockneys would stand all night long outside the great houses while
balls were in progress, just to see these "beauties" as they came
out onto the porch between rows of footmen, indifferent to the
staring crowd, as the barker called for their coaches: "Lady
Dudley's carriage! Her Grace, the Duchess of Leeds!" Bitterly
referred to as "professional beauties" by the ladies who went un-
photographed, they were all wealthy or had wealthy admirers.
And though some led immoral lives, for preference on the Riviera,
immorality was never the key to their position. There were none
of them without worthy husbands and respectable homes. By the
end of the century they were not above turning a few pennies by
selling their smiles for toothpaste advertisements. Their fortunes

and their rank put them as far beyond criticism as the stars of the cinema screen.

No professional beauty had arrived until she had been seen sufficiently often with the Prince and been permitted the shallow curtsy known as the "half Sandringham" (it was made when meeting royalty in a garden, when presumably they have no intention of speaking to one). The Prince would spot the more attractive ladies when standing in for his mother at presentation parties at St. James's Palace, and then observe them at leisure during the balls. He required them to be not only elegant and *au courant* with all the gossip, but also indefatigable; Edward loved dancing jigs and quadrilles and fast German waltzes. He would show his favour by an invitation to Covent Garden, where he had a stage box known as "the omnibus" because he shared the cost of it with three intimate friends. At the back of this box was a large mirror that enabled the occupants to see everyone without being seen themselves. An invitation to dinner at Marlborough House would then put the seal on the young lady's position. The season reached its climax on the last Friday in July, just before Goodwood, when the most elegant ball of all would be held.

It was at Goodwood that the Marlborough House set enjoyed itself most. The professional beauties would rent little houses at the edge of the forest and bring their horses with them. Every morning the Prince would go riding with one or another of them, and they would meet for enormous breakfasts before the races; they would pile themselves into their coaches to go and have tea with the neighbouring châtelaines, and they did not dress except for the Duke of Richmond's party with which the week always ended.

The most celebrated of these beauties was the daughter of a clergyman, who had married a rich Irishman called Langtry. Invited by chance during a visit to London to a party at which the painter Millais and a few men of fashion were present, she was launched with breathtaking speed. Her beauty, it is true, was astounding: her profile and her proportions were those of a Greek statue, her complexion was of the whitest, her hair of the blondest; she was only twenty years old and her charming manners were untouched by puritanism. Within a few months of her début, no party could possibly have been a success without her. In Hyde Park the crowd would gather to see her ride by, and would climb on to the benches and applaud. Mr. Langtry retired to his yacht. The Archduke Rudolf came expressly from Vienna to meet her, but the Prince of Wales had forestalled him. One of her earliest admirers, Wilfred Scawen Blunt, who had given her a very fine horse, wrote: "I had the happiness of seeing her on my horse as she rode by with His Royal Highness," and he added, with a very doubtful play on words: "In any case lilies can be very dull if they are not bedded out." She was in fact known as the Jersey Lily, for Millais had painted her with these flowers in her hand. Oscar Wilde declared his admiring and desperate passion for the reigning beauty, dedicated poems to her, and threatened to sleep on her doorstep. Her beauty distinguished her age just as that of the Princess of Wales had distinguished the preceding one. The Queen, who had herself had to remove the Millais drawing which her youngest son, the Duke of Albany, had hung up in his bedroom, expressed a wish to see the phenomenon, and on the day that Mrs. Langtry was to be presented, she herself was on the throne. We can picture Victoria, her little fat hand extended coldly and her eyes still swollen with curiosity as the famous beauty curtsied before her, and the slightly raised eyebrows as, with too ravishing a movement, Mrs. Langtry picked up her train to join the other ladies. Half a century later a similar scene brought Mrs. Simpson to the feet of Queen Mary.

Almost as beautiful as Mrs. Langtry and further up the social scale were Millicent, Duchess of Sutherland, and her sister Frances, the Countess of Warwick, two striking blondes, who were in the very first rank of the professional beauties. Lady Warwick, who was then Lady Brooke, held the first place in the Prince's affections throughout the 'eighties, for far longer, in fact, than Mrs. Langtry, and he showed her a devotion far more serious than that with which he pursued the transient Americans. This devastatingly attractive woman, whose ample wealth put all the ostentation that was expected of her rank at her disposal, was of an impulsive and adventurous disposition. Even when she was eighteen she resisted

Queen Victoria's attempts to persuade her to marry her youngest son. She was already completely at home in the world of fashion, as she was to be later in the world of politics. If the important correspondence recently unearthed is to be believed, Lady Warwick and the Prince were lovers for many years. Did he not call her "my little wife," and did he not try to appease the jealousies aroused under his own roof by this liaison? He managed to get the Princess of Wales to stop making scenes and to be nice to his beautiful friend whenever she had to receive her. In recognition of her forbearance he once described her in a letter as "a perfect lady." To amuse her lover, Lady Warwick got up lavish week-end parties at her historic country house, and dressed herself in the most extravagant creations. Twenty-five years later she had cause to regret this expense; the good-hearted George V also regretted it when she was forced to hawk her letters around, with the threat of selling them in the United States, in order to get some of it back.

Kindhearted, impulsive and spoilt, Lady Warwick nearly lost Edward's friendship when she became a socialist. Angered by a newspaper article that had upbraided her for the money she had spent on a lavish ball, she rushed to the editor's office to remind the perpetrator of this libel that luxury is a duty, since so many honest men live off it. After two hours of discussion Lady Warwick emerged convinced. Several doors were closed to the "red peeress" but not those of Marlborough House; the Prince always listened to her with a smile on his face, certain that it was no more than the childish babbling of a pretty woman. It was a scene straight out of one of Shaw's plays: the sable-clad lady trading paradoxes, which today would seem commonplaces, with an idealistic journalist.

While the ladies of fashion were gaining the sort of celebrity enjoyed by actresses, actors were entering Society. The Victorian theatre, which was utterly barren until Wilde revived the style of Sheridan, could boast some admirable actors. The Prince and Princess of Wales would go several times a week to the theatre and have plays produced at Sandringham, then dine afterwards with the actors. The Queen brought down a few companies to

Windsor to give performances for the family, and knighted such actors as Bancroft and Irving. The stage was becoming more respectable, but there were a number of drawing-rooms of which this could not be said. Opera remained in the Italian tradition with stars like Patti or Nilsson, who were paid extravagant fees without anyone worrying very much what was paid to anyone else. It was under the influence of Lady de Grey, an intimate friend of the Princess's, that it became Wagnerian; she brought over the de Reszke brothers once a season to Covent Garden. They were Polish gentlemen who caught so exactly the tone of international elegance that a luxury brand of cigarettes was named after them.

The year 1880 opened with a complete *volte-face* by the English public. Disraeli, who was absorbed with the Empire and diplomacy, remained at heart a foreigner and never understood public opinion. By seeking fresh elections, he thought he would increase the Conservatives' majority, but there was a Liberal landslide. "I cannot have Gladstone!" was the Queen's immediate reaction. This talkative, awkward man got on her nerves; his speeches, which had been violently hostile to the Turks during the Balkan crisis, had very much upset her. As for the Prince, he had known Gladstone since his childhood, for Mrs. Gladstone was related to his governess, Lady Lyttelton; he admired his integrity and the ardent faith that complemented his extraordinary capacity for Parliamentary duplicity. Gladstone could not have been more different from Disraeli, whose resemblance to Shylock meant that the slightest act of loyalty on his part won him enormous admiration. Gladstone, on the other hand, had the appearance of a prophet, and his cleverness was held against him as though it were a crime. Strachey has described his speeches in a vignette that illustrates their obscurity:

> Speech was the fibre of his being; and when he spoke the ambiguity of ambiguity was revealed. The long, winding intricate sentences, with their vast burden of subtle and complicated qualifications, befogged the mind like clouds and like clouds, too, dropped thunderbolts.

Disraeli behaved with the greatest courtesy towards the Prince, but he valued the Queen's friendship too highly to give him any part in government. It might be otherwise with Gladstone. Victoria would have liked Granville or Hartington as Prime Minister. But the latter's indolence was too much even for "my dear Duchess." When the Prince of Wales, on his mother's instructions, met the future Duke of Devonshire at the Turf Club, in order to sound him out, he was told in a sleepy voice: "It's too boring, really, why should I be Prime Minister? Only Gladstone knows what's going on. The nation doesn't know me; tell the Queen not to count on me."

The Prince transmitted the result of his inquiry in political circles through his equerry, Knollys, to his mother's secretary, Ponsonby. This indirect route was often the best way of gaining a hearing at Windsor. Rumours were of more value there than letters; they got repeated and they were commented upon. The Prince of Wales is sure, his message ran, that if the Queen would consider Mr. Gladstone as her and the royal family's friend instead of believing him to be her enemy, as Prince Leopold (the Duke of Albany) is persuaded, she will find him everything that she could wish.

On April 23 the Queen finally summoned Gladstone to Windsor and received him coolly in an unheated room. For five years Victoria was to battle against her Prime Minister; far from weakening her, this antagonism gave her strength, and her taste for life returned; obstinate on matters of importance, she became even more tyrannical over details. Disraeli had charmed and lulled her to sleep. Gladstone stung her to wakefulness. They agreed on nothing: Gladstone wanted Home Rule for Ireland and would countenance colonial wars only if they were fought to protect established possessions. When Gordon launched his expedition against the Sudanese he appealed to the Commons: "These people are struggling to be free, and they are rightly struggling to be free." Victoria, the Prince, and the public were furious when, due to the Government's inertia, the heroic Gordon was stranded in Khartoum and encircled by the Mahdi's hordes. Reinforcements arrived too late and were crushed. It was thought that Egypt would be lost. The Queen sent Gladstone a telegram in clear so that everyone should know what she thought of her Government. The Prince was present at all the ceremonies held to perpetuate Gordon's memory and made it clear that he had joined the imperialist camp. The English called their patriots "jingos."

The House of Commons in the 1880s contained three remarkable young men, the most brilliant of whom was Lord Randolph Churchill, an aristocrat, who hotly opposed the Liberals' policies; Austen Chamberlain and Sir Charles Dilke, the former republicans of the 'seventies, were the other two. Sir Charles achieved a great ascendancy over the Prince during the first half of the decade, and then it was Lord Randolph's turn once more to bask in the favour of Marlborough House. Her son's friendship for Sir Charles gave offence to the Queen. A large, ruddy, bearded man with an Olympian presence, self-assured and utterly lacking in humour, he had in him the stuff of a Gambetta. He applied himself first to modernizing the army and had no difficulty in convincing the Prince that the Duke of Cambridge, who was at its head, was hanging on to methods whose inefficacy had already been proved by the Crimean War, with a stupidity that amounted to senile decay. But Dilke was only an Under-Secretary at the Foreign Office as the Queen refused to give a portfolio to an ex-republican. His views were not far from those of Lord Hartington, but the latter's vagueness made him unsuited to Parliamentary intrigues and he could therefore be of little use to the Prince. The influence of Marlborough House did not transform Sir Charles into a courtier. He noted in his diary:

> It is worth taking the trouble to talk to the Prince, even if he seems not to be listening at the time; he does in fact hear what you say and, when speaking to somebody else later on, brings out everything that you have told him.

He encouraged the Prince's Francophile policy and interested him in the question of workers' dwellings. If the Queen had died, Sir Charles Dilke would have been a great prime minister. But she lived, and during her reign even the most brilliant careers were not immune from scandal.

The Dilke scandal recalls the Mordaunt affair in which the Prince had been compromised fifteen years earlier. Now his loyalty to another victim of puritanism was put to the test throughout an even more unsavoury trial. Following the pattern set by Lady Mordaunt, Mrs. Crawford, the wife of one of Dilke's colleagues, admitted to having had culpable relations with Sir Charles, after some anonymous letters had opened her husband's eyes. During the divorce case brought by her husband, remorse giving way to a desire for vengeance, she volunteered all the most compromising details of her liaison with Dilke. The politician, she said, had seduced her when she was still a young married woman, in a low hotel in the Tottenham Court Road, and had compelled her to share the bed with a certain Fanny, whom he was keeping. The confession, reproduced in the press *in extenso*, is one of those rare documents that reveals what went on beneath the surface in Victorian society:

> Sir Charles taught me every sort of French vice, and then in moments of intimacy he would whisper: "You're very like your mother."

The court refused to credit such allegations against a statesman, although Crawford did obtain his divorce, but public opinion had been stirred up by the press. Gladstone, who was then reshuffling his Cabinet, refused to include Sir Charles Dilke in it. In order to clear himself, the latter demanded a retrial, an imprudence similar to Wilde's in his second action against Queensberry. Crawford then produced some witnesses who confounded Sir Charles; the most violent was Mrs. Crawford's mother, whose daughter so closely resembled her in "moments of intimacy." To the court it appeared evident that she had been his mistress. It was she who had sent the anonymous letters to her son-in-law. She had tracked down the hotel in the Tottenham Court Road and had persuaded or bribed the chambermaids. Sir Charles was condemned for adultery and his political career was at an end. Marlborough House did not desert him after the trial and the Prince continued to treat him in a friendly manner.

The attitude of the Victorians to women was that they were children constantly menaced by the male sex. The law, which allowed them no political rights, protected their virtue with severity.

One imprudent word and you were pursued for breach of promise, one unconsidered gesture and you were condemned for outraging modesty. Sons would be advised by their fathers never to enter a compartment in which there was a woman alone. The latter could pull the alarm cord and the young man would have to choose between marriage and paying enormous damages or other forms of recompense. One of the Prince's intimate friends, Colonel Valentine Baker, had to pay dearly for an adventure of this sort. The scene must have taken place in a non-corridor train, as the young lady in question took refuge on the running-board outside, to escape from his over-ardent compliments. Screaming and di-shevelled, she had the colonel arrested at the next station. Valentine Baker, now dishonoured, accepted a commission from Turkey and, being also in the pay of the Intelligence Service, continued to serve his country in the Near East.

It seemed that there would be no end to the scandals that broke out in the Prince's entourage; the morally upright members of Society were deeply disturbed at seeing young couples becoming *ménages à trois* and debutantes dancing with officers who had rich mistresses, or mothers who married their daughters to their lovers. A delegation of ladies, led by the Duchesses of Leeds and Beaufort, went to Lambeth Palace and asked Archbishop Benson to organize a campaign of purification. They felt that a *cordon sanitaire* had to be established around Marlborough House, as the whole of Society was menaced by its licence. The Archbishop, wishing to remain on good terms with the Prince, suggested prayer meetings, feeling that he could leave to a higher authority the trouble of bringing the guilty back to the straight and narrow path. He then suggested that the Queen should be enrolled in this crusade. "That's no good," replied the ladies. "She's not smart enough. But if the Princess of Wales . . ." The prelate approached the Princess, who consulted her mother-in-law. "This idea of prayers in the middle of the week seems to me most extraordinary and I do not see why the Princess should go to Lambeth Palace, which is a purely sacred domain," replied the Queen. Although they failed to secure the patronage of royalty, the ladies did pray, and, with the consolation of divine support, disdained to proffer more than two fingers to the young ladies who were straying down the path of dissipation; if the name of a habitué of Marlborough House was mentioned they would bite their lips. Victoria had no wish to encourage a movement directed against her son, but she never lost an opportunity of teaching him a lesson. When she was about to publish *More Leaves from a Journal of Our Life in the Highlands*, the Prince suggested that she might tone down the effusiveness of her remarks about John Brown and drew the following reply: "These comments are really rather curious coming from someone who only lives for a world in which indiscretion is the rule rather than the exception and in a circle in which there is not the slightest uprightness of principle."

The English love the members of their great families to exhibit the traits characteristic of those who made them famous and they admire in them eccentricities of behaviour which would seem odious in the common man. Lord Hartington, with his superb indifference, his almost studied carelessness, was still the *grand seigneur* of the eighteenth century. The Marquess of Salisbury, scholarly and untidy, recalled his ancestor, Elizabeth's minister. The Churchills' insolence and their gift for improvisation was inherited less from the Marshal than from his wife, the ambitious Sarah. Once Lord Randolph Churchill had become a success in Parliament and Marlborough House had ended the ostracism which he had suffered in Society since the Aylesford affair, he and his wife became the most fashionable young couple in London. Sir Charles Dilke's place in the Prince's circle was now taken by this younger son of the Duke of Marlborough. The attention paid by the heir to the throne to promising M.P.s was much the same as he paid to possible Derby winners in his stable. Unfortunately he was to derive less satisfaction from Parliament than from the turf, and the two remarkable men whom he backed had but brief careers.

Lord Randolph was a member of the Conservatives. Small, tense, perfectly, if slightly eccentrically, dressed, he resembled a greyhound, ready at a moment's notice to spring upon those who displeased him. He attacked Gladstone with bitter mockery and showed not the slightest respect for his moral conscience or the least fear of his eloquence. Stroking his delicate moustache and nonchalantly leaning on the dispatch box, the young Member would harry the Grand Old Man. His head sunk into his vast stiff collar, his arms crossed, the prophet would listen with the air of an old ram disdaining to face an importunate mongrel. Lord Randolph soon became impatient with the Conservatives' flabbiness; gathering around him a few admirers, he formed a fourth party whose policy, though chiefly destructive, was distinguished by a benevolent attitude towards Ireland. Impressed by his success (nothing like it had been seen since the younger Pitt!), the Queen had summoned the Churchills to a reception and the Prince had accepted their invitation to dinner. The Duchess of Manchester, with her baccarat parties that so shocked Parliament, had been behind all this: like the Prince, Lord Randolph was a passionate devotee of cards and racing. His mare, named for some curious reason L'Abbesse de Jouarre in homage to Renan, brought him in considerable sums. He had need of them in order to support his grand style of life and his new party.

His wife was his best electoral agent: she brought to his meetings both her prestige as a professional beauty and her American vitality. She owed her jet-black hair, her striking teeth, and her matt complexion to her Indian blood. Her liaison with an Austrian diplomat did not prevent her from being completely devoted to her husband's career. Eighteen eighty-five was the year of Lord Randolph's triumph: a year of *Sturm und Drang,* Gladstone noted when his Ministry fell. He was replaced by Lord Salisbury, and Lord Randolph now became Chancellor of the Exchequer. Salisbury was his own Foreign Minister as well as Lord President of the Council. To a friend who thought he had taken on too much he replied, "In fact I have the work of four Ministries to deal with: the Presidency, Foreign Affairs, the Queen and Lord Randolph, and their burdens increase in that order."

In December 1886, however, the Prime Minister was relieved of the most difficult of his charges. Unable to acquiesce over a detail in the Budget, the Chancellor of the Exchequer resigned from Salisbury's cabinet in a headstrong gesture and sent a copy of his letter to Lord Salisbury to *The Times*. It was from this paper that Victoria first learned of the discord in her Government; the Prince then sent her a letter of explanation which he had received from Lord Randolph. He thus compromised himself on behalf of the man who would probably have been the great figure of his own reign. The Queen's reply to Marlborough House ran:

> That strange unaccountable man, Lord Randolph Churchill, who has been a perpetual thorn in the side of his colleagues since he has been in office. Why did he take office if he thought there was such a 'chasm' between him and them? The fact is *he* expected all to bow to him, as indeed some were inclined to do. It is regrettable and even dangerous that the Prince should maintain his relationship with him.

Embittered, Lord Randolph now launched out on a course that was to cost him his supporters; his health declined; at forty he was a ruined man. In a last effort to play the great man he took it on himself to go to Berlin and St. Petersburg to speak in the name of England. He took with him the Prince's warm commendations. For all that Lord Salisbury might warn the Chancelleries that "This journey is a purely private one, Lord Randolph in no sense represents Her Majesty's Government," he was received as an ambassador extraordinary by both Bismarck and the Emperor of Russia. Following the example set by the Prince on each of his visits, Lord Randolph wrote letters from St. Petersburg full of euphoria, demanding access to the Mediterranean for Russia. The Queen, who was insensible to Slavic charm, hauled her Ambassador over the coals for having entertained Lord Randolph and wrote her son one of those letters which at forty-five he still could not open without trembling:

> I cannot understand why you should make so much of this unprincipled and impulsive man with his dangerous ideas on foreign policy, on whom *absolutely* no reliance can be placed.

But the Prince continued to quote from the traveller's letters and to air his ideas. The Queen wrote again:

> We must not alienate our allies. We are, I am happy to say, on the best possible terms with Germany, Austria and Italy, and this, as you well know, is the only means of containing the aggressive spirit of the Russians.

With the Dilke scandal and Lord Randolph's resignation, Edward saw his hopes of an interesting political life disappear. Lord Salisbury, who was too intellectual to take him seriously, willingly listened to him when he recommended a few of his friends for official positions. To quote from a biography of Edward VII that was written with some naïveté:

> Although they did not have remarkable political capacity, Lord Londonderry and Lord Cadogan, who were both very wealthy and honourable men, and both fond of racing and entertaining on a large scale, were perfectly adapted to public careers.

Before he could emerge to play a more than purely formal rôle, the Prince had to wait till his friend Lord Rosebery became Prime Minister.

And so the Prince of Wales continued his habitual style of life. In June 1885 he wrote to a friend from the country house of the Marquess of Ripon, where he was spending a couple of days:

> We lead a very social life; last week I was at Newmarket. Splendid weather. Monday the Westminsters' ball. Yesterday the Princess and I arrived here from London. The inauguration of the college in Leeds went off very well, and the reception was enthusiastic. Tomorrow I am going to Preston for the Agricultural Show, spending the night at Latham, and I come back on the following day to Town. From Saturday to Monday I shall be at Ferdy Rothschild's place, or rather his palace at Waddesdon. In a week's time we are going to Cowes for my sister Beatrice's wedding [Battenberg]. From there to Goodwood (with the Duke of Richmond) for the races. The 17th we return to Cowes.

The Prince kept his friends informed with the same accuracy about his shooting:

> In two days at Wynyard, we killed 7,790 head of which 5,817 were rabbits and 1,973 were pheasants.

Armies of beaters were employed to make these massacres, which seem so un-English and unsporting, possible. They recall Cranach's painting of the Elector of Saxony shooting stags, at bay in a pool, at point-blank range.

A malicious journalist wrote that in eight months the Prince had been to thirty plays, twenty-eight race meetings, forty-five dinners, balls, or garden parties (official or philanthropic and not counting private receptions!), while he had been only eleven times to the House of Lords.

The great nobles no longer took Edward seriously. In the Stanley family he was known as Tum-Tum on account of his large stomach. "Everybody was there: Tum, Mrs. Tum and the five little Tums," said the future Lord Derby in a letter describing a wedding he had been to. Old friends were having a hard time of it trying to keep up with the Prince and the Princess; ruin and scandal had decimated their ranks. The most faithful, Christopher Sykes, had got through an enormous fortune entertaining the Prince. "Christopher, I have nothing to do this evening, why don't you arrange a little dinner party?" the Prince would say to him, or, "Possibly twenty of us will be coming to stay with you for the St. Léger," or even, "Well, Sykey, it's a long time since you gave a ball."

In between times the Prince would pour bottles of cognac down his courtier's neck. Occasionally this martyr to snobbery would dare to protest. "Well, Sykey, who do we take ourselves for to-day?" his illustrious friend would ask in his raucous, hearty voice.

"For the most faithful and most severely tried servant of your Royal Highness," Sykes would reply.

When he was on the eve of bankruptcy the Prince was heard to murmur, "Bad, bad." The victim's sister-in-law went to Marl-borough House and explained to the Prince that Sykes' ruin had been his doing. The most pressing debts were paid.

The public was kept ignorant, apart from a few indiscretions in the press, of the liberty which reigned in Marlborough House. Everything took place in private; in London in the 'eighties there was only one night-club at which society women could sup and dance after the theatre, but they still had to be accompanied by their husbands. When the famous Skittles put in an appearance, the place suddenly emptied. It was there that the Prince of Wales gave a small party to relax after the official functions that marked the fiftieth anniversary of the Queen's accession to the throne. The King of Greece and the Archduke Rudolf, who had come for the Jubilee, were of the party, as were also the Duchess of Manchester, Lady Randolph Churchill, and a few young people. After supper, at about two o'clock in the morning, the Prince asked the orchestra for the quadrille from *La Belle Hélène* and, with "my dear Duchess" as partner, danced a can-can as though possessed. The Archduke was not amused; turning to his friend Kinsky, he said, "Tell the waiters to go, they must not see their furture King making such a clown of himself."

CHAPTER EIGHT

Fin de Siècle

A PROFOUND *malaise* weighed upon the last ten years of the nineteenth century. The optimism with which colonial expeditions and industrial development had been undertaken gave way to discouragement and unrest. Observers became anxious over the mounting perils: "yellow," over-population, atheism. Every country had its bogy: France, nationalism; Russia, nihilism; Germany, socialism; and Italy, its Freemasons and its Jesuits. As the century neared its end, financial scandals became rife among the ruling classes, now gorged with gold and property. England was exempt but the conflict between her imperialists and her intelligentsia worsened. To her bourgeoisie, the aesthetic movement seemed a ridiculous affectation which, after the Wilde scandal, became odious.

The Prince of Wales tipped the balance towards imperialism with the weight of his overnourished fifty years. The 'nineties were to be the most troublesome period of his extended youth. Although almost an old man, he still trembled before his mother; his nephew laughed at him, the public did not take him seriously, and soon even those of good family would despise him. Still wandering in the mists of her eternal childhood and cut off by her deafness, the Princess of Wales preserved her husband's dignity by the example she set of happy family life; if he did not become openly unpopular, it had much to do with his wife.

A scandal, which was nowhere near as serious on the moral

level as the Mordaunt affair or the row with the Churchills, brought the Prince into public disfavour. When those who live for pleasure get into trouble there are always people of different inclinations ready and waiting to make things worse. In September 1890, the Prince went to the Doncaster races. As his old friend Sykes, with whom he usually stayed, had been ruined, he accepted the hospitality of a rich shipbuilder called Wilson, at Tranby Croft. He brought with him a few friends, one of whom was Lord Edward Somerset and another Captain William Gordon-Cumming. It was not easy to keep the Prince amused; the Wilsons, who had set much store by their guest's visit to secure their position in Society, could not help feeling slightly apprehensive. What happened before dinner reassured them. The Prince deigned to mix a cocktail, the recipe of which had been sent him by a friend in Louisiana. Surrounded by a gay but respectful circle, he filled a champagne bucket half full of whisky, threw in some crushed ice, a slice of pineapple, two glasses of maraschino, and a few drops of angostura, and then poured some champagne in on top of it all. The dinner, which was excellent, was spent discussing who was going to win on the following day. But how were they going to get through the rest of the evening?

Mr. Wilson proposed a game of baccarat. "Excellent," said the Prince. "I happen to have brought some counters with me; all we have to do is to throw a cloth over a couple of whist tables." They played very late and Captain Gordon-Cumming was particularly lucky. After they had said good night, one of the Wilsons' sons went to his mother in a state of agitation. "Gordon-Cumming cheated," he told her. "When the players called their cards I saw him slip some five-pound counters out of his sleeve."

"We can't have a scandal!" exclaimed Mrs. Wilson. "Keep an eye on the captain tomorrow and whatever you do don't say anything." Thereupon she rushed off to tell her daughter and her son-in-law all about it. Her son, for his part, confided his indignation to one of the guests, a lieutenant in Sir William's regiment, who vehemently defended his superior. The next evening the Wilsons, who had obtained a green cloth and some proper counters, kept a close watch on Gordon-Cumming. The Prince held the bank.

Lord Kitchener

The Wilson son-in-law saw the captain slip a three-pound counter over the line where he had placed his stakes whenever calls that were favourable to him were made. He also noticed, during another game, the captain glancing at his neighbour's cards and then increasing his bid by ten pounds. The Prince paid him out five. "There's another ten to come," he said.

"I am so sorry, here you are," Edward replied. The Wilsons found themselves caught between their desire for respectability and their fear of hurting the Prince by accusing one of his friends. They told the two most distinguished guests what was afoot. In the course of a third game, these also observed the captain and were equally convinced. Without asking the Prince for his opinion they decided to speak to Gordon-Cumming the next morning. The latter got on his high horse and demanded to see the Prince. But Edward, who had spent the day at the races, was not prepared to see him until after dinner. Lord Edward Somerset eventually told him what had been happening. The delay was fatal; they should have acted quickly and in the greatest possible secrecy.

The Prince would not accept his friend's explanations. "Very well," said Gordon-Cumming, "I shall insult the Wilsons at the races tomorrow."

"There were five people who saw you," he was told. One of the guests suggested that the cheat should sign a document in which he would commit himself never to touch cards again as long as he lived. The Prince advised him to agree, otherwise everyone at the races the following day would get to hear about his indiscretion. "If you sign, those who saw you will swear never to breathe a word of what has happened." Continuing to protest, Gordon-Cumming signed; the witnesses countersigned the document, which was then confided to the Prince's secretary.

A month later the baccarat game at Tranby Croft was a wide open secret. Gordon-Cumming received anonymous letters, doors were closed to him, and his superiors cut him dead. In desperation he started proceedings for defamation against the Wilsons, and once again the Prince had to step into the witness box. Gordon-Cumming's counsel had cited him in the hope that so august a friendship would impress the court, but the Prince did not attempt to defend him; he contented himself with saying, "It is difficult for the banker to keep an eye on all the players at once and, in any case, such an idea would never enter one's head in a friend's house." Gordon-Cumming lost his case; he resigned from the guards and on the day that he did so married a very rich American girl called Florence Garner. Despite her parents' opposition she had remained faithful to the cheat; after the marriage, she buried herself with him for the rest of her life in a castle that he possessed in Scotland, a touching end to a sordid affair.

The Tranby Croft scandal made a catastrophic impression on the country. Was the future King of England no more than a croupier who played with cheats and with people who were unable to keep their word? The Nonconformists organized meetings of protest. One journalist calculated that since the Prince's birth, 880 million prayers had been offered for him in church. So much wasted time annoyed the shopkeepers, and the devout saw irreversible condemnation in the Lord's deafness. *The Times* made the same demand on the Prince as he had made on Gordon-Cumming, that he should promise never to touch another card. One town to which he went for an inauguration soon after the trial strung up a banner in the main square with the inscription "No gambling," instead of hanging out flags.

The foreign press, delighted at this opportunity to humiliate proud Albion, was unleashed and *La Vie Parisienne*, which should have known better, devoted a whole of one number to planning Edward's future kingdom on the lines of a casino. The Queen, more hurt than angry—after all the Prince had acted with correctness—advised her son to seek support from the Established Church against these puritanical attacks. She turned to Benson, the Archbishop of Canterbury and an experienced man of the world. He was of the opinion that an open letter would redeem the Prince's position and close malicious mouths. A republican crisis seemed once more to be in the offing. "It is the press," wrote the Prince, "that is trying to set me at loggerheads with my future subjects. They take no account of the time which I devote to my official life." He added: "I have a horror of gambling, and should always do my utmost to discourage others who have an inclination for it, as I consider that gambling, like intemperance, is one of the greatest curses that a country can be afflicted with. Horse-racing may produce gambling, or it may not; but I have always looked upon it as a manly sport which is popular with English-men of all classes, and there is no reason why it should be looked upon as a gambling transaction. Alas! Those who gamble will gamble on anything."

Never was there better proof that hypocrisy is the homage which vice renders unto virtue. The Prince's passion for cards had often embarrassed his closest friends. When Madame de Pourtalès lost a hundred louis in one evening, she was far from amused. In order to avoid exposing her less wealthy guests to such reverses at the Prince's table, she preferred to pay considerable fees to actors who would come for the evening when the Prince dined with her at Rue Tronchet. The Arthur Pagets acted as Edward's bookmakers, and he would readily send them cheques for a thou-sand pounds and more to settle his bets. He also wrote and asked Mrs. Paget to gamble for him on the Stock Exchange so that his name would not figure in the stockbrokers' books:

> Thank you for Mr. K's information . . ., but as I hardly know him I do not feel any obligation towards him. However, one can never be sufficiently grateful for good tips in these difficult times. Since he suggests Rands, buy as many of them as he tells you.

The Prince loved the power bestowed by money; his need for it increased as he grew older since he was spending very heavily. His understanding of all financial operations was such that some people were convinced that he had Jewish blood. But this instinct for money existed in that other Coburg, Leopold II: the more old-fashioned sovereigns, however, clung to their traditional ideas. A friend and almost an agent of the Rothschilds, the Prince loved peace, for it allowed money to circulate and multiply. Victoria was a landed proprietor, Edward a man of finance; she was provincial, he was international.

As is the case with rich people, the Prince's belief in imperialism stemmed from patriotism as much as from the thought of the material gain that would accrue to the City. He increasingly distrusted the abstract ideas that caused trouble and the slogans that distracted the people from their work and incited them to war. As King he was the incarnation not only of monarchy but also of capitalism; the Marxist iconography was not mistaken in depicting the capitalist with his attributes; top hat, cigar, and paunch. For one cannot get involved in business and altogether avoid vulgarity and dubious friends.

Towards the end of the 'eighties two financiers assumed an important position in the Prince's circle. They supplanted the Rothschilds, and, though of less good stock, they were almost as rich if not as honourable. The first of these gentlemen was the Baron de Hirsch, a Hungarian Jew, who had made his money speculating in Balkan railways. The Prince had met him in Paris. Hirsch had great social ambition, but his career had started at a bad time. Society, in part ruined by the Union Générale crash (he was thought to have been responsible), gave him the cold shoulder. In vain did he give two and a half millions to the Duchess d'Uzès for the Boulangist Party; his town house in the Rue de l'Elysée (today the Maison de la Pensée Française) remained empty, and he was blackballed for the Rue Royale Club. The Panama scandal did nothing to help either. The Baron was treated in the same way as were Reinach and Hertz. Gyp's anti-Semitic caricatures and the figure of Julius Herzen, whose struggles to enter high life are portrayed in Paul Bourget's *Cosmopolis*, were based on this financier.

Hirsch had a shoot in Hungary; the Prince accepted an invitation to go there and was thrilled by the hecatombs of game which were beaten towards his gun by hundreds of peasants. Although the doors of the Hofburg, like those of the Faubourg Saint Germain, remained closed to him, the Baron now found those of Marlborough House opening wide before him. He settled in England. The Prince's friendship was not a passport into every circle. So the banker decided to become a "sportsman" and bought a string of horses; a friend of the Prince's became his trainer, and in his first year he won the four biggest races. He was also extremely generous to charitable works patronized by duchesses.

It was Hirsch who introduced to the Prince another baron of

high finance who was endeavouring to become an Englishman, Ernest Cassel. With his beard, his paunch, his large nose, and his big eyes, he looked like a caricature of the Prince. This resemblance, and the intimacy into which the banker was almost immediately accepted, revived an old piece of gossip. The Prince Consort, it was said, had been the son of an official who, long after having abandoned the Duchess of Saxe-Coburg, fathered the financier in a legitimate marriage. It is no more than one of those endless myths about the origins or tastes of sovereigns that existed long before the Sunday press discovered them for its readers.

Sir Ernest, the son of a Cologne money-lender, started in the City as an employee of Bischoffsheim and Goldschmidt. In close touch with the Stock Exchange, he had an income of £5000 a year from his working capital, at the age of twenty-two. He later started up businesses of his own in Egypt, where Lord Cromer's protection was very useful to him, and in Uruguay and Morocco. The farther off one's enterprises, the more money they bring in, but a strong hand has to control them. Although there remains no trace of the business transactions which the Prince carried out with Cassel's assistance, his gratitude, even before he became King, was in proportion to their size. The financier was made a Baronet and a Privy Councillor; the Prince even arranged for him to be received by the Tsar, something that in principle was impossible for a Jew. Like the Baron de Hirsch, Sir Ernest pretended to be a sportsman and a country gentleman; the political world eagerly sought admission to his splendid house in Park Lane. The ease with which he gained favour irritated the Prince's older friends. Edward had taken the financier with him to the premiere of Wilde's play *The Importance of Being Earnest*; when he asked Soveral if he had seen it, the diplomat replied, "No sir, but I have seen the importance of being Sir Ernest." During a ball at Marlborough House one of the Prince's partners, a member of the intimate circle, bowed low before him after a dance. "And what does Salome desire?" he asked, laughing.

"Sir Ernest's head," replied the lady. Edward turned on his heel and for a long time would not speak to her.

Hirsch and Cassel did not have the right tone, and Society,

although not anti-Semitic as in Paris, would not accept them. The Prince let it be known that he would refuse to go to those houses that remained closed to his friends. Only the very great, those whose position put them above smartness and money, held out against the millionaires' invasion. Once, when invited for a week-end to a historic country house, the Prince added the Baron de Hirsch's name to the list which his hostess had proposed to him. The latter expressed her regret at not being able to ask someone whom she did not know and by the same post resigned from her position in the Princess's household. Marlborough House replied by return that the name of the Baron de Hirsch would not have been suggested if they had known that she had never met him, and she was begged to withdraw her resignation.

Thus the 'nineties saw the future King's Court forming at Marl-borough House. Respectable people did not feel that it augured well for the future. Hirsch and Cassel might have had a certain in-fluence in internal politics, but, unlike the Rothschilds, they had no widespread family connections and were not on friendly terms with numerous sovereigns in a way that would have enabled them to intervene abroad. The politics of the Rothschilds diverged from those of the Prince during this decade. They showed hostility to Russia and were so pro-German that in 1898 Alfred, with a view to preparing an alliance with Germany, brought Chamberlain and von Hatzfeldt, the Ambassador, together as often as he could. The official classes, the colonial governors, the bishops, the gen-erals, everyone in fact who belonged to what is now known as the Establishment, regarded the Marlborough House set with distrust at this time. Lady Monkswell, the wife of a high official, expressed the general trend of public opinion in her diary:

> Our Royalty is so German that yesterday evening at Buckingham Palace I thought I was at a ball in the Court of Dresden. The Princess of Wales had false hair and, I am afraid, powders her face, but how right she is to be so pretty in a very English style. The Duke of Clarence is a stupid fool.

Before he died, poor Clarence was a great anxiety to his family. He was quite characterless and would soon have fallen a

prey to some intriguer or group of roués, of which his regiment
was full. They indulged in every form of debauchery, and on one
occasion the police discovered the Duke in a *maison de rencontre*
of a particularly equivocal nature during a raid. Fifty years before,
the same thing had happened to Lord Castlereagh, and he had
committed suicide. The young man's evil reputation soon spread.
The rumour gained ground that he was Jack the Ripper (others
attributed the crimes committed in Whitechapel to the Duke of
Bedford). Paul Feval's *Mystères de Londres* was far outdone by
popular imagination. Clarence's sister, Princess Victoria, was also
for a moment a victim of *fin de siècle* giddiness. She fell in love
with a Society painter who had a perfumed beard and long ringlets
and would in no way have been a suitable husband. The Prince
soon put an end to this ridiculous affair, and the young girl returned to being her mother's shadow, copying her dress, hair style,
and mode of make-up.

During the 'nineties, Marlborough House, saddened by Clarence's death and emptied by marriage, was to see less and less of
the Prince. The wind of dissipation was blowing through London;
a statue to Eros triumphant was raised in the centre of Piccadilly
Circus on a modern-looking pedestal. All around this statue, in the
theatres, in the Café Royal where artists and writers met, at the
Amphitryon where millionaires gave fabulous dinner parties, and
in the drawing-rooms of Mayfair, London was in a state of
singular effervescence, avid for rare pleasures and new crazes.
Victorian dignity tottered before the temptations introduced from
Paris or the Orient.

In Phil May's sketches we can still see the crowd that thronged
Piccadilly Circus after the closing of the theatres: flower sellers
in large hats; peers, some with monocles and gold-headed canes,
strolling about with chorus girls from the music-hall (some of
them even married them); guardsmen in their tight-fitting red
tunics, guttersnipes slipping pornography or an address that
catered for every taste into the hands of rich Australians or
prospectors returning from South Africa; bookmakers and stockbrokers; Jews and their beplumed wives; Hindus; sailors walking
arm in arm singing "Ta-ra-ra boom-dee-ay" as they looked for

adventure; the last of the flashy *demi-mondaines*; girls sought by the police; red-faced provincials, the easy prey of pickpockets; salvationists standing shoulder to shoulder before this tidal wave of immorality; and enormous policemen. Here Oscar Wilde bought up the whole of a flower seller's stall to fill Lord Alfred's cab, a flamboyant gesture that earned him the ungrateful abuse of the other stall-holders. Max Beerbohm, small and precise, would dash off caricatures on his top hat; the tall, pale Aubrey Beardsley would order an absinthe at the Café Royal. His exquisite and morbid drawings for Wilde's *Salomé* and for the *avant garde* review *The Yellow Book* were the most characteristic products of these "mauve" years; their influence on European taste was profound.

The "mauve 'nineties" wilted in the mud stirred up by the Wilde case; Kipling and the Empire were to triumph over the decadents. Puritanism always exacts the severest penalties from pleasure-seekers. The Prince, who had had his share of them, did not hide his sympathies for Wilde, who was a subtle flatterer and an amusing and convivial companion. Edward had often been to have tea with the poet. Before his marriage Wilde had shared a house with an artist whose very young girl friend used to do the honours. For all its importance in the history of ideas, the aesthetic movement had had little influence in England. It was confined to a small area of London, to Oxford, and to a few wealthy people. The Souls were too involved in politics to be bothered with the *avant garde*, but they were not against it. No one doubted that Balfour and Asquith would be prime ministers, and meanwhile the ageing Salisbury was slowly getting rid of the accretions of a long reign. The machine of government had become ossified by routine. The Queen's voice was becoming increasingly cracked with age and, like her administration, she was sinking into the grave. The Boer War revealed the army's unfitness and the Government's ineptitude.

There was nothing Victorian about the literature of this period. Wilde's plays with their intriguers, millionaires, and dedicated adulterers, are a portrait of Edwardian Society, facile and ostentatious. In style they resembled those of Sheridan and their appearance was accompanied by a return to eighteenth-century tastes. Wilde knew the professional beauties well. One episode in Edward's life during these years might have been taken straight from *Lady Windermere's Fan.*

Lord Charles Beresford, an extraordinarily good-looking Irishman with a difficult nature, had for some time been Lady Brooke's lover (she was later Lady Warwick); the Prince also found her attractive and started to pay court to her until eventually she gave in to him. This betrayal came to Lord Charles's ears; during a ball given by Lady Brooke, he lost control of himself on seeing the Prince and approached him with his fist clenched. "Do not strike me," was all his Highness said and his sang-froid avoided *lèse majesté* and scandal. It was a comedy turn but its consequences were considerable, since Beresford was an admiral and had very great influence at the Admiralty; he did his utmost to oppose all Edward's plans when the Prince became King and tried to reorganize the fleet. Edward VII on the other hand refused even to consider the often remarkable suggestions that came from his former rival.

Equally worthy of Wilde is the following anecdote. The Prince could not bear to sit down thirteen to table. Once, when dining in a castle in Germany, he noticed early in the meal that there were only twelve other guests and this upset him very much. But then his face suddenly cleared. "Everything is all right, Princess Frederick Charles of Hesse is pregnant," he said. One can imagine these Society figures sweeping through the palm-filled Louis XV drawing-rooms in which Wilde's comedies were set, awaiting their destined moment of triumph when the new reign dawned: Lady de Grey, tall and beautiful as a goddess; Margot Asquith, small and erect like a fighting cock, responding to Mrs. Hwfa Williams' long guffaws with a sarcastic laugh; and "my dear Duchess," more imposing and more diamond-studded than ever, patronizing the more promising of the new generation. "They sailed in" was an expression used by the survivors of this period, comparing those proud and gracious ladies, beplumed and riding high, to sailing ships entering port.

Among the beauties who had achieved fame already, and who

succeeded in retaining their renown right up to the 1914 war, was the young Mrs. George Keppel. As elegant as she was beautiful, and as amusing as she was subtle, she was presented to the Prince in 1896, during Newmarket week, by one of her admirers, a cousin of the Churchills. Hardly had the eyes of the ageing and blasé Highness rested upon this superb creature than they burst into life. The Prince of Wales completely took her over and she assumed a place in his life which no woman except the Princess had ever had. The young woman's gaiety thrilled the old egotist. He could not bear to be separated from her for more than a week throughout the thirteen years of life which remained to him. Alice Keppel was the daughter of a Scottish baronet and the granddaughter of a Greek beauty. Her husband, the younger son of Lord Albemarle, came from a family which already owed much to royal favour. The first Albemarle, a handsome Dutchman, owed his title and his fortune to the patronage of William III. Ever since, the Keppel family had filled high positions at Court. It is said that the husband acted with a tact that retained for him the Prince's friendship and the esteem of his friends.

Where racing was concerned, '96 was a great year for the Prince; his horse Persimmon's victory in the Derby won him not only an extraordinary recovery in popularity, but also £30,000 in prize money and bets. The humiliated gambler had had his revenge! He was now the king of sportsmen, and that term included a very large number of his future subjects. He owed his triumph, one of the greatest that England can offer, not only to chance, which he called the glorious incertitude of the turf, but also to his profound knowledge of horses: as he brought in the winner, top hats and canes were thrown in the air. The acclamations rang out again that same evening in the large dining-room at Marlborough House, in which he gave, as every year, a banquet to celebrate the Derby. The wheel had turned full circle; everything was now going to be all right and he would be a popular king. Lord Esher, one of his most faithful friends, saw in the victory of Persimmon (by Saint Simon out of Perdita II) the happiest event of the Prince's life. At the height of this triumph, the Prince found time to write Lady Warwick a very long letter that

was both tender and prudent. Beresford had insisted on congratulating him, and Edward had been unable to refuse him his hand,
but "my little wife" should not worry, the scandal would never be
forgiven.

About this time he achieved a victory in diplomacy which in
any other country would have won him considerable esteem, but
in England it had little effect on public opinion for it struck at the
arrogance of the imperialists. The Prince was very sympathetic
towards the United States and included numerous Americans
among his friends, such as the Senator and banker Chauncey
Depew, whom he had met at Marienbad, and Whitelaw Reid, an
extremely wealthy businessman who was the Ambassador to London. (In the United States embassies were once the homage which
Government paid to riches, rather like peerages in England.) It
is a little-known fact that in 1895 the United Kingdom and the
United States were within an ace of war over a frontier question
involving Venezuela and British Guiana. Brandishing the Monroe
Doctrine, President Cleveland was delighted to have a pretext for
getting a foothold in South America and energetically took
Venezuela's side. The English press's response to his interference
was howling defiance. Ambassadors found themselves delivering
messages that were hardly diplomatic. The editor of *The New
York World* became alarmed at the proportions that this trivial
incident was assuming. He knew the Prince well and telegraphed
him to ask his advice. Marlborough House replied "that the crisis
will be succeeded by the same warm feeling of friendship which
had existed between [the two countries] for so many years."

When the telegram was published in *The New York World*, it
immediately had a soothing effect. Lord Salisbury, who had
originally asked the Prince not to send it, had to admit to its
being very opportune. A commission drawn from both sides of the
Atlantic was sent out to establish the shadowy frontiers, and the
public realized the absurdity of such a quarrel. The Prince's happy
intervention recalled, though in less dramatic form, a similar action
by his father thirty years before, when he had prevented war with
the Northern States by going over the Foreign Minister Granville's head.

In 1897 the Diamond Jubilee, which marked the sixtieth year of the reign, gave Edward the opportunity to exhibit his talents as an organizer. It was Victoria's farewell to a public that now adored her, to an Empire which believed itself invincible, and to a family which was established on most of the thrones of Europe. It was all done very simply, without any sentimentality, or a word out of place, and with all the discretion of someone who has no further illusions. The curtain was falling on an earnest, honest, often narrow but sometimes generous, sentimental, and pious epoch. The play that was to follow was being rehearsed in the wings, and had been for several years past; the Edwardian era had already begun at Marlborough House, with its professional beauties, its Jewish grandees, its actors. The Season of 1897 was extraordinarily brilliant. "My dear Duchess," who had by this time been widowed and married to her lover Hartington, now the Duke of Devonshire (hence the nickname "double-duchess"), gave an enormous fancy-dress ball at Devonshire House. Dressed herself as Zenobia, she decked out a beauty that was as crumbling as the proud Palmyra's with chokers of diamonds and ropes of pearls. The Prince of Wales came in the striking costume of a Commander of the Templars, and the Princess as Marguerite de Valois. Some of the more promising members of the younger generation were also invited: Lord Derby, whose mother was Clarendon's daughter, and who had just married the Duchess's daughter; Balfour, who was continuing the Salisbury tradition; Rosebery with his Rothschild wife; Winston Churchill, who had both his father's genius and his manners; and the Asquiths. The plebs, too, were not forgotten: free meals for 330,000 paupers spread the party spirit into the suburbs.

Despite Persimmon's victory and Mrs. Keppel's influence, the Prince's temper became worse. He was cruelly aware of the ridiculous side of his position and became very difficult to amuse. Staying at Waddesdon with Ferdinand de Rothschild in 1898, he slipped on a staircase, fell down a few steps which fortunately were thickly carpeted, and broke his knee. The excitement among the domestics, the host's consternation, and the horror of his entourage can be imagined. If he had to spend two months in plaster, the Prince would become intolerable. They persuaded him to go off on a cruise; he would be able to stretch out and avoid such temptations as the theatre and the races.

"Let's ask Sykes," he said, knowing full well that his poor friend was alone capable of putting up with his bad temper. Sykes, who was very ill, was taking a cure at Homburg; on his doctor's orders he begged the Prince to excuse him. A telegram reminded him that such an invitation was an order. The courtier interrupted his cure and, after a difficult journey, joined the yacht. The Prince found him listless and a few days later gave him leave to disembark. A week later Sykes died. After his death, as after his ruin, Edward's behaviour was impeccable. With his leg still in plaster he attended the funeral, the one sort of ceremony that he did not appreciate. He ordered a plaque to be engraved to the memory of his faithful friend: "Where is it to be put?" he was asked. "In the stables," said the Prince with a smile. "No, in the Royal Chapel, that would be more suitable." And from a paradise which, let us hope, resembles Marlborough House but is inhabited by angelic Highnesses, the martyr to snobbery could look down and see his name immortalized in company with royalty of many generations.

One disagreeable incident had an unfortunate effect on the Prince's temper during the final year that remained to him before he reached the throne. On April 3, 1900, as he sat in a train in the station in Brussels with his wife, on his way to Copenhagen, he was fired at by a young anarchist named Sipido. The bullet passed between the Prince and the Princess, grazing on its way the hat worn by Miss Knollys, their lady-in-waiting. Everyone remained perfectly calm. It was at this time that the cry "*Vive les Boers*" was to be heard at every street corner on the Continent. Sipido's ambition was "to strike down Kruger's hangman." The Belgian police, who no doubt shared his opinions, allowed him to escape, and their negligence incurred the Prince's displeasure. He took his cousin Leopold to task for it. The Belgian King went to Paris himself and with the aid of his friend M. Lepine tracked Sipido down. The Belgian courts gave the anarchist a very light sentence.

"Ah! my dear," his Russian sister-in-law said to Edward, "do not take it too seriously. In my family we are so used to assassinations." The Kaiser and the other sovereigns sent telegrams of congratulation. The English were more reserved, and their joy that the heir to the throne had escaped death was less evident; Parliament neglected to vote an address of sympathy. Marlborough House discovered that the popularity brought by Persimmon's victory had not percolated through to the political world. After this attempt on the Prince's life, the Queen gave orders that members of her family should be carefully guarded. An excellent detective, called Melville, was attached to the Prince and followed him everywhere. Assassination attempts were on the increase during the 'nineties and in the group photographs royalty has a hunted look, as though fearful that the camera might conceal an infernal machine, but the anarchists had very little success in England. The Grand Duchess of Mecklenburg-Strelitz (Cousin Augusta) wrote to her niece, the Duchess of York:

> My plan against the anarchist monsters is to suppress all associations, to muzzle the press, and then to seize any man or woman who expresses anarchist opinions and to whip him daily; as for the assassins, they should first be tortured and then strapped to the mouth of a cannon.

The Princess of Wales was not impressed by such refinement and would have preferred that they be lynched by the mob.

Queen Victoria's reign reached its apotheosis with the Jubilee and should have ended there but, as it dragged on, England became increasingly isolated in consequence of the reverses suffered in South Africa. In the wings, the rehearsals for the following reign still continued. A treaty of no very great importance indicated that Edward VII's policies would be based on his personal prejudices. The Marquess of Soveral negotiated an arrangement by which England would refloat the finances of Portugal (her ally for three centuries) and also arranged an exchange of islands in the Pacific, of which a few went to Germany. This appeased William II, who was aware that he had become a laughing stock over the Coburg succession. These negotiations were conducted over dinner by the fat King Don Carlos, the Prince, and Soveral, without reference to their Governments. Everything was so well arranged that the Chancelleries had nothing to do but subscribe to the proposals that came from Marlborough House.

In 1901 the Queen's health rapidly declined, but her personality remained so powerful that the future King was still left in the shade. The Government also ignored him and the red dispatch boxes piled up on the tables at Osborne.

CHAPTER NINE

The Widow at Windsor

THE QUEEN'S POPULARITY, nurtured by Disraeli and deepened by the struggle with Gladstone, had reached its triumphal apogee in the Golden Jubilee of 1887. Victoria had settled the smallest details; she no longer objected to appearing in public or to bedecking herself in lace and jewellery. She even opened her palaces to her guests, the representatives of every Court in Europe. Only the royal houses of Austria, Spain, and Italy were not related to her now. The Prince of Wales, who knew them all personally, was a marvellous host. Marlborough House was never without its quota of ambassadors extraordinary, crowned heads, and maharajas. When the procession set out to cross London from Buckingham Palace to St. Paul's, with the heir to the throne at its head, it consisted of thirty-two princes, all relatives of the Queen.

The most handsome, wearing on his head the golden, eagle-crested helmet, was Prince Frederick, the heir apparent of Prussia and favourite son-in-law. The Dukes of Clarence and York, who had just returned from a world cruise, were the darlings of the crowd; the Duke of Connaught could be recognized by his aquiline nose and enormous moustache, and the old Duke of Cambridge was unmistakeable in his marshal's uniform. But the populace of London was confused by such a plethora of royalty: their beards made all the princes look alike, and it was hard to tell the difference between Prince Christian and the Duke of Edinburgh or to distinguish between the Hesses and the Battenbergs. But that hardly worried the people. They were waiting for the simple landau in which Victoria, who regarded gilded coaches as vulgar, was riding slowly along Fleet Street and the Strand. The jingling accoutrements, the glittering medals, the serried ranks of plumes, these meant little to them, but the little lady in black, with osprey feathers on her head, received an incredible ovation. Opposite the Queen, slender and still beneath her sunshade, sat the Princess of Wales, smiling like a wax mannequin, and the Princess of Prussia, who, overcome with emotion, was wiping away her tears. The Queen's daughters followed in other carriages, their dresses embroidered with jet, and rows of medals upon their breasts, the slender Helena, the sad Beatrice, and poor little Louise, whom the Duke of Argyll treated so badly. Now that Victoria had passed, the crowd stared silently at them; a few princesses, blond hair showing beneath the lace confections on their heads, still attracted an occasional cheer, but the procession from this point on was really a circus parade consisting of Indian potentates and delegations from the lands of the East. The Queen stood up well to the fatigue and emotional strain of these days; her people's enthusiasm gave her strength. As the Prince bowed to kiss her hand after the *Te Deum* in St. Paul's, he must have thought that she still had a lot of life left in her.

But there was one young man who remained aloof from these family festivities: Victoria's favourite grandson, William of Prussia. He had little affection for his parents and it annoyed him to see them take their place in the front rank of royalty while he himself was just one of a crowd. He would not have long to wait. Shortly after the Jubilee the Crown Prince developed cancer of the throat and went off to San Remo, with his wife and a small suite, thus further removing himself from the seat of power. A whole network of spies surrounded them, controlled, through their Chamberlain Radolinski, later to be Prince Radolin, by Bismarck. The Chancellor watched their mail and persuaded the old Emperor to forbid them to visit the Montpensiers, who were at Cannes. (Bismarck was afraid of an Orléanist coup, which he thought would have strengthened France.) The young Prince William never once went to his father's bedside. He had other cares. His grand-

H.M.The Queen.

father could refuse him nothing and invited him to a meeting with the Emperors of Russia and Austria which took place at Gastein on August 8, 1886: "Do I need to tell you that he will only commit stupidities," his mother wrote to his grandmother. "Willy is as much a novice, and as headstrong and violent in politics as it is possible to be. He swears only by Reuss* and he is Russian to the tips of his fingers."

After the meeting, the future William II engaged in a correspondence with Tsar Alexander III in the mystical tone so dear to Russian sovereigns since the great days of the Holy Alliance:

> The Prince of Wales's visit was extraordinarily fruitful and its effects will be increased by the influence of my mother and of the Queen of England. These English forget but one thing: my existence, but I swear to you, my dear cousin, that I shall do everything for both you and for your Empire.

Rash comments such as "sooner or later England and Russia will be at war" alarmed Queen Victoria's daughter and added to her anguish. The only being who could have supported her, her husband, Frederick, reigned for a mere hundred days in 1888 and then died through the negligence, so the Germans said, of an English doctor. He left his wife to the mercy of a son who laughed at her, and of Bismarck, who hated her. On the day of Frederick's death, the Empress's palace was surrounded by troops, and her papers were confiscated.

All her ambitions and hopes now frustrated, a foreigner in both Germany and England, Victoria's daughter found consolation only in the long letters which she wrote to her mother:

> Willy never speaks to me about you any more or about any of his English cousins. It is so wounding and disappointing after all the trouble I have been to for him!

The Prussian Court's indifference to the Emperor Frederick's obsequies was all the more painful to the Prince of Wales in that this heartlessness often took the form of bad manners. He even went so far as to say, so angry was he, that his brother-in-law, had he lived, would have given Schleswig back to Denmark and

---

* A German prince, the Kaiser's Chancellor.

Alsace back to France. It was a most improbable supposition, and in any case it was an unwise thing to say, for it helped to make Edward hated in Germany: but then his family was more important to him than matters of state. The Princess also expressed her indignation:

> Instead of consoling his mother, William is entirely on Bismarck and company's side, and they treat her as if she were of no importance.

Her brother's rash comments only weakened the Empress's position: "Why does Bismarck make me responsible for what Alix and Bertie have said about Ernest of Cumberland?"* she said. (The Prince and Princess had wanted the latter's Hanoverian possessions returned to him.) The Empress Frederick retired from Berlin to her château at Friedrichshof, where she devoted herself to her enormous collection of *objets d'art*. She had inherited this passion from the Prince Consort and its spirit is to be found in such vast museums as the Victoria and Albert and the Kaiser Friedrich.

Now that she was a widow the Empress seldom risked a visit to Berlin, and her health declined: she was subject to a sort of ague which gave her nervous tremblings, but she still retained a sublime smile on her lips. The reports that she sent to Windsor of her son William caused nothing but alarm.

> I still hope that since he is your grandson and dear Papa's, the antediluvian ideas of the Hohenzollerns will be modified by a broader and more humane spirit, but unfortunately he is at the mercy of a military clique.

The Junkers, who disapproved of the Empress's friendships with Jews, regarded the Jewish grandees with which her brother, the Prince of Wales, surrounded himself, with horror. The young Emperor spoke of them with insensate passion. He believed himself to be chosen by God to crush socialism and to repulse the barbarians of the East. In one of her rare moments of humour the Empress described her son's romantic ideas:

---

* The husband of Alexandra's youngest sister.

Everything has to be done at top speed so as to create surprise. The ideal Minister for William would be a combination of Jules Verne, Lord Randolph Churchill, and General Boulanger, plus a few explorers and of course Richard Wagner if he were still alive.

Chancellor von Bülow could also be quite amusing on the subject of William II's frenzied way of doing things:

> The Emperor was at his most excitable when contemplating a meeting with another sovereign or when treading on foreign soil. His feelings were a mixture of impatience, joyful anticipation, and nervousness; he was like a young girl entering a ballroom for the first time, anxious about how it would all turn out. But as dance succeeds dance without mishap, and as the keepsakes mount on her chair the young girl becomes radiantly happy, as she sees her fondest wishes coming true.

And the Chancellor added:

> In Russia, he behaved like an aide de camp of the *ancien régime*, or like one of the Princes of Oldenburg or Altenburg at the Imperial Court; in England, he was the Queen's grandson and an Admiral of the Fleet; but in Italy he shone with a different light: at the Quirinal he was completely *Casa Savoya*, and at the Vatican he believed himself to be the protector of the Papacy.

The Emperor would speak of his grandmother, Queen Victoria, with tears in his eyes but he would turn his back on his mother. He could be both excessively affable and excessively reserved, almost to the point of loutishness: everything the young man did proved an irritant to his uncle. William II's idealism (he saw himself as Lohengrin), and his self-assurance, which was caused as much by his desire to cover up his infirmity—a withered arm —as by the adulation of the Court, dazzled the less percipient Germans. They saw, in this proud, fairly handsome and chaste young man, the reincarnation of medieval emperors. But all this Wagnerianism remained incomprehensible to the Prince of Wales, who was more of an Offenbach character himself. The young man regarded his uncle as a debauchee, an intriguer, a Francophile, and a spy; he nicknamed him "the old popinjay." The antipathy was deeply rooted, almost physiological; Edward adored the company of women; William, whose mother had brought him up very strictly, was more of a misogynist. Though he did not take his fondness for his soldiers as far as did Frederick the Great, he felt at ease only when dining with his General Staff. Both Bismarck and von Bülow distrusted their master's muddled genius, his passion for the theatrical, and his acute but hasty intelligence. Once they had been driven out, he was a toy in the hands of his Prussian officers. "Willy is mad, absolutely mad," his mother kept repeating. With his uncle he had but one point in common, his passion for changing from one uniform into another. When Edward sent him a tartan kilt, William lost no time in having himself photographed in it and sending a copy of the portrait to his uncle; the intention was kind, but he wrote at the bottom: "My hour will come." This provided food for thought—something of which they had a horror at Marlborough House.

The Prince of Wales was soon to realize how lucky he was that Bismarck was still in office; the Chancellor would probably be able to put a brake on the young Emperor's folly. Even his accession to power was marked by an affront to the English royal family. He forbade his sister to marry a Battenberg, an incident that delighted the Russians since the victim was Prince Alexander, who had been such a nuisance to them as King of Bulgaria.

The rise of the Battenberg family, which acquired among the monarchies of Europe a position of far greater eminence than that recognized by the Almanach de Gotha, is worthy of a short digression. Prince Alexander of Hesse, Tsar Alexander II's brother-in-law and an officer in the Russian Army, was a handsome man (his great-grandson, the Duke of Edinburgh, resembles him). He had married a certain Countess von Haucke, who was of both Polish and French blood. The Grand Duke of Hesse, having ascertained that this match had gained his powerful brother-in-law's approval, granted Prince Alexander the title of Battenberg but, since the Tsar Alexander III treated the children of this morganatic union with the utmost contempt, they turned for protection to the English Court. Ever since Prince Albert had expressed his opinion that "We are too fair, we must have some warmer blood for our children," Queen Victoria had sought sons-in-law of a darker complexion and more amenable nature. Her youngest and favourite daughter, Beatrice, married Henry of Battenberg in 1885. Her granddaughter Victoria of Hesse married Prince Louis of Battenberg, a British Admiral of the Fleet. The third brother, Alexander, was designated by the Congress of Berlin as the ruling Prince of Bulgaria under Turkish sovereignty, although his only knowledge of that country was derived from his experience as an officer in the invading Russian Army. However, Rumania had been given a Hohenzollern and Greece a Dane and they had both done very well. On one occasion Alexander had saved the Tsar's life;* a bomb had been placed beneath the dining-room in the Winter Palace, timed to go off between the dessert and the cheese courses; as Alexander arrived late, however, it only blew up an empty table while the guests were still waiting in an adjoining room. At Darmstadt in 1884 the Battenbergs made a big impression on the romantically inclined Queen Victoria. It was there that the youngest daughter, Beatrice, fell in love with Henry and the eldest of the good Vicky's daughters developed a passion for the handsome Alexander. This Prince had already visited London before gaining his Bulgarian domain; such was the prestige of the English Court, and the effect of Disraeli's friendship, that he was rash enough to forget his debt to the Russians. When he arrived in Sofia he paid more attention to his subjects than to the directives he received from St. Petersburg, and always consulted London before making decisions. But Russians are not possessed of great patience: during the autumn of 1886 Tsar Alexander III ordered the Battenberg to be removed from his palace by a commando of officers. Taken prisoner, he was obliged to abdicate at the point of a pistol. Queen Victoria wrote to the unhappy young man:

> My indignation against your barbarous, Asiatic and tyrannical cousin is so great, that I don't wish to write to him any more.

There was a frenzy of excitement amongst royalty; those who had ties with St. Petersburg were cautious, but Alexander was allowed to return to Germany. In Berlin he once more met the Emperor Frederick's daughter and was presumptuous enough to ask for her hand. London was behind him, but the young girl's

---

* February 17, 1880.

brother became Emperor at this point and expressed his disapproval violently. "What! a Battenberg!" he stormed and forbade the betrothal. Her mother was not to be put off: Russia made protests and the Hesses, who were divided between St. Petersburg and London, kept silent for fear of compromising themselves. Letters flew in all directions and the chancelleries were in a fever. Queen Victoria herself came to Berlin. Bismarck unreservedly supported his Emperor:

> It is clear [he said] that by this marriage the Queen wishes to embroil Germany with Russia, and as she is not in the habit of being opposed in family matters, she will put the priest in a sack, the husband in a trunk, and have the marriage instantly celebrated.

The Chancellor sought an audience with the Queen of England. After their interview, she was to persuade Alexander to renounce the Prussian Princess's hand. The young man went to Osborne to get over his upset. "How I envy you having Sandro with you," wrote the girl's mother to the Queen. "It will be as good for him physically as it will morally." She must indeed have been taken with him.

Having set Europe by the heels for more than ten years, sowing discord among the ruling families and practically starting a war, Alexander of Battenberg now retired from the political scene and married a singer of no consequence.

The young Emperor, who at the time of his accession was as irritated by his uncle's remarks at the Emperor Frederick's funeral as he was by Edward's friendship for Alexander of Battenberg, now made it impossible to keep up even the appearances of politeness that the Prince was so anxious to retain. On one occasion the Archduke Rudolf had invited the Prince of Wales to shoot in Austria. No sooner had he arrived in Vienna than the Emperor of Germany invited himself to Franz Josef's Court and demanded that he should be the only visitor of mark in the capital. His Ambassador called on the English Ambassador to tell him that the Emperor "would prefer the Prince's bedroom to his presence." Suffocating with rage, "the uncle" went off to stay at the dismal Court of Rumania for the duration of his nephew's visit. Rudolf was too great a friend of the Prince for Franz Josef to be able to uphold his guest's dignity with conviction, and Queen Victoria expressed her indignation unreservedly. Bismarck found himself obliged to supply an explanation: the Prince, he said, was treating William as an uncle would a nephew, and was forgetting that he was now the Emperor. The Queen's indignation was redoubled, and she wrote again, this time underlining her words:

> The idea that the Prince did not treat his nephew as an Emperor is really too *vulgar* and *too* absurd . . . almost to be *believed*. We have *always* been very attached to our grandson and his pretension to be treated in *private* as in *public* as an Imperial Majesty is pure folly. He has been treated *exactly* as the Queen herself treated her dear uncle, King Leopold. If he has *such* notions, he had better *never* come *here*. The Queen will not swallow this affront.

Lord Salisbury, and Bismarck himself, somehow managed to patch things up, but William II had cruelly wounded his uncle, a mature man in a difficult position that was only made worse by the least lack of respect. Thus the 'eighties finished on an unfortunate note. Right to the end of his days the hatred which he felt for William II was to have a large place in Edward VII's thinking. "The old popinjay" would now refer to the Emperor only as "my illustrious nephew," but humour does not have much currency in Germany. At one time the qualifying adjective had been taken for a proof of admiration, but very soon the irony became insulting. In time, however, William wrote some sentimental letters to his grandmother and she softened towards him as she had softened on his eighteenth birthday. When she sent him the Order of the Bath, he sulked: it was the Garter that he wanted and shortly afterwards a duke was sent to Berlin to confer one on him. The Kaiser now expressed a wish to visit England with great pomp and the Queen accepted the request with pleasure. He arrived with an impressive-looking fleet, displayed affection for his family, and was full of consideration for the members of the Government. The Prince and Princess managed to be nice to him, and the visit was a success. Victoria loved treating this powerful Emperor as a little boy, in the same way that she loved giving advice to the charming young couple Alix of Hesse and Nicholas II.

She had a preference for her German relatives, for she saw them only on formal occasions and found them more serious-minded than her English descendants. The Prince and Princess's children were still the same sickly infants that had so disturbed her as she had bent over their cradles. The eldest seemed rather abnormal with his long, narrow head and his drooping shoulders. It was impossible to interest him in anything serious but he adored dancing and fell madly in love all over the place, with debutantes or with friends of the family who treated him like a little boy.

Yes, it was going to be a problem to find the Duke of Clarence a wife; neither the public nor his family was particularly keen on the idea of a Russian or a German alliance. He was nearly thirty when he fell violently in love with the Princess Hélène of Orléans, the daughter of the Count of Paris. His parents, who admired the young girl's beauty and intelligence, approved this choice, but she was a Catholic. What would the Queen say? What would the Pope say? the Count of Paris wondered. The Queen softened when the young couple threw themselves at her feet and she decided that, if the Princess did cling to her religion, the throne would have to pass to Edward's younger son. Was this indulgence or prudence? Prince George was after all a better choice than his elder brother. But Pope Leo XIII forbade a mixed marriage and the Pretender took his daughter off to Italy, where she married the Duke of Aosta. Prince Eddy would have to be married off without further delay before he made some irreparable mistake.

There was a young girl who was "suitable from every angle" living outside the orbit of the Court, but she was a bad match on account of her parents' eccentricities. Princess Mary (May) of Teck was the daughter of a cousin german of the Queen, the fat Mary of Cambridge, and of a friend of Edward's and Alexandra's, the Prince of Teck, the son of a Württemberg and of a pretty Hungarian woman. This pair, who were very much beloved in Society, had to spend long periods abroad to escape their creditors, although Victoria was eventually to pay them off with a bad grace. Princess May had a reflective rather than an intelligent nature and was fresh-faced rather than pretty; she was reserved in the presence of her relations and her rowdy brothers; but she was descended from George III. The Queen summoned her to Balmoral and found her perfect. It was arranged that she should go and stay a week-end with a Danish diplomat who was also entertaining Edward and his family. Prince Eddy had known May all his life, but now he wisely fell in love with her. The betrothal was joyfully announced: a sensible woman would keep the heir to the throne on the right path. But a month before the marriage a congestion of the lungs removed Clarence from the scene; in his delirium, as the end approached, he called for Hélène of Orléans. Princess May returned to the shadows, and the whole process had to start again from the beginning, this time with the younger brother. George, Duke of York, was a sailor and a handsome, serious-minded man, passionately attached to his mother. "Let him marry May," the Queen decided. The Princess was recalled and the marriage took place on July 6, 1893, in the chapel at St. James's Palace. As the future Queen Mary advanced to the altar, Victoria shed tears beneath her veil. The Prince and Princess of Wales were smiling, the Princess of Teck was triumphant, and dear Cousin Augusta and all the royals from Rumpenheim were there. Following the bride were ten princesses dressed in white lace and carrying bunches of that very *fin-de-siècle* flower, the orchid, instead of the conventional little bouquet. It was not long before the affection in which the Prince and Princess of Wales were held by the people was extended to the young Duke and Duchess of York.

But it was not so easy to marry off the daughters. It was said that they were backward and infantile and their mother would not allow them to be taken away from her. The Empress Frederick, who never had enough to worry about, wrote to her mother with a note of concern:

On the subject of the marriages of our dear Bertie's adorable daughters, I do not believe that Dolly Teck [the Duchess of York's brother] or Ernie Hohenlohe, charming as they may be, are quite the thing for your granddaughters. Max of Baden, who will perhaps be the grand duke, or the young Lippe, who at least is not mediatized, would be much better. I am going to write to Bertie about it, but I am afraid of irritating our dear Alix and of interfering in their family affairs; it isn't wise to leave the destiny of these dear little ones "in the void."

Louise, the eldest, was eventually married to a great friend of her father's, the Duke of Fife. He was very rich and he shared the Prince's tastes for business and racing. A timid girl, she spent the rest of her life in the most solitary of his Scottish castles, fishing for trout. The Government asked the House of Commons for a dowry, which gave rise, as had always happened with her aunts, to disagreeable scenes in Parliament. Maud, the youngest, married a Danish cousin who later became King Haakon of Norway. Victoria never found anyone suitable.

The Jubilee in 1897 brought to the Queen's door representatives from every part of the Empire; it was like an immense family celebration, an apotheosis organized by Kipling; regiments of every colour marched behind the royal coach. No foreign sovereign was invited; Ferdinand of Bulgaria, priding himself on his Coburg cousinage, was the only one to come to London. Coldly received, he took offence. The Queen's carriage was escorted by her sons and grandsons on horseback. So as to avoid tiring her, the thanksgiving service was performed by clergy and choristers on the steps of St. Paul's Cathedral while she remained seated in her carriage; fortunately the weather was fine. It was Victoria's last appearance. Shortly afterwards her sight declined, her memory became feeble, and she fell totally under the influence of her daughter Beatrice, whose opinion of her brother was not a high one. Edward received no thanks for his help in organizing the Jubilee; he was still only rarely received by his mother, but their views on politics were at last drawing closer; they were at least agreed on the decision to carry the African war on to victory, and on distrust of Germany.

After the triumphal Jubilee, Queen Victoria sank back into old age, or rather into a sort of immortality. The etiquette which surrounded the sovereign became almost sacerdotal. Her silent and rheumatic Court lived in terror and in adoration. The diary of a

lady-in-waiting, Lady Lytton, suggests the atmosphere of Balmoral
during the 'nineties:

> The Princesses play patiences but the gentlemen stand at the end
> of the room in a very stiff way and very tiring to themselves. . . .
> The evening was very dull as usual. The Queen went away to see
> Princess Beatrice part of the time, and Princess Christian was very
> sleepy. . . . Princess Beatrice got annoyed with the Queen because
> she interrupted a game of halma. The Princess complains of having
> to give up so many things. . . .

This atmosphere weighed heavily on the Prince and robbed
him of all his vitality. He would go for weeks without seeing his
mother. One of Max Beerbohm's caricatures, entitled "The Rare,
the Rather Awful Visits of Albert Edward, Prince of Wales, to
Windsor Castle," shows the Queen in the foreground, her lips
tight, a white mob cap on her head, and in the corner, like a child,
a fat and bald old gentleman. "Why should I go and see the
Queen?" the Prince asked a confidential friend. "She listens to all
her children except me."

Beatrice, the Queen's youngest daughter, and her husband,
Henry of Battenberg, who was known as Liko, never left her;
they helped her to receive her visitors; it was they who persuaded
her to bring down singers to Windsor. Her beloved son-in-law
even managed to convince Victoria that a room, one of course that
was as far as possible from those which she occupied, should be
set aside for smoking. The Battenbergs' influence might have been
resented by those close to her, but there was one person whose
position in the inner circle of the Queen's household positively
exasperated her family and caused alarm in the official world.

The Empress of India had decided to learn Hindustani and for
this purpose had engaged a bearded and turbaned Indian called
Munshi Abdul Karim. He quickly became as indispensable as John
Brown had been. One can see him as a shadow in the background
of all the Queen's portraits: he acted as her guide when her sight
started to fail, and was always close at hand when, seated in an
armchair, she received her Ministers or her children. He brought
over his wife and mother and insisted on having Indian servants;

the wholly Oriental smell of roast sheep spread out from the apartments which they occupied, and percolated through the courtyards of Windsor. The India Office became anxious; secret information was being spread, and they begged the Queen not to ask Abdul Karim to read the Delhi dispatches.

To her offspring, it was no little cause for anxiety that the head of the family should fall into the hands of a servant while at the same time retaining full control of the reins of power, and the Government was equally alarmed. Victoria had to do everything for herself, to see everything, and to sign everything, and although she worked hard late into the night, the red boxes piled up on the tables. Beatrice assisted her but, stupid and muddle-headed as she was, she often forgot to open the most important boxes. She was too absorbed in the water colours which she painted for charity sales. As the Queen's sight gradually deteriorated, the secretaries had to copy the dispatches for her in larger and larger handwriting.

The old lady's obsessions took up as much of her time as did the care of her Empire. Such was her respect for the function of royalty that nothing that had ever belonged to her was thrown or given away; everything had to be arranged and catalogued and, if it was an *objet d'art*, photographed. She treated people in exactly the same way; they had to write their names in visiting-books with the dates of their birthdays. There was one for highnesses, one for diplomats, and one for artists. She took as much interest in the teeth of a newborn baby on a farm at Balmoral as in a reform proposed by her Viceroy that might affect the lives of millions; in either case she had to be kept precisely informed on developments in the situation.

From her bereavements she extracted a tragic joy. Her Battenberg son-in-law died in South Africa, and he was followed by a Schleswig-Holstein grandson: a photograph of the dead man would take its place on one of the tables, and these portraits crowded around the busts of Albert like tombs around a cenotaph. The Duke of Albany, Alice of Hesse, the dear Prince Imperial, Eddy Clarence, and the dear son-in-law Fritz, all dead. . . . She had survived, and her robust good sense seemed to draw strength from this fact. A lady-in-waiting said to her, "Isn't it nice, Madam, to know that we shall be meeting our loved ones again in Abraham's bosom?"

"I shall certainly not be meeting Abraham," replied the Queen, who on that day noted in her journal: "Poor Leila is not much consolation in these trying days."

But she found no more consolation in politics than she did in Leila. With the fall of Salisbury's Ministry, Gladstone returned to power for a short time. Then Lord Rosebery formed a Ministry. He was too young and too brilliant to gain the Queen's entire confidence. Her cherished policies of imperialism were held in check both in Afghanistan and in the Transvaal and were giving England a bad name among other nations. It was necessary at all costs to remain on good terms with Germany, and if possible not to fall out with Russia. Possibly Victoria had dreams of a family pact that could save the peace and assure the monarchical order. In September 1896 she invited the Tsar and his wife to Scotland. The Prince of Wales was also asked, to help put the members of the imperial suite at their ease, since they would find the atmosphere of Balmoral rather austere. Had he not just come back from Russia, where he had been attending the imperial wedding in a mood of considerable optimism? He would be able to lead the conversations, keep an eye on the seating arrangements at table, and organize the walks. As for the Queen, she would remain with her grandchildren, dispensing copious pots of tea in the Scottish manner.

Everything went off very well: the Queen and the Tsar discussed the world, of which, between them, they possessed over half. Her guest told his grandmother that the treaty with France was the best he could do to counterbalance the Triple Alliance. "Those ghastly Republicans are driving the priests from their churches and sending the Princes into exile." The Tsarina would slip in with a sigh: "I should simply hate to meet such people! Their newspapers wrote such horrible things about you, Granny dear! Their Society has no responsibility and is quite corrupt." Unfortunately the Queen of England did not have an autocrat's liberty to choose her own alliances, but this visit certainly helped to improve relations between the two countries and fostered in Englishmen's minds illusions of a youthful imperial couple brimming with sincerity and good-will.

The Prince of Wales clung to this impression without ever suspecting the way in which politics and mysticism were confused in his young relations' minds. Uncle Bertie, on the other hand, inspired them with the admiration that simple people often have for the sophisticated; and the Tsar adored his Aunt Alexandra. A photographer had been procured by the Queen to provide them with a souvenir which, thanks to a recent invention, was an animated one. The film was shown, to the great approbation of the Court, in the red drawing-room at Windsor three weeks later.

Next to this colourless autocrat, William II certainly seemed the dominant figure of the end of the nineteenth century. A good actor, with a feeling for publicity well in advance of his times, he was determined to keep his name, at whatever cost, on the front pages of the newspapers. Although his reign ended in disaster it should not be forgotten that, even in France, the young Emperor's ideas and approach made a deep impression on thoughtful people. The extravagance of his behaviour did not become evident until after 1900. The English admired his serious intent and found it hard to understand the Prince of Wales's hostility where the Emperor was concerned.

After his official visit in 1889 the Kaiser returned every summer to spend a few weeks with his grandmother at Osborne. There, in an effort to erase the impression made by his previous display of bad manners, he would treat his uncle with jovial familiarity, slip him advice on politics and sport, and in brief give everyone the impression that he regarded him as a kindly if faintly ridiculous old man. His great English friend, a man whom the Prince could not abide, was the great sportsman and yachtsman, Lord Lonsdale, who, although crippled with debts and very stupid, nevertheless believed himself destined to play a big role on the political stage. The Kaiser, on the other hand, found some of the habitués of Marlborough House, whom he met at the Royal Yacht Club, very distasteful, particularly the Jews, the complaisant husbands, and "the grocer," as he called the great tea merchant Sir Thomas Lipton. The members of this club, the most exclusive in England, soon found the Kaiser's visits, accompanied as he was by an enormous suite, to be extremely trying. Baron von Eckardtstein, an attaché at the German Embassy, who had an English wife and was a friend of the Prince, did his best to salve English *amour propre*. But the Kaiser's tendency to win the regattas did not increase his popularity. "Cowes was such fun before he used to come, but now it is a bore," sighed Edward.

William's offhand attitude often made his uncle's position a difficult one. In 1893 the Prince, who was on board his yacht *Britannia*, signalled the Emperor, who was racing him in *Meteor*, that they ought to go home, otherwise they would be late for dinner at Osborne. "The race must be finished," replied the Kaiser. "My dear Eckardtstein," said the Prince to the diplomat, who happened to be on board with him, "his Majesty has got to understand that the Queen will be very angry if we are late." Eckardtstein's only reply was a strained smile. "I can see that if you do as I ask, you will wake up tomorrow morning as the Minister to Zanzibar," said the Prince, and the race continued. Uncle and nephew arrived at Osborne, followed by their equerries, just as the Queen, who had finished dinner and was in a very bad temper, was going into the drawing-room. The Kaiser approached to kiss his grandmother's hand and excused himself in a very cavalier manner, but the Prince, who had changed his clothes with lightning speed, did not dare let his mother see him and for the rest of the evening remained hidden behind a pillar, mopping his brow.

When away from court, the Prince made no effort to hide his feelings for the Emperor, feelings that were often caught on the raw. If by chance they found themselves in the same house, their hosts would be in constant trepidation lest the slightest *contretemps* should give rise to an international incident. On one occasion a young and beautiful American girl, Consuelo Vanderbilt, who had recently married the Duke of Marlborough, saved a situation created by her husband's pig-headedness with admirable tact. The Kaiser had been asked to dinner at Blenheim Palace and the Duke had decided that the Prince and Emperor would be fetched from the station in the landau. He would ride alongside it, while his

wife would sit inside with the Kaiser on her right and the Prince
of Wales on the knifeboard. And so it turned out, as the Prince
refused with a rather bad grace the seat beside the Emperor which
the Duchess offered him. William blossomed forth in response to
the cheers of the crowd and admired the flags floating over the
baroque palace. But the Prince's smile had vanished, only to return when the Duchess asked for his leave not to accompany him
back to the station, thus enabling him to share the place of honour
with his nephew. His position in the kingdom was an exact
parallel of his seat on the knife-board, for neither afforded sufficient
room for his imposing figure.

As long as the Queen remained alive, this hostility did not
impinge on government policy. During the 'nineties large exchanges
of territory were effected between the two countries: England ceded
Heligoland in return for Zanzibar and the Samoa Islands; and the
embassies were kept busy by the Coburg succession problem.
German opinion was aroused when the Queen of England arranged
with the local diet, without consulting the Emperor, that her
grandson, the Duke of Albany, should become the Grand Duke
of Saxe-Coburg-Gotha on the Duke of Edinburgh's death. And
there were dissident elements in England who saw that Heligoland
could protect the Kiel Canal and consequently the German fleet,
which was now becoming sizeable. But Chamberlain expressed
the general opinion when he said, "Germany has the largest army
and England the largest navy. An army cannot fight a navy. Therefore they must agree to keep the peace." The Prince of Wales,
who had seen the German fleet at Cowes and at Kiel, was irritated by this oversimplification. He even wrote to his sister to
express his regret that Germany was spending so much money
on warships. Once again the Empress Frederick poured oil on
the fire. Calling on the Foreign Minister's wife, she read out her
brother's letter. A few months later, Prince Henry of Prussia,
who had boasted about the new fleet even more violently than his
brother, was given a cold reception at Windsor. His uncles and
cousins went out of their way to show their displeasure, although
they were a little more discreet in front of the Emperor. In a
letter to Princess von Bülow the Empress said, "Henry is a darling

boy, but he does say such stupid things." She should have reserved such comments for her mother.

The Prince's feelings about the Kaiser were to be justified in the public's eyes by one particular piece of insolence. Imperialist elements in South Africa, with Cecil Rhodes behind them, invaded the Boer Republic. A civil servant called Dr. Jameson rode in at the head of a party of roughnecks, employed by Rhodes to protect his mines, with the intention of returning with President Kruger as their prisoner. Such aggression can only be justified by success. Jameson was humiliatingly defeated. The Cabinet disavowed him and a semblance of a trial took place. The Kaiser sent to President Kruger the following telegram:

> I express to you my sincere congratulations that you have, supported by your people and without appealing for help to powerful friends, succeeded in your energetic action against the armed bands who invaded your country.

The Prince of Wales hurried down to Windsor; William would have to be put in his place. He could not be allowed to adopt such a tone unless he was prepared to accept a diplomatic rupture. The Queen reflected and then wrote to her son:

> Unpleasant letters and wounding remarks can only add to the damage. Sovereigns should avoid them with great care: William's mistakes stem from his impulsive nature and his vanity. In this case calm and firmness are the most powerful weapons.

The Cabinet accepted Victoria's advice. The Prince, who had not disguised his sympathy for Jameson, made his friendly feelings for Rhodes even more obvious by resigning from the Travellers' Club when the latter was blackballed for it.

When, three years later, war was declared against the Boers, the Kaiser's views were shared by the rest of Europe. The aged Queen, baffled by a war that had been lightly undertaken, was to end her reign beneath a torrent of abuse. But she resolutely refused to consider the possibility of defeat. Because of the hostility that existed towards her in France, she decided on a visit to Ireland instead of her usual holiday in Cannes. Victoria and her son were brought closer together by these difficult years; she listened to his anti-German comments; she discussed business with him and even allowed Lord Rosebery to let him have a key to the dispatch boxes, the little gold key that had belonged to the Prince Consort. After the incident of the telegram the Kaiser did not return to England for some time.

In November 1899 the Kaiser's affection for his grandmother triumphed over his pro-Boer sentiments and he was once more back in England with a large suite. It went against the grain for the Germans to have to "bow before Mammon" and their Emperor did nothing to attenuate their feelings when he exclaimed on seeing Windsor Castle, "So it is from there that the world is governed!" But they found the silence that reigned during the ceremonies impressive, and the briefness of the toasts contrasted with the endless speechmaking that went on in Berlin, where conversation was always completely drowned by music. The Queen liked Chancellor von Bülow, and they conversed together on a number of occasions: he had an elegance and a cosmopolitanism that was rare among his compatriots, and at Sandringham, where the visitors spent a few days, he was in his element:

> The Prince and Princess are the best hosts in the world; their table, their stables, and their gardens are all perfect.

The only slight imperfection was the English accent which the Prince affected when speaking German. Von Bülow was aware that the Princess referred to her visitors, among her intimates, as "those beastly Germans" and that she could not abide the Empress, whose house had taken the opposite side to hers on the dispute over the Duchies. Narrow of mind and large in body, the Empress personified everything that the Prince meant when he referred to the Germans as "the three K's": *Kirche* (church), *Kinder* (children), and *Küche* (kitchen). The Empress, Dona, for her part, tended to put on airs and, as her husband said, it was easy to see that his wife had been brought up at Primkenau (the residence of the Duke of Augustenburg) and not at Windsor. The atmosphere was strained; to the English, the German ladies were provincial and their husbands noisy: "Don't speak so loud," the Empress Frederick had often said to her son. But to their guests the simplicity of the English seemed offhanded, and both the level of conversation and the moral tone appeared rather low.

William II wanted to start a political correspondence with his uncle. For Christmas, at a time when things were going extremely badly in South Africa, the Kaiser handed him, with seasonal good wishes, a dossier on the war that had been drawn up by his military advisers. It contained suggestions of a strategic nature and some remarks on armaments, and its conclusions gave little encouragement as to the outcome of the campaign. The Prince thanked his nephew coldly: two months later his nephew sent him a few more *Gedankensplitter*:

> My very dear Uncle, You received my aphorisms so kindly, that I am taking the liberty of sending you a new series, which may interest your entourage. After all I have been the head of the German Army for twelve years. I hope that dear good Mama is not too upset by the bad news. One must have patience and lots of it as the end is still far off and it does not seem that the Lord has responded to the prayer for peace that was offered in St. Paul's.

The Kaiser finished by comparing the war to a cricket match and suggested that England should be able to accept defeat in a truly sporting spirit. Such a conclusion, on so serious a matter as the South African war, was too much for the Prince. The English Ambassador was ordered to deliver a curt reply. But it was not long before Edward saw his "illustrious nephew" again.

In January 1901, the Queen's health rapidly declined; shocked by the news, the Kaiser expressed his determination to be present when his "beloved English Granny" drew her last breath. In vain did the Empress, who hated England, remonstrate. She was supported by Chancellor von Bülow, who was terrified at the *gaffes* which his master would commit under the stress of emotion, and by the Duke of Connaught, who was horrified at the idea of the Emperor and his numerous suite intruding on an overwrought Court. But it was all to no avail. "England," the Kaiser replied, "will be moved by this gesture." He was right: as he wept at his grandmother's bedside, his tears did much to wipe out the memory of the telegram and the impression made by this powerful sovereign's bellicose speeches.

The eyes of the entire world watched as the Queen drew her last breath beneath the flower-patterned cretonne draperies in her simple bedroom. The Prince arrived at Osborne on the nineteenth, and was followed by the Emperor the next day. Soon the family was complete. The hotels in Cowes filled with journalists. Victoria was rapidly weakening; to her son-in-law, the Duke of Argyll, her death resembled the sinking of a three-masted vessel as it slowly submerged, and then reappeared again above the waves. On the twenty-second the Prince, who had returned to London, was back. The Queen took and held his hands. "Bertie," she said and kissed him. Then she sank into a coma from which she did not emerge except to ask for her little white dog. The German Emperor held her in his arms for several hours to help her breathe more easily. The Princesses, anxious for the future, left the room in tears. They were getting in the way of the doctors and nurses; they went to their apartments, where they closeted themselves in vain little secret meetings with various newcomers and replied to hundreds of telegrams. In their distress the ladies-in-waiting upset the servants by giving them orders that conflicted with those of the equerries. The Marlborough House secretaries were soon observed to be increasing in importance. Balfour arrived requesting in the name of Parliament that there should be a meeting of the Privy Council. The Archbishop of Winchester appeared when the Queen had completely lost consciousness. The railings by the gate were crowded with reporters and inquisitive people and, as the carriages went to and fro between Osborne and Cowes to pick up the waiting dignitaries, they had to plough their way through hordes of people. A soft rain fell in showers on the green lawn, while ladies in black bustled about and colonels stood around looking concerned.

Since no sovereign had died for over sixty years, the exact protocol to be followed had been forgotten. The Prince of Wales's dignity had a soothing effect on the senile and feminine Court. On the twenty-second, at half past six in the evening, the Queen died. Those who were present knelt before the new King to kiss his hand. The Princess of Wales refused to receive this homage: "There will be only one Queen until the day of the funeral. Until then I shall remain a princess." The Prince's household felt that he ought to take control of the situation but the King wisely decided to leave the arrangements for the funeral to his mother's household.

A catafalque was erected in the dining-room at Osborne. Surrounded by Winterhalter's portraits of her children, and of Albert, painted during the happy years, Victoria lay in state in her bridal dress for eight days. Then, when the delegations had all arrived, the yacht *Albert* crossed the Solent with the coffin on board. The Kaiser and the new King, each dressed in the uniform of an admiral, followed in the *Victoria and Albert*. The next day the coffin was taken to London and across the capital, through crowds of mourners, from Victoria Station to Paddington. There were forty European and Oriental princes on foot, while the Princesses followed in closed carriages. At Windsor, the King, the Kaiser, the King of Greece, and the King of the Belgians, in their military uniforms, capes, and white plumes, and the Princesses, their faces hidden by long pieces of crape, walked up to the chapel. For a moment the calm order of the procession was nearly disrupted: the horses that were to pull the gun-carriage on which lay the bier reared up and refused to start. The cavalry was about to provide substitutes when Ponsonby ran up to the King and suggested that sailors should be used instead of horses. The Kaiser thought this an excellent idea.

"All right," said the King to the equerry, "but if anything goes wrong I shall never forgive you."

Order restored, the procession moved on to the mausoleum at Frogmore and the coffin was lowered to lie beside Prince Albert's. A recumbent white figure in marble, representing Victoria on her wedding day, had been waiting for her for thirty years.

In no way did the King appear to be in a hurry to assume power. He regarded himself as no more than the organizer of the ceremony. All who saw him at this time were impressed by his tact, but the lack of enthusiasm which the nation felt for the new reign was expressed by *The Times*:

> We would not pretend that there was nothing in his long career that those who admire and respect him would have wished otherwise.

And Henry James wrote to a friend:

> We all feel without a mother now that we no longer have the mysterious little Victoria, but only the fat, vulgar, and terrible Edward.

CHAPTER TEN

The King

"WE HAVE DECIDED to be known by the name of Edward, a name carried by six of our ancestors." Strong and guttural the royal voice rose beneath the vaults of the banqueting-hall in St. James's Palace in which, on January 23, 1901, the Privy Council was meeting. The King was speaking with the tones of authority. The Councillors exchanged surprised glances; some of them were even shocked. What! Was he dropping the sacred name "Albert" so dear to his mother? Without notes, but with perfect ease, the speech carried on. It contained not one word that could possibly have caused anxiety in Parliament or surprise in Europe, but the air of command unknown since the time of the Stuarts, and its extempore nature, gave food for thought. While the Heralds at Arms, in emblazoned and quartered tunics, were proclaiming, "Long live King Edward the Seventh!" Lord Redesdale and two equerries were hurriedly trying to write down the text from memory, since no one had remembered to take it down in shorthand, so as to be able to give it to the reporters waiting in the blackened courtyard of the brick-built palace.

Yes, changes were certainly taking place, even in the holy-of-holies at Windsor. Ponsonby was horrified, when calling for orders, to find the King, the Kaiser, and the King of the Belgians smoking enormous cigars in the former Queen's drawing-room. Sixty years of single rule had turned any number of sinecures and forms of procedure into hallowed privileges and established customs and they had multiplied around the throne like mushroom growths around a tree trunk. Routine had ossified the monarchical machine. Few people thought that a man who had become King at the age of fifty-nine would want to alter the way things were done or refuse to be bound by entrenched habits: it was put about that he was too frivolous to take much interest in the official side of his life and too tactful to make reforms. No one doubted that he would now at last be able to have the time of his life, but neither his friends nor the public imagined that there would be so much political emphasis in the way in which he blossomed forth.

Intimates such as Esher and Redesdale were astonished at the royal zeal; Marlborough House was indeed still open to them and they could still chat with the equerries and pay their respects to the Queen, while waiting to be received by the King. He would receive them with the same cordiality, talk to them about racing, or question them on the latest piece of gossip with the same curiosity that he had shown in great and small things alike, but conversation with him became increasingly brief. One evening, after having chatted with Lord Redesdale, Edward rose and said, "Now I must say good night, as I have work to do." And he pointed to a pile of red boxes.

"Surely your Majesty is not going to get through all that to-night."

"Oh! I must, and anyway I find it very interesting!"

To a man in a position of authority, to whom curiosity acts as a spur, duties are an agreeable occupation. They were no longer the burdensome performance that he had had to go through as Prince of Wales, like an automaton, but duties that he could throw himself into with a passion that made of him an imposing and impressive King. The manner in which he accomplished them suggested that he was putting some grand over-all policy into effect. His feelings during the nine years of his reign can be compared to those of a man who at last inherits a long-coveted house: on obtaining the keys from the solicitor, he rushes in, opens all the doors and all the cupboards, lets air and light into the mildewed rooms, engages servants to dust and polish, removes the dust sheets to discover exquisite pieces beneath them—and the occasional horror which he banishes to the attic—and then chooses his bedroom and invites his friends. For a sovereign whose authority is curbed by an enormous fabric of law and custom it is not, of course, quite so simple. So jealous was the Government of its prerogatives that the King, who, in the days when Dilke and Churchill were his protégés, must have plotted far-reaching reforms, did not feel inclined to take the risk. He showed no anxiety to change the personnel of his staff, and he paid close heed to the aged Lord Salisbury's advice and to all his mother's counsellors, but he made up for it in his own domain. The old lady's palaces were thoroughly refurbished without any regard for the feelings of the Princesses, who now found themselves thrown out of Osborne and seldom invited to Balmoral or Windsor, or indeed to Sandringham, which was much too smart for them; in the elegance of the Court they were now no more than unfashionable figures.

The King was a tyrant in nothing save matters sartorial. Now that he was the dominant figure on the stage, the dress and deportment of all those responsible to him were scanned by his eagle eye. An Order worn a little too high, or a button badly sewn on a uniform, would attract an Olympian frown, and any Minister who was unwise enough to appear in tails when he should have been wearing a frock coat found that the King's opinion of his capacities fell considerably. As Virginia Cowles, his American biographer, said with some pride:

> The only foreigners whom the King had no control over were the Americans. He had given up worrying about them. They could never understand the difference between breeches and trousers.

One evening when Lord Rosebery appeared at Windsor wearing trousers, Edward said to him sharply, "I presume you have come in the suite of the American Ambassador."

At diplomatic receptions, both at home and abroad, he managed things perfectly. He would work his way through the ambassadors, the Ministers, and their suites, in the following manner. First he would speak to A and then bring B into the conversation; withdrawing faintly and imperceptibly but still appearing to listen to B, he would attract C into the conversation; thanks to his extra-

The Archbishop of Canterbury.

ordinary knowledge of decorations and of uniforms, he never once confused the Argentine military attaché with a counsellor from the Rumanian Legation; his voice would rumble agreeably down the length of the gallery, but when he got annoyed it would make the glass chandeliers tinkle. To someone who suggested to him that he should invite forty writers who had contributed to the *Encyclopaedia Britannica* he exclaimed: "For-r-ty w-ri-ter-rs. I won't have forty w-ri-ter-rs at Mâlbrough House." There were some words that he found impossible to pronounce on account of his guttural "r" and he once nearly choked himself trying to say "guerrilla warfare" during a speech from the Throne.

Despite the difficulties of the South African war, the constant irritation of his nephew William, and his pained surprise at all agitations for social reform, Edward blossomed; being King changed everything; he could still unbend, but it was now with an admirable simplicity; he still had his moods, but they expressed a will that would not be denied. His acts of politeness, that almost equalled those of Louis XIV, became a talking-point. On one occasion an Indian prince astonished the other guests at his table by throwing some asparagus over his shoulder; the King, showing not the least surprise, did the same in the most natural possible way, and everyone followed suit. His outbursts of temper became rarer; there were few people more delightful as long as everything was going well, but at the slightest mishap he became odious. The life of the King of England, however, does tend to run smoothly. And if he wanted to vent his spleen there was always his faithful valet, Chandler, on whom, if some Minister had proved truculent or some report had upset him, he would pour out his wrath on the most trivial pretext. It was like a blood-letting.

Ponsonby was once the victim of one of these outbursts in Paris. He had taken it on himself to observe that the present which had been bought for a member of the Jockey Club was too small: the intended recipient had been to a great deal of trouble to arrange for the King to visit some stables, including some that belonged to Monsieur Blanc, who was not a member of the Club. As all the gold boxes had already been given away during this trip, Ponsonby suggested that it might be better to send a present from London when they got back there:

> The King entered and immediately I realised that he was furious, despite his efforts to master himself. He slowly put his hat, his gloves, and his cane down on the table: "Are you telling me that this box, which I chose myself, is not good enough?" Trembling, I replied: "Yes." His voice then rose to a pitch that shook the entire hotel. What did I know about Paris? How could I judge what should be given to Du Bos? A torrent of words reduced me to mute terror. Finally, I took it on myself to say that he usually gave such beautiful presents to his friends . . . that Du Bos would show it to everybody. . . . Instead of calming him, this raised a fresh storm. He then dictated a letter to Du Bos, begging him to accept a small souvenir from His Majesty. Triumphantly the King picked up his hat, his gloves, and his cane and went out slamming the door.

Later he tacitly acknowledged his mistake, and often left Ponsonby to choose his presents.

Nothing could be denied him now that he was King, although he sometimes had to press for what he wanted. Paris was also the setting for a scene that took place in the Hôtel Meurice, where he was staying incognito with his aide-de-camp, Arthur Paget. On the evening of their arrival, Edward gave Paget his freedom and went off on his own but came back early. Walking through the dining-room, he saw Paget enjoying the company of an attractive woman. The King joined them at their table and was charming. Over the coffee, he said, "Dear boy, I have worked you much too hard today; go and get some rest."

"I am feeling fine, sir," replied Paget.

When they had drunk their cognac Edward turned to Paget again and said, "You are looking *very* tired."

"But I assure you, your Majesty . . ."

A second cognac was called for. "I *advise* you to go up to bed immediately." This time the penny dropped and, leaving the King alone with his conquest, the aide-de-camp reluctantly disappeared.

He conducted his affairs now with more discretion but the stories that circulated in the clubs would have done justice to

Henry VIII; it was said for example that one of the officers on the yacht heard, as he passed the porthole of the royal cabin, the guttural voice saying, "Stop calling me sir and put another cushion under your back." To keep him in a good temper there had to be pretty women around him; Mrs. Keppel became a sort of Pompadour. Victorian morality bowed before her graciousness. That most correct of ambassadors, Sir Arthur Nicolson, who had been invited to join a cruise, was heard exclaiming, "Thank God, Alice will be on board!" By this he meant that the King would be in a good humour and that the work of his entourage would not be upset by his moods.

But it was not simply the satisfying of his vanity that brought harmony to Edward's life. His profound sense of royal dignity, which had deepened with the advancing years, made it possible for him to avoid those situations which had compromised his reputation as Prince of Wales. The majestic and epicurean tastes that he cultivated in his later years symbolized the best that life has to offer: women, horses, champagne, and cigars. The Crown has a certain mystique that can turn some unlikely people into popular sovereigns, giving them often a greater appeal than their Ministers. Only the strong-minded or the cynical are impervious to it; and such people had little importance in England at that time, even among the intellectuals. To Madame de Pourtalès, who met the King in Paris soon after his accession, he was a different person from the Prince of Wales she had known, and she distinctly preferred the King; but she found the majestic air with which he held out his hand to be kissed by old friends like the Marquise de Jaucourt, who was English by birth, a little excessive. The very contrast between Edward and his mother impressed his subjects' imagination. His experience served as a substitute for intelligence, and his generosity, which stemmed from the egotist's desire to be surrounded by smiling faces, passed for good-will. Although in his life, and in his manners, he was his mother's opposite, he had inherited a political instinct from Albert, more international than that of his Ministers.

The now ageing Salisbury respected, rather than esteemed, his sovereign, but Edward had several personal friends in the Cabinet:

there was, for instance, the Duke of Devonshire, who was becoming increasingly vague. Lord Lansdowne was not sufficiently respectful and the King disliked Chamberlain's stilted manners, although he shared his imperial beliefs. His first brush with the Cabinet came when he wanted to suppress a few lines in the Declaration drawn up in 1689, which he had to read before Parliament:

> I repudiate as idolatrous and superstitious every invocation of the Virgin Mary, and the sacrifice of the Mass such as it is practised in Rome.

Edward was convinced that his numerous Catholic subjects would be offended. But the Government, whose power depended on a predominantly Protestant electorate, would not give way. There was not much problem over the Civil List. The King tactfully proposed a few economies at Court and then asked for a larger sum that his mother had had; he could be relied upon to spend it to good effect. Parliament voted him £543,000 with a good grace.

To the members of the Government it was a cause for reproach that the King took no interest in the colonies and was bored by social problems, although they appreciated his tact and his knowledge. As he lacked application, the work had to be simplified by a number of secretaries before it could be submitted to him. His comments in the margins of Cabinet papers lack significance when compared with his mother's. He found paper-work a nuisance; in August 1901 he gave the Kaiser a memorandum prepared by the Foreign Office for his eyes alone without having read it himself. His attitude to the Empire was paternalist, and he would very often support the native chiefs against the colonial governors appointed by the Crown. Although he liked neither repression or oppression, he could at times be extremely intimidating. A delegation of African Kings who had come to London seeking reforms was received in the palace. Edward VII read the text, refusing their requests, prepared by the Government; but the Africans, who were not satisfied, made no effort to leave the audience chamber. Taking his seat on his throne, Edward said in a voice of thunder,

"Chiefs, the King has spoken!" The Africans bowed and left the room.

The King wanted to get the Boer War over and to get on with the preparation of his palaces for the Coronation; it was set for a date eighteen months after the Queen's death. In order to give the ceremony the desired éclat, one had to allow an interval of this sort. Those who owned the finest houses in London were asked to put an apartment at the disposal of royal guests. An official from the palace was attached to the person of every prince or ambassador extraordinary and saw to his comforts, acted as a liaison with the Court, made sure that he was treated with respect and provided with sufficient entertainment; he also performed the same services for an often excessively large suite, the size of which established the visitor's importance among the competing royalty. Sir Lionel Cust, a Curator of the royal collections, a charming and erudite man, was put in charge of Prince Danilo of Montenegro, a character straight out of *The Merry Widow*: he wore a hussar uniform with a heavily frogged slung jacket, had waxed mustachios and a magnificent shako. He arrived with an attractive woman he had picked up *en route*, who was passed off as the lady-in-waiting of a nonexistent princess. He made the most of his holiday in London, was always late, and put some spirit into even the stuffiest occasions.

Priests and dignitaries busily rehearsed the ceremony in Westminster Abbey. An equerry stood in for the King and humourlessly informed the Archbishop and the Dukes that they should not *really* kiss him when they paid homage. The antique dealer Duveen, who lent or rather sold the trappings of magnificence to the King's wealthy friends, was put in charge of the decorations. The banners and flags could not be left to the different municipalities; throughout the length of the procession there had to be a uniformity of colours: red and gold. Hardly had the carpet-layers put in the last nail in the apartments in Buckingham Palace than the first of their Highnesses started to arrive. But there were no crowned heads staying at the palace; the King had to be a solitary figure of majesty. There was a continual coming and going of carriages between the palace and the stations. From the time that the first delegation arrived, a red carpet was rolled out as every boat-train from the Continent pulled in, and there was always a member of the family on hand to represent Edward VII. The important arrivals were entitled to an escort of the guards. The Ritz, the Savoy, and Claridge's, which had been booked out for months in advance, were filled to overflowing with maharajas and millionaires. César Ritz, who had just opened his new hotel in Piccadilly, had laid in tons of salmon and pâté de foie gras, and had brought in train-loads of roses. The weather was wonderful; visitors from the provinces, who had not found anywhere to put up, were already camping in the parks. In every town firework displays were prepared; the most popular set-piece, after the royal portraits, was "England opening her arms to South Africa."

But at the Aldershot Review, on June 20, the guests on the stand noticed that the King was listless and perspiring freely; as the Dominion troops marched past beneath the floodlights he remained slumped in his chair without taking any notice. "He doesn't tease me in the way he used to," said the Grand Duke Michael to Princess Victoria. She told him not to worry, he was just not feeling very well. But the Queen, who was fascinated by the spectacle, paid no attention when her daughter said to her, "Papa is being too boring, tell him to take more interest." The royal family returned very late to the palace. As the Princess went to say good night to her father, she found him leaning heavily on a table. "Quickly, undo my belt, I'm suffocating," he breathed. He was so swollen that the Princess could not get the buckle undone. She ran down the corridor to call the valet, but he was too drunk to be able to help her. The Queen finally arrived and cut the belt with a knife that she found on a tray that was always put out, in case the King had midnight starvation. Edward could easily have died in that deserted palace without managing to summon help. Luckily the equerry on duty answered the telephone and dashed off to fetch a doctor. Despite the fact that he was in considerable pain, Edward would not hear of a postponement of the Coronation. He could not, however, attend the great banquet at Buckingham Palace on the twenty-first, to which all his guests were invited. It was held in an atmosphere of hushed awe, and the latest news which anyone could obtain from the Queen, or her daughters, or from the doctor himself, was passed on in whispers. The only person able to raise a laugh was Danilo.

A rumour spread through London that the King was dying; the Coronation could not take place. Monsieur Cambon heard the news from his chef, who knew the palace chef well. At one o'clock in the afternoon the dining-room of the Ritz was crowded with royalty, peers, Americans, and Italian princesses. Suddenly they saw César Ritz come in, as white as a sheet. He asked for silence. "The King is seriously ill; the Coronation is postponed indefinitely," he announced. In one of those buzzes of conversation in which false news quickly takes root, the guests went back to their rooms to pack. Ritz withdrew, a prey to a nervous depression from which he was never to recover.

The King had been suffering for several weeks from an infected appendix. Now his condition was critical and an immediate operation was necessary. In no time the darkest possible rumours were going the rounds, that the surgeon, for whom the excitement had proved too much, had had to give up in the middle of the operation, or that Edward had already been dead for two days. It was jealously suggested that the appendix bug had been brought into the palace by Lord Esher, whose daughter had just been operated on. The bulletins remained curt for several days. An enormous crowd gathered outside Buckingham Palace, their eyes fixed on the standard whose lowering would have been a signal of death. Tons of venison, salmon, and lobster, which had been stacked in the ice-rooms for the banquets, were distributed by the royal kitchens. By June 25 the bulletins were striking a more optimistic note. The Prince of Wales wrote to his wife:

I found Papa smoking a cigar and reading a newspaper. The doctors and the nurses say that they have never had such an extraordinary patient.

With the success of the royal operation, appendicitis soon became fashionable. Edward spent his convalescence on his yacht. He was delighted by the scores of congratulatory messages that poured in from every part of the world, and he himself answered the more important among them, declaring, "When I nearly died in 1871, exactly the same thing happened. Suddenly my sins were forgiven and I found that everybody loved me. It is a good idea for Kings to be ill from time to time."

In a message to his people he regretted the inconveniences which the delay had caused but he added:

> My people's prayers for my recovery have been heard, and I offer my profound gratitude to Divine Providence for having saved my life.

The Coronation was fixed for August 9; most of the foreign princes were unable to wait as long as that; and for this reason the position of the princes in the King's own family increased in significance. Cousins Augusta of Mecklenburg and Frederika of Hanover had three weeks of being very important. Edward's sisters may have deplored the people with whom their brother had surrounded himself and the childishness of his family, but they were not going to lose this last opportunity of taking a front seat. The Prince of Wales and his wife did everything that was expected of them with unobtrusive devotion. They looked after the children, they performed at official functions, and, since there was no one else to do it, gave dances for the least important guests. The King insisted that the fairest of his friends, even if they were not peeresses, should witness his apotheosis, and he spent hours working out the seating plans in the Abbey with the Duke of Norfolk, just like a painter arranging his pictures before an exhibition. He decided that the ladies should wear ball dresses beneath their ermine-bordered purple robes, and all their jewellery. He even contemplated going to the Abbey by car, but these machines were still unreliable and the horses might have taken fright if they had backfired.

One of the King's godchildren, Olga Alberta, had no official right to a seat in the Abbey; she had recently married, at her god-father's instigation, a moderately rich and very talented photographer called Monsieur Meyer. Edward suggested to the King of Saxony that Meyer be made a chamberlain, in order that the Baron and Baroness de Meyer could be sent invitations.

From seven in the morning London shook to the sound of artillery salutes; thousands of people spent the night by the side of the route, which, on the day, was lined by troops from India and all the overseas Dominions (the Sikhs with their fan-shaped beards and conical turbans were particularly appreciated by the crowds). It was to be a day of triumph; the venerably traditional and the fabulously exotic were the ingredients of a ceremony that no other sovereign could possibly have provided for his subjects.

Carriages went by, laden with footmen and coachmen in powdered wigs, their gilding refurbished for the occasion, and they helped the crowd to pass the time. Through the windows one could catch glimpses of a blue cloak worn by a member of the Order of the Garter, of the Duchess of Marlborough's tiny head set on its long neck, and of the beautiful Duchess of Portland. But the great day was to leave the Marchioness of Londonderry with some unfortunate memories. Things started to go wrong even in the early morning as she was driving down Park Lane. Her carriage horses became excited. As she leant out of the window, her head heavy with diamonds, to order people out of the way, she heard a taxi-driver shout, "Go and f——— yourself, you and your f——— Coronation!" This could hardly have put her in a good temper. On reaching the Abbey, the Marchioness thought it prudent to retire before sitting through a ceremony of such length, but she stayed for hours in the only convenience provided for such precautions. A queue of peeresses formed outside the door, displaying an increasing lack of patience, when suddenly her voice was heard calling for a pair of forceps. Had the excitement gone to her head? they wondered: she was, after all, well over sixty. Slightly dishevelled, she finally emerged. As she had been readjusting her train her diadem had fallen into the pan. To retrieve it without damaging the stones, nothing less than a gynaecological instrument had been required.

The ushers went to work and the velvet-covered stands were slowly filled. Surrounded by children and Court Officers, the King at the palace was drawing on his purple velvet robe, with its ermine lining, over his Court dress; steel corsets held his stomach in, helping him to throw out his order-laden chest. The

Queen, as always, was late; Edward paced up and down and then sent one of the equerries to find out what was happening, and ordered the pages to ginger up the ladies-in-waiting. Finally he could contain himself no longer and with his robes flying out behind him ran over to the Queen's apartments to say, "Alexandra, do you want to go to the Coronation or do you not?" But when the Queen eventually appeared she was quite unabashed and smiling happily. She was covered from head to foot in diamonds and wore a gold-embroidered robe. Together they came down between two lines of royal servants. These had come from all the royal castles and houses and they formed a lane right to the door of the coach as it stood with its eight cream-coloured horses.

To the crowd, Edward and Alexandra seemed like something out of fairyland; it was as if the King and Queen in *Alice in Wonderland* had come to life. Their progress from Buckingham Palace to Westminster Abbey was greeted with the most tremendous cheering. The Duke of Connaught was riding in close attendance. Guardsmen, in their bright red tunics, marched ahead, and the Beefeaters came behind. They were followed by glittering Indian aides-de-camp and by the Maharajas of Cooch Behar and Gwalior. Kitchener and Roberts drew great applause. In the Abbey everyone was seated and waiting. Aged peeresses in yellowing ermine, who were thought to have died thirty years before, scrutinized the ravishing young creatures that were already old friends of the King. In one of the stands in the transept, their breasts strung with decorations, Victoria's daughters and granddaughters were striking the attitudes of stained-glass saints, although their eyes missed nothing of what was going on. Princess Beatrice produced an enormous prayer book, the gift of the Society for the Encouragement of Needlework. The firing of a cannon announced that the procession had arrived. The Queen, surrounded by the Duchesses of Sutherland, Portland, Montrose, and Marlborough, all of them tall and beautiful, entered first beneath a canopy. She took her seat to the left of the altar. As the King entered, the boys of Westminster School shouted, "*Vivat Rex Eduardus*": he advanced slowly and proudly, smiling and nodding almost imperceptibly to right and left; then came the Bishops, their tiny heads atop their gilded copes, officiating throughout the ceremony with a slowness that was due as much to their rheumatism as to their anxiety not to omit the slightest detail of the complicated ritual. At times the King's sonorous voice could be heard making the responses; four Knights of the Garter supported the canopy over Edward the Confessor's throne. During the paying of homage, the eighty-year-old Archbishop of Canterbury had difficulty in rising to his feet again and the King had to help him. The Archbishop's hand was trembling so much that as he was anointing the Queen he allowed a small drop of oil to fall on her nose. Not daring to wipe it off, she turned to the Duchess of Marlborough with an anguished look and asked, "Is it a disaster?"

As the crown was being placed on the Queen's head the peeresses, with one delightful movement, raised their coronets to their own heads, their white-gloved arms resembling a hundred swans' necks. Some of the younger ones, anxious lest their coronets should have disarranged their coiffures, produced little mirrors. The dowagers shuddered. Mirrors in public! At the most solemn moment of all, Princess Beatrice managed to drop her prayer book on to a table laden with gold plate which clattered to the flagstones with the most frightful noise. The end of the ceremony was marked by another crash. The Duchess of Devonshire, who had tried to join the royal procession as it was on its way out of the Abbey instead of remaining with the other Duchesses, got caught up in her train and fell down the steps of her stand, scattering her coronet and her bracelets on to the carpet. As she was picked up she rapidly checked that her red wig was still in place, quickly covered up her bruises with clouds of face powder and banks of pearls, and dashed after the royals, knocking the ushers aside. Scarcely had the King left the Abbey than the Duke of Norfolk became aware of a series of detonations that appeared to be coming from one of the vaults. Followed by policemen and Beefeaters, he gathered up his robes and rushed down to discover Lord Esher and his family having a picnic; the "plot" was nothing more than the popping of champagne corks. Lord Esher was too much of an epicurean to think of changing the hour at which he took his lunch.

Despite the fact that the ceremony took place so soon after his operation, the King, as he said to a courtier who expressed anxiety for his health, felt "not the slightest fatigue. Marvellous, isn't it?" When the Queen took off her crown, her Greek nephews amused themselves by trying it on. On the following day the newly crowned King and Queen drove in a landau through the poorer quarters of the capital, where, at the suggestion of Sir Thomas Lipton, a meal was provided for more than a hundred thousand people.

In this era that now seems so distant, society was still patriarchal and the monarchs of Europe did, in a very real sense, still represent their people, whose emotions, which were later to be exploited by various forms of fascism, were canalized by loyalty to them. Stupid or mad though the kings may sometimes have been, they did less harm than the dictators. Court routine and the influence of their brother monarchs helped to mitigate their mistakes. Edward, now that the Coronation was over, was a considerable figure in Europe, and of all the sovereigns he was perhaps the foremost. None were so well informed or had such style as he. The relationships which he had established with the various heads of states were of considerable importance, since his attitude to any one country tended to be governed by his feelings for its sovereign. For all that his distrust of Russia might persist, the fact that the Tsar was his nephew, both through Alexandra, whose sister was his mother, and through Alice of Hesse, whose daughter was the Tsar's wife, filled Edward with strong feelings of sympathy for that potentate. The Slav side of the Tsar's nature, the mysticism and stubbornness, were so much outside Edward's own experience that he could see nothing except a virtuous young man who had been brought up by English governesses, but who was unfortunately surrounded by eccentric grand dukes and dishonest Ministers. His feelings for Nicky and Alix were made known through the Ambassador, his old friend, Lord Hardinge.

What Edward had thought of his other nephew, the Emperor of Germany, when Prince of Wales, we already know. On becoming King he found that he was treated with more consideration in Berlin, but behind the exchanges of politeness it was clear to everybody that the old hostility still existed. On the other hand his feelings for the Habsburgs were of nothing but respect and kindliness. He referred to the Emperor Franz Josef, whose egotism remained unimpaired despite the tragedies of his life, as "that dear old man." Count Mensdorff was the Austrian Ambassador in London, and he often had to accept the responsibility for the Emperor's duplicity.

In Italy, Edward reserved his respect for Victor Emmanuel's mother, Margaret of Savoy, and for his wife, Helena of Montenegro. They were a pair of proud and majestic queens. As a kingdom, Italy was still young and suffering from violent political crises. Italians, who are touchy people, resented the offhand way in which the British Government treated them, but the King's attitude did much to put this right. He even wanted to bring them into the *Entente Cordiale*, although Cambon was of the view that they would do more good by staying in the Triple Alliance. They were already creating difficulties there and in the end they were to betray it.

To Alfonso XIII of Spain, Edward VII, with his Parisian tastes, his sporting instincts, and his way with the ladies, was the ideal. Edward was very fond of him and had a great respect for the Queen Mother, Maria Christina of Austria. They often met and their friendship was to prove of some importance during the Algeciras crisis. Both Victor Emmanuel and Alfonso were unimpressed by the way in which the Kaiser treated them. Edward's friendship for Don Carlos of Portugal was, however, less auspicious. In order to emulate his English cousin the latter embarked on a series of extravagancies that were not appreciated in that already ruined country, and the result was revolution and his own assassination.

In Denmark, the King was virtually amongst his own family. He did not find them very amusing but they were useful as a source of information and helped him in his intrigues against the Kaiser.

In Norway, he had a son-in-law on the throne; Edward was not entirely in favour of that country's establishing its independence of Sweden but, rather than have a republic, he acquiesced. Of all the sovereigns, the King of the Belgians was alone in earning his contempt. Possibly he saw in him a tasteless caricature of his own interests in women and money. The methods that the elderly King used in the Congo and the way in which he treated his daughters left Edward with feelings that he did not attempt to conceal.

To Edward, as to the rest of Europe, the Balkans were a constant source of irritation; Greece, where his brother-in-law reigned, had a place in his affections, but he found King George, who was constantly making demands, rather importunate. The decline of Turkey afforded her neighbours a temptation to expand, but Bulgaria and Serbia had to be discouraged. English diplomats were horrified by Balkan political customs. The widow of the former Bulgarian Prime Minister, Stambulov, put her husband's fingers, which had been cut off by Ferdinand's agents, in a bottle and displayed them in her window. In Serbia the bodies of King Alexander and Queen Draga were flung through the palace windows. "One doesn't throw kings out of windows," remarked Edward and for a long time he refused to recognize Peter Karageorgevich, the instigator of the plot. But the most remarkable individual in that part of the world was Ferdinand of Coburg, King of Bulgaria. He had managed to obtain complete independence by 1907. The English were alarmed by his intellect and the Germans were shocked by his manners, but it was the Bulgarian Tsar's own extreme ambitions that were responsible for the downfall of his boldest schemes. Had he not dreamed of being crowned Basileus in Santa Sofia? Ferdinand was by far the most astute of the European monarchs, but the effect of his machinations was often ruined by his cynicism. Having negotiated a loan through Alfred Rothschild, who was on his way through Belgrade, the King did his guest the honours of the capital. "Dear Baron," he said to him, "what do you think my subjects are saying as they see us pass?" "Sire," was the reply, "they must surely be saying: 'There is a sovereign who is congratulating himself on the progress of his people.' " "Not at all, they are saying: 'Look at those two old Jews, each of them rubbing his hands because he thinks he has got the better of the other.' " (Ferdinand's Coburg grandmother, a Hungarian heiress, was said to be a Jewess.)

King Edward's headstrong niece, the hereditary Princess of Rumania, of course saw herself as the Basilissa. She had adopted her future subjects' easygoing morals, and her uncle had to defend her reputation more than once. No one admired Queen Marie's beauty more than she did herself. On one occasion she was asked by one of her nephews for a portrait. She signalled to a lady-in-waiting, who immediately produced a salver piled with photographs. The Queen examined them one by one: "This one is divine. . . . The beauty of that profile . . . the nobility of that pose. . . . Oh! those eyes . . ." The effect of these theatrical gestures at the Greek Court, which was very unpretentious, was explosive. The Greek Queen (the Empress Frederick's daughter) was once heard saying a few hours after Marie of Rumania's arrival, "If that woman doesn't leave tomorrow, I will kick her out of the palace myself."

The King's opinion of the Sultan, Abdul Hamid, most probably coincided with that of Lord Hardinge, who wrote to him during the 1909 revolution:

> I must confess to some sympathy with a man who, despite the brutality of his methods and his lack of scruple in politics, has succeeded for so many years in playing one power off against another with a cynical indifference to the consequences, other than for those which would directly affect himself.

Relations with President Roosevelt were cordial despite the role which he had played during the Spanish war. The President started his letters with, "My dear King Edward" and ended them with "Sincerely yours." The millionaires, the royalty of the New World, were always very welcome at Court. The Dukes of Roxburgh, Newcastle, and Manchester all married Americans, and the Astors became English.

The King's attitude to France was slightly ambivalent for, whatever his feelings for the France represented by Monsieur Loubet, he

never forgot the Empress Eugénie. Through her and through Paléologue, who was attached to Delcassé's Cabinet, he had a direct
link with the French Government, and she was to play an un-
official though statesmanlike rôle at the English Court from the
very beginning of the *Entente*. Even the Orléans princesses, for
all that they were in exile, remained patriotic. Queen Amélia and
her cousin, Princess Waldemar of Denmark, often helped to
smooth down the King's feelings when they were ruffled by representatives of the Republic.

Thus, for nine years, the heads of state all turned their eyes
towards the English Court, and London in consequence enjoyed
an incomparable prestige.

CHAPTER ELEVEN

The Court

"NOTHING IS MORE irreproachably perfect in every detail than the King of England's Court and household, a sort of staid luxury without ostentation, a placid, aristocratic ease and opulence which has nothing showy about it. Everything is run on silent wheels that have been perfectly greased; everything fits in, there are no spaces between, no lapses, no false note. From the polite, handsome and superlatively groomed gentleman-in-waiting who receives you in the hall, to the magnificently solemn and yet welcoming footman who walks before you down the corridor, everything pleases the eye, satisfies one's fastidiousness. When I call before my mind the royal English abodes I always have the vision of softly carpeted, picture-hung corridors, with a silent-footed servant walking ahead of you, discreetly impersonal and yet belonging to the whole; I have the feeling of mounting shallow-stepped stairs leading towards rooms as perfectly 'groomed' as were the horses of the royal carriage which brought you up to the front door, as perfectly groomed also as the tall sentry presenting arms before the gates."

Such was the impression that the King's niece, Marie of Rumania, brought away with her from England. No one who had been received at the Court of Edward VII ever forgot the perfection of its luxury or the magnificence that helped to counteract the boredom of the official ceremonies. If literature and the arts had had a place there, the prestige which the King's Court enjoyed would have been worthy of Versailles. His travels and the time which he had spent with his mother had given him ample time for reflection on the ways in which to give the English Court an éclat which it had not known since the days of the Stuarts, with the brief exception of George IV's reign. The first necessity was to air and repaint the royal residences. Sir Lionel Cust, the Curator of the collections, was adviser to the King on matters of taste. "I don't know anything about pictures, but I know how they should be hung," Edward said.

Scarcely was Victoria laid to rest in the marbled and faintly Byzantine surroundings of Frogmore than her various mansions were invaded by an army of workmen. Osborne was given over to the removal men, and when each of the Queen's children had taken away whatever he chose, case upon case of portraits and souvenirs were sent off to the German courts. Not many of the cousins took the trouble to express their gratitude for being thus encumbered. John Brown's statuettes were melted down and the upholstered chairs and massive mahogany furniture were sold off. A stack of mouldering elephant tusks, the annual tribute of an African chief, was discovered in an attic. Beatrice and Louise were given cottages in the park and the enormous villa became a naval school. Electricity and bathrooms were put in at Windsor but the historic atmosphere was retained. Pieces of porcelain were placed in the Gothic galleries to brighten up the suits of armour, the banners, and the tapestries. The drawing-rooms were depopulated of the hordes of white marble figures of every shape and size that had been made of the Queen's grandchildren, cousins, dogs, and of course John Brown. In the cupboards, priceless pieces of jade that had come from the Court of China or been pillaged in the Summer Palace were discovered, together with steel cod-pieces prudishly removed from suits of armour, whole services of Sèvres and Meissen, silver trowels used for laying foundation stones, jewelled caskets that had once held loyal addresses or the ceremonial keys to cities which the Queen had visited, and the vast centrepieces, usually allegorical in design, presented to her on the occasion of her Jubilee. Pieces of panoply that had come from India yielded scores of moths, and Austrian feathers crumbled into dust as soon as they were touched. (The indiscreet Munshi, and the other Indian servants, were sent packing with the same dexterity, and the courtyards were no longer filled with the stench of curry.) The Van Dycks and the Rubenses were revarnished and their frames regilded; the Boulle furniture and the enormous vases with their bronze mountings were set off against the finest damask. Charles II's gold plate was set up on the sideboards in the vast Waterloo Room* in which hung Lawrence's portraits from the Congress of Vienna. The terrace, which provided a view of the entire Thames Valley, was planted with richly variegated flowerbeds, filled with begonias and tulips, whose bright colours contrasted with the austere castle walls. Windsor, which was to give its name to the royal family after 1914, became a worthy sanctuary for the Crown.

"Get this tomb cleaned up," the King said, referring to Buckingham Palace. Under Victoria, whose London palace filled her with horror, the soot-laden air had been allowed to blacken the gilding, tarnish the mirrors, and encrust the mouldings. The beautiful Regency furniture was brought out from under the dust covers, and the wonderful things with which the Brighton Pavilion had once been furnished were brought out of store. The staircases and the galleries were carpeted in bright blue, and enormous mirrors, which doubled the length of the rooms, were put in. The chandeliers, which had been blackened by the gas lighting, were now electrified so that their crystal cataracts glistened. The King gave orders that the façade of the palace should be redesigned; the colonnade that one sees today is reminiscent of the Louvre in much the same way that the public rooms in the Ritz remind one of Versailles. Richly gilded wrought-iron gates, carrying allegorical designs, were set up around a vast square in the middle of which the Victoria Memorial, in white marble, rose like an enormous wedding cake covered with sugar icing.

Balmoral remained rustic and Scottish although central heating was now put in. As for Sandringham, everything was already so

---

* The Waterloo Room is so called because the annual dinner celebrating Wellington's great victory is held in it. The King made it a rule that if there were any French present it should be called the banqueting hall.

H.M. Queen Alexandra

comfortable and adapted to the King's tastes that no changes were necessary.

Having set the stage without regard to expense, the King now felt that he could play his rôle in a suitable manner. The members of his admirable entourage, with their tact and lack of personal ambition, were ready to help him. Sir Francis Knollys, his Private Secretary, and Sir Dighton Probyn, whose beard was so long that it hid his decorations, had served him as Prince of Wales since the year 1870. They remained at their posts, taking over from the officers of the Queen's household, who were almost all men of very advanced years. The youngest of them, Frederick (Fritz) Ponsonby, stayed on to become Edward's Assistant Secretary. A ready wit and an amusing raconteur, he has left us an entertaining diary. The secretaries and equerries performed their duties on a roster system. They would lunch with the ladies-in-waiting and usually dined at the royal table. Other officials were attached to the various Ministries to act in a liaison capacity between Whitehall and the Court. Of these, the most remarkable were Lord Crewe, who, because he was a liberal, never entirely gained the King's confidence; Lord Hardinge, the diplomat; and Admiral Sir John Fisher. But the King reserved his greatest respect for Lord Esher, the Clerk of the Works. Many of the happier changes that were made in the palace were due to his highly developed taste.

The qualities that Edward expected of his courtiers were an impeccable sense of dress, the ability to play a good hand at bridge, some knowledge of the turf, fluency in both French and German, and powers of conversation capable of preventing a lapse into silence. He gave them his confidence and something of a free hand, and he was perfectly willing to accept advice.

Edward VII gave much more thought than his mother ever did to the comfort of those around him. When a guest left Balmoral, a footman would hand his valet a hamper containing a half-bottle of champagne, fruit, and a venison pie. In the Queen's day departing guests had had to rely on the restaurant-car throughout their journey.

Admirable manners and total loyalty diminished the number of intrigues inseparable from Court life, or at least mitigated their effects. Coming from the same background and sharing the same tastes, those dictated by their sovereign, the courtiers had a perfect understanding of one another. Factions did not exist. The only danger came from the attractive women with whom the King loved to surround himself, for they were constantly carrying on intrigues with ambassadors and leading politicians in order to increase their sense of self-importance.

The high quality of the personnel who, to this day, surround the English monarchy can be traced to Victoria's highly moral Court, but its members were well able to adapt themselves to Edward's more worldly ways. They understood exactly the extent to which the Crown can benefit or suffer from a sovereign's intelligence or mediocrity and they were able to moderate the effects of either of these traits if they became too marked. The King's immediate entourage was very swift to detect the slightest suspicion of scandal and to nip it in the bud. It is only in recent years that what went on behind the impeccable front presented to the public has come to light. Thus in 1907, when the King and Queen were making an official visit to Ireland, it was discovered that the jewels belonging to the Order of St. Patrick had disappeared on the eve of the knightly ceremony. Since the jewels were the property of the Crown, the King was furious and gave orders for a thorough inquiry into the matter. It was learnt that the king-at-arms who had charge of these gems was in the habit of giving masculine parties in the room in which the strong box was kept. One obvious adventurer, who had been received in Society, was immediately suspected, but the King's advisers warned him against pursuing the matter as this young man had been a close friend of his brother-in-law, the Duke of Argyll (poor Louise's husband), and he would undoubtedly have compromised the royal family if the matter had ever come to court.

Whereas Edward inspired confidence, was capable of taking the initiative, and knew how to deal with a difficult situation, William II was suspicious and, being more of a soldier than a diplomat, had a tendency to blunder. The difference between the two can be illustrated by one dramatic incident. In November 1901, the King heard that his sister was far from well and went over to Friedrichshof; Fritz Ponsonby went with him. Edward found the Emperor with his mother in a pseudo-English country house full of Italian *objets d'art*. The atmosphere of suspicion could have been cut with a knife. The Empress sent for Ponsonby. As soon as he reached her room the nurse was sent out and she whispered to him confidentially, "There is something that I want you to do for me. It is to take all my correspondence back to England. No one must know that it is being taken away. Someone will bring the letters to you in an hour's time." The nurse returned and the Empress composed herself for sleep. In the middle of the night four men suddenly appeared in Sir Frederick's bedroom carrying four large packing-cases covered with black oilcloth. They were bound to be something of an embarrassment, but then it occurred to Ponsonby to label them *Porcelain—fragile* and to have them placed beside his real luggage so that everything would be collected together in the morning. The Emperor came to the station with the King, and the secretary was in some fear that he might notice these strange pieces of luggage, but everything went off well. The letters arrived safely in London, but the incident could have been an episode from *The Prisoner of Zenda*. There were sixty volumes of them, for all her letters to her mother had been returned to her with a view to eventual publication.*

The Empress died in August 1901, and the King and Ponsonby set off for Germany once more. She had wanted her body to be wrapped in a flag and returned to Windsor but her funeral took place in Potsdam, with all the military pomp of the Hohenzollerns.

The courtiers noticed that the King and Queen became almost different people after they had succeeded. Alexandra became visibly younger. As though to thank her for all the patience which she had shown as Princess of Wales, Edward insisted that she share all the honours. Despite the fact that she often irritated him, he took pride in her unfading beauty. One evening, the first on which she wore the Garter, she arrived as usual, late but radiant, with the diamond-encrusted insigne over her heart. The King leapt to his

---

* The correspondence was published in 1927, greatly to the annoyance of William II, who had never suspected what had happened; nor did the British royal family particularly enjoy having their personal affairs revealed.

feet. "It should not be worn on the left!" he shouted indignantly. "Go and change it at once."

"But Bertie, it looks better on that side," she replied.

"We shall not go in until you have put it on correctly," said the King, resigning himself to wait with a martyred expression on his face.

The faithful Miss Knollys did her best to organize Alexandra's life and keep her on time, but she always took the blame if things went wrong, as Alexandra's cheerfulness dissipated every feeling of irritation the moment she arrived. Deaf and stupid though the Queen was, an infallible instinct enabled her to hold her own in conversation with all the appearance of vivacity. Nor had she lost her taste for practical jokes. On one occasion, according to her nephew Prince Christopher of Greece, when the Empress of Russia was in bed with flu at Marlborough House, the Queen decided to pull her leg. She dressed Prince Christopher up in the clothes in which Queen Victoria had met Napoleon III:

> It was a horror in tartan taffeta. I thrust a plumed bonnet on my head and armed myself with a lace umbrella. Thus equipped I was conducted by the Queen along interminable corridors, in which we passed horrified servants, right to the Empress's door. Then in a solemn voice she announced: "Her Majesty, Queen Victoria."

The shock, followed by convulsive laughter, turned a mild case of flu into a severe attack of bronchitis.

Queen Alexandra was the inventor of royal fashion. It parallels but is distinct from worldly fashion, and subsequent queens of England have followed her example: she went in for clear colours that showed up well from a distance, toques, osprey feathers that lengthened the face without hiding it, and jewellery both on her clothes and on her person, even during the day. She was particularly fond of mauve and silver embroidered cloaks trimmed with lace and, thus caparisoned, she would open workers' dwellings looking as though she had just left a ballroom. Queens, she realized, were really actresses and their apartness produced the same effect as the footlights in a theatre. Long before it had ceased to be frowned on she was wearing make-up, applying a mask of cold cream, face powder, and rouge to her cheeks. Her slender umbrellas, their handles made of Fabergé enamel, usually the gifts of grand dukes, became an indispensable adjunct of royalty. Her daughter-in-law inherited her collection of them and added to them at least a hundred more.

The Queen had a very kind heart but those around her were troubled by the way in which the undeserving poor benefited from her largesse. As her response to every begging-letter was always a five-pound note, somebody pointed out that only individuals who had swallowed all their pride could write such letters. "Well, if that is the case," she replied, "it means that nobody ever sends them anything." The King could only sigh. "Thank God," he said, "the crown jewels are in the Tower, otherwise the Queen would have auctioned them all off for her charities."

Once, when walking through a fair-ground, the Queen saw a miserable little stall in which an elephant-man was being ex-hibited; he was a monster with grey and calloused skin whose nose hung down like a trunk. She went in, sat down beside the freak, and chatted gaily of this and that. The unfortunate man, who had never been treated as a human being before, was quite dumfounded. Every year, afterwards, she sent him a Christmas card.

The Queen was particularly generous towards her own com-patriots, and there are dozens of letters still kept at the Danish Embassy, from Miss Knollys, that start thus: "Another Dane . . ."

But it was only with children that Alexandra was ever really happy, for she enjoyed childish things. Once, at a reception given by Lady de Grey, she heard that a Punch and Judy show was taking place in the nursery and ran off immediately to join the infants. She took a great fancy to Lady de Grey's daughter—Lady Juliet Duff—and used to take her with her in her carriage simply because the little girl wanted to go through the arch at the top of Constitution Hill that is reserved for royal coaches.

Such kindness of heart, such unsystematic charitableness, might almost have been mistaken for mental backwardness. One little boy,* at any rate, had no doubts about it. He happened to be

---

* Anthony Butts, an eccentric of the 'twenties. The following extract is from *Curious Relations* by William d'Arfey, edited by W. Plomer (London: Jonathan Cape, 1945; New York: William Sloane, 1947).

staying at Lord Allington's country house, Crichel, at the same
time as the King:

It was a dull, drizzling morning, but after luncheon a watery sun
made its appearance. The Royal Party were packed into cars and
driven off to a large field, at some distance from the house, where
the Scouts were in attendance. Owing to the condition of the road
it was found to be impossible to approach the field, and some
seventy yards had to be covered on foot, much to the disgust of
His Majesty, who remarked in awe-struck tones to his companion,
the Junoesque and bosomy Mrs. Fanshawe, tones very reminiscent
of those of the Red Queen's Consort: "My feet are *wet!*" So
firmly did his voice disassociate his treacherous and unreliable
members from the rest of his anatomy that one felt that they were
no more part of his essential ego than were his gaiters and would
be as easily changed as the latter when he got in. . . . As soon as
Royalty was seated the Boy Scouts started to do their stuff; there
was a great deal of it and their lack of inventiveness was matched
only by their dogged persistence. They seem to have been wound
up like so many automata, and their principal lacked the tact or
the authority to stop them. . . . A settled look of unutterable boredom touching on despair settled on the Royal faces.

It was just before the singing of the National Anthem that a drop
of water fell on Mrs. Fanshawe's hat. That lady turned to His
Majesty, saying in a loud voice with the greatest air of disgust
and irritation: "I must have left my umbrella in the car, Sir."

Before anyone of those in a position to do so had had time to
stir (and none of them, it must be confessed, displayed the slightest
evidence of intending to do so) King Edward gave a grunt, and
the Queen, of all people, jumped to her feet, an exquisitely neat
figure in a beautifully cut and not very fashionable coat and skirt
and a heavily veiled toque of Parma violets. She was hurrying up
the muddy slope towards the cars as fast as her high heels could
carry her, followed at some distance by her daughter, Princess
Victoria. Lady Allington had sketched a vague gesture of rising,
but it remained incomplete. In a few minutes Her Majesty reappeared, carrying Mrs. Fanshawe's umbrella, which the latter accepted
with cool graciousness, but quite without surprise. As for the King,
he never so much as looked round.

A little later, the small boy found himself alone in a large
drawing-room:

Someone had come into the room: the someone was a short and
slender lady whose appearance seemed vaguely familiar, but whose

identity I couldn't absolutely place. Her golden-brown hair lay in tight curls low on her forehead, rising high on the crown of her head in a square compact mass, like the flattened coiffure of a caryatid; her dress was mauve and had orchids pinned on to her bosom, while her pearls even outclassed, if possible, those of her hostess. But it was neither her rather brittle grace nor the splendour of her accoutrements which caused me to remark on her as she wandered from occasional table to occasional table, picking up small objects, examining them cursorily and putting them down again. What caused me to regard her with a certain apprehension was the fact that she kept shaking her elegant head from side to side with the automatic precision of a metronome and murmuring in staccato syllables, over and over again, like the response in some litany:

"God save the King! God save the King! God save the King! God save the King! God save the King!"

Almost as candid as the small boy is an elderly lady called Baroness von Stoeckel, who published a book of memoirs on the Courts that she used to know. She came from one of those families that once supplied confidantes and youthful companions for princesses, and equerries or chamberlains for grand dukes, those indispensable supernumeraries that were always to be found at Livadia or Sandringham, forever busy and good-tempered. The following is an account of her departure from Sandringham:

After lunch Sir Arthur announced that the special train would leave at 1:55. The Grand Duchess Alexandra and Princess Victoria made a movement as though to leave the table but her Majesty, who had not finished drinking her coffee, told them to wait. She drank her coffee slowly and then, when it was finished, rose from the table. As I was rushing to get into the carriage, the Empress (of Russia), who was suffering from lumbago, sent for me. I was wearing a veil as there is nothing more vulgar than going out without a veil, but one is forbidden by etiquette to appear veiled before a sovereign. I therefore had to take out the pins that held the veil in place although I was late and knew that the train was waiting.

The Baroness has much to say about Princess Victoria, who, like her mother, was kind but quite tactless. There is a certain quality of burlesque in her story of her visit to an old ladies' home that makes it worth repeating:

The Princess arrived with some presents and went round to talk to the old-age pensioners. "Well, my dear," she said to one, "happy?"

"Oh yes," replied the old lady, "I have been here for twenty years."

"They must miss you very much at home."

"But I haven't got a home."

"You must be very lonely!"

"Oh, but I have friends."

"You poor dear, how very brave you are!" she said, leaving her in floods of tears as she moved on to the next. Here she was equally successful and when she left, the ladies who ran the place begged her never to return.

Princess Victoria and her brother George, who shared the same babyish sense of humour, were great friends, and the Princess of Wales was often irritated by their childishness. The sort of education which princesses could expect—and this applied particularly to the King's sisters—inevitably stifled their talents. Ponsonby often found himself in his capacity as Secretary having to straighten out their affairs, and he noticed that they had no judgement and easily fell victim to intriguers. The ladies of Edward's family played a purely decorative role at his Court and of them all the young Princess of Wales, who now lived in Marlborough House, was the most successful at it.

Mrs. Keppel's position was of equal importance. It was her opinion that the Ministers sought, and her friendship that the Ambassadors courted. The Court counted on her to keep the King in a good temper. Alice Keppel was essential to her dear Bertie's happiness, which explains why the Queen went out of her way to be nice to the favourite. Vita Sackville-West, daughter of the celebrated Lady Sackville, describes her, in the character of Mrs. Cheyne, in her novel *The Edwardians*:

Mrs. Cheyne . . . had a real spaciousness in her nature. . . . She brought to everything the quality of the superlative. When she was worldly, it was on the grand scale. When she was mercenary, she challenged the richest fortunes. When she loved, it was in the highest quarters. When she admitted ambition, it was for the highest power. . . . Romola Cheyne, for all her hardness, all her materialism, was no mean soul. She had, however, one weakness: She could not allow anyone to be better informed than herself. Whether it was

politics, finance, or merely the affairs of her friends, the last word,
the eventual bombshell of information, must proceed from her
and no other. On the whole she preferred her information to be
good; and although she was quite prepared to invent what she
could not ascertain, she would first make an assault on the main
and most reliable source of knowledge.

Sir Osbert Sitwell, who knew Mrs. Keppel well, wrote the
following passage in his admirable memoirs.

> I liked greatly to listen to her talking; if it were possible to lure her
> away from the bridge table, she would remove from her mouth for a
> moment the cigarette which she would be smoking with an air of
> determination, through a long holder, and turn upon the person
> to whom she was speaking her large, humorous, kindly, peculiarly
> discerning eyes. Her conversation was lit by humour, insight and
> the utmost good nature: a rare and valuable attribute in one who
> had never had—or, at any rate, never felt—much patience with
> fools. Moreover, a vein of fantasy, a power of enhancement,
> would often lift what she was saying, and served to emphasize the
> exactness of most of her opinions, and her frankness. Her talk had
> about it a boldness, an absence of all pettiness, that helped to make
> her a memorable figure in the fashionable world.

When in London the King would have tea with Mrs. Keppel
practically every day. Her friends knew better than to ring her
doorbell if there happened to be an extraordinarily smart coupé
standing in front of her house with a coachman whose hat bore
no cockade. The King always took his fox-terrier, Caesar, with
him. This was a very badly behaved dog. It was almost as if he
could read the legend on his own collar: "I am Caesar, the King's
dog." He ran all over the house, to the fury of the Keppels' French
governess, who gave vent to her republican ardour by kicking the
sacred animal. The King would amuse the Keppel children, who
called him "Kingie," by allowing them to slide pieces of toast
down his trousers with the butter side down, while betting on which
piece would arrive at the bottom first. Sometimes Mrs. Keppel
would take her eldest daughter, Violet, to the palace; the child
would play in the garden while the grown-ups had tea. One day
she espied a tricycle in a coach-house, leapt on it, and careered
across the lawn, unable to steer or stop her mount, while footmen

and gardeners dashed after her, shouting, "The King's tricycle, the King's tricycle."

Not long after the coronation, the Keppels' house in Grosvenor Street started to fill with beautiful pieces of furniture, with tapestries and precious carpets. Some of them, like the two porcelain pagodas that had once stood in the Brighton Pavilion, came straight out of the royal furniture stores. Others were gifts from friends of the King and from American or other foreign ladies who were seeking access to the sovereign. But money and birth were not sufficient to penetrate the magic circle. The women had to have beauty (Mrs. Keppel had the sense never to be jealous), they had to be able to play a good hand at bridge, and they were expected, from time to time, to throw an amusing party. But, most important of all, they had to be *au courant* with the little items of gossip that the King found amusing. "For the love of heaven," Lady de Grey once said to Ponsonby during a cruise, "suggest a topic of conversation, because I am being put next to the King for the third time."

"Tell him all your friends' and relatives' secrets," he replied. She answered with a laugh that she had already done so the first evening.

Sir Ernest Cassel, who had formed an alliance with Mrs. Keppel, obtained an incredible ascendancy over the King's mind. He had been of some assistance to him as Prince of Wales, but there was more than recognition of past services rendered in Edward VII's affection for him. It was an absolute trust of a kind that suggested that this powerful and wealthy man had nothing to gain from his sovereign. His position exceeded that of even the most faithful courtiers, and the King saw him every day, which was far more often than he saw his own family. In looks the financier closely resembled a hairy hippopotamus. His mansion in Park Lane was a monument to the worst in Edwardian taste. He had bought eight hundred tons of Carrara marble and even the kitchens were lined with it. His dining-room, with its antique oak panelling, could seat more than a hundred guests. In the hall four van Dycks, which he had commissioned Duveen to find, were hung between lapis lazuli pilasters. A cart-load of flowers would come up every day from his place at Moulton Paddock. With people that mattered he was very generous. Mrs. Asquith was given a pair of hunters, Mrs. Keppel a chinchilla wrap, and the Duchess of Devonshire's favourite charities benefited to the tune of tens of thousands of pounds. Those who had some standing at court were given a share in his business operations. Sir Ernest financed the building of the London Underground and, for this, considerable political influence was required. On his death in 1921 he left eight million pounds. The King often went to stay at Moulton Paddock, for he continued the habit he had when Prince of Wales, of inviting himself to his subjects' houses, and would arrive with a retinue of guests, servants, and detectives. Sir Ernest's daughter married a politician who was related to some of the greatest families in the land. His granddaughter was later to marry Prince Louis of Battenberg (the last Viceroy of India, Lord Mountbatten).

Second only to Sir Ernest in political importance was Lord Esher. Of him Margot Asquith wrote:

> Esher is a man of infinite curiosity and discretion, what the servants call "knowing," and has considerable influence at Court. His good spirits, fair judgement and frank address make him plausible and popular, and he has more intelligence than most of the Court pests. Slim with the slim, straight with the straight, the fault I find with him is common to all courtiers, he hardly knows what is important from what is not.

The Marquess of Soveral remained the most intimate friend. He also acted as confidant to all the ladies and to the Queen herself. Alexandra would complain to him when Edward went too long without seeing her.

With the exception of the two Jubilees, the English had been deprived of the pomp of monarchy during the preceding reign. But now they would have plenty of opportunity to admire the activities of royalty, what one might disrespectfully refer to as the royal circus. The photographs in the new glossy magazines with their colour supplements were to convey to their readers, year in year out, the pageantry that the King was so good at arranging. In November, the Opening of Parliament, with the fog muting the cheers and the fanfares and dimming the golds and purples as

the carriages roll towards Westminster and its blackened lattice-
work of stone. It is a day on which the House of Lords resembles
a scene from some vast Gothic opera, the galleries filled with
ambassadors and peeresses in full court dress, while on the floor
the peers in their purple robes contrast with the bishops in black
and white. From the corridors outside, where the heralds-at-arms
and the mace bearers are stationed, a cry is heard: "The King!"
and then another sound, the tapping of the Beefeaters' halberds on
the flagstones as they approach. In a long robe of velvet lined with
ermine, the King enters, giving his hand to the Queen, who as always looks slender in a dress that shimmers with jet-black dia-
mante. Her arms and her neck sparkle with diamonds, and on her
head is a small crown set lightly like a boater without disarranging
a single curl. She hardly seems to notice the weight of the enormously long velvet train which the two pages, specially brought up
from Eton, carry behind her. Preceded by the crown and sceptre,
which have come under escort from the Tower, the Sovereigns
mount the throne. Behind a door can be heard a murmur: it is the
Members of Parliament, waiting for the King to send for his
"faithful Commons." As they enter, the bewigged Lord Chancellor,
in his gold-embroidered robes, hands the speech to the King, who
proceeds to read it in a firm voice. After a suitable pause, in which
the two chambers absorb what he has said, the King extends his
arm to the Queen, descends from the throne, and departs amid
the same ceremonial. One year, the procession was half an hour
late in arriving. Alexandra's necklace had been caught in the
coach door and had broken: the pearls had all rolled under the
horse's hooves. The King refused to leave until he had been assured by the lackeys that they had found every one.

In June, it was the debutantes queuing in the Mall to get into
the palace that attracted the crowds. There they would sit in their
carriages, with three white ostrich feathers on their heads, their
mothers in attendance. As no photographers were allowed into the
palace, the magazines' artists would depict an idealized scene,
although it must, in any case, have been a wonderful sight: the
swan-like necks of the ladies and the superbly turned calves of the
men, the glistening cuirasses and the pyramids of flowers.

These presentation parties were held in the evening with the object of providing a spectacle more theatrical than the dull levées held at St. James's Palace. On such an evening the royal family would gather in the white drawing-room and then proceed to the throne room to the sound of "God Save the King." Once they had grouped themselves in order of precedence around the red-velvet-covered dais, the file-past would commence. One by one an usher would call forward the young girls as they waited tense with excitement in an adjoining room. Each would have a card that would be passed from one gentleman usher to another. The final one, who was armed with a tall ebony cane, would call out her name as she curtsied low, three times, before the throne. For her, the most difficult part was to hold up her train as she walked backwards, across a wide expanse of floor, in order to rejoin the others. For months beforehand these curtsies would be practised under the instruction of former ballet-dancers, of which the most famous was Madame Moufflet. The same functions were the occasion for the wives of ambassadors to present their distinguished compatriots who happened to be in London at the time. There was no honour more sought after by the Americans. To brighten up the proceedings, an orchestra would play light music: tunes from *The Merry Wives of Windsor*, overtures by von Suppé, and selections from Gilbert and Sullivan. The Master of the King's Music would sometimes suggest something a little more serious, but the King always firmly refused; the keynote had to be gaiety. Wagner and Mascagni were allowed during banquets, but he didn't listen to them.

During the great balls the Beefeaters, in their scarlet tunics, would come from the Tower to mount guard on the staircase, halberds in hand. Red-coated footmen would receive the guests in the hall.

There was no Court in Europe, not even in St. Petersburg, that could offer such an array of beauty, or such exotic uniforms. The tiaras, the decorations, the epaulettes, and the jewellery provided a shimmering backcloth against which the Indian princes stood out like uncut diamonds. The principal guests would open the ball with a solemn quadrille or a polonaise. The King and Queen would then separate and, preceded by gentlemen ushers, circulate amongst the guests. The bowing of heads as they passed would be like the wind travelling through a field of corn. Their tour of the room completed, the orchestra would break into a waltz or a double Boston. The King, who had once loved dancing, was now content to sit with an ambassador and watch. If he started tapping with his cigar-holder it was a signal that he was being bored and one of his intimates would rescue him by joining in the conversation. At midnight the royals would follow the King and Queen into the dining-room through a press that was only just held back by the ushers' staffs of office. In another room there would be a buffet for the guests. Between pyramids of roses and mountains of exotic fruits were laid out boars' heads, pheasants, and peacocks with their tail feathers in array. On the sideboards, the gold plate and the silver gilt trophies would be displayed. The orchestra would have orders to play until dawn, by which time the King would long since have been in bed.

Equally lavish (a very Edwardian word) was the hospitality at Windsor if another sovereign was being entertained. Thirty people would come for the week-end and the King would himself plan the programme hour by hour: the details of dress, the decorations to be worn, the seating arrangements, and the allocation of apartments and bridge tables—nothing escaped him. A tour of the royal collections led by the courteous Sir Lionel Cust would occupy the morning. The Curator has preserved the comments of many of these visitors. Young Alfonso XIII, who had come with the intention of getting engaged to the ravishing Princess Patricia of Connaught, was heard sighing: "*J'ai un creux là dedans. A quand le lunch?*" (I am absolutely starving. When are we going to have lunch?) France's official painter, Bonnat, who came over with President Loubet, particularly admired the Lawrences. The German princelings were always looking for resemblances and trotting out family trees. The royals would have lunch without their suites, in the oak dining-room. In the afternoon they would pay a visit to Eton in landaus or go by car for a picnic in some bogus ruins near Virginia Water. After tea there was bridge. They would dine in the Waterloo Room, usually deafened by the bagpipers who marched around the table. A theatrical performance would occupy the rest of the evening. The plays were not always very well chosen. *Le Courrier de Lyon*,* for instance, was performed before the King of Portugal, who had just been a witness to his father's and his brother's assassination. The King of Greece expressed a desire to hear the singer Mary Garden, although Melba had been booked for this performance some time before. She was engaged, and the two prima donnas found themselves seated on the same sofa as they awaited their turn to go on. Looks of hatred were exchanged.

It was from Windsor that, in each day of Ascot week, the royal party would set out in landaus, with postilions and outriders dressed in old-fashioned, gold-embroidered liveries. Other landaus would follow with the members of the family and the Court, the ladies with their umbrellas open to protect their finery from the dust raised by the preceding carriage or in case there was a shower. To the sound of a fanfare the procession would drive on to the course and draw up in front of the stand. Here the assembled throngs of Society people, dressed in their most extravagant best, would applaud the royal family.

It was a reign in which the keynote was one of splendour rather than of taste, and it was at its most aesthetically successful on occasions of this sort.

---

* A well-known melodrama of the time, very popular in England.

CHAPTER TWELVE

The Edwardians

"EDWARDIAN PAGEANT!" The English, or to be more precise the
Conservatives, still dream nostalgically of the first ten years of
the twentieth century: they see it as a cavalcade passing into the
distance in a cloud of golden dust, having in its passage filled
London with all the finest and rarest things in the world. It was
the sort of parade in which decorations and orders abound and
every kind of osprey plume and oriflamme is to be seen. Here are
all the races of the world come to pay their homage in England,
an England that like some high-mettled steed prances like a
circus horse to the tunes of *The Merry Widow*. "Quite a high
stepper" they would say of someone who had style. For nearly
eight years from the time of the Coronation at the end of the
Boer War, the festive spirit lasted, and then Lloyd George's
speeches and the international crises struck their false notes. The
popular heroes of the procession were not only Kitchener and
Baden-Powell, the maharajas and the ambassadors, but also the
bankers and the ship-builders whose wealth symbolized the riches
of Empire.

Leading the way, a King and a Queen ride past in a coach: they
are as well known and symbolical as their playing-card counter-
parts, and the crowd, which applauds them, knows its place; behind them come landaus and motor cars festooned with flowers,
in which sit opulent women and the professional beauties, more
beautiful than ever, blooming like those heavy roses to which they

gave their names: Lady Helen Vincent, Lady de Grey; mingling with them are the great singers; Melba, Lina Cavalieri; and the actresses; Ellen Terry, Irene van Brugh. They are followed by the great families, their ranks filled with generals, bishops, and ambassadors; and finally, the City. Large avenues are pushed through the labyrinth of streets in order to make way for the procession. Government buildings and banks erect colonnaded façades and adorn themselves with imperial symbols. This fatal word, Empire, is indicative of megalomania, but although the procession is a triumph of almost Roman proportions, the vanquished are tactfully included as guests. But even the Boers are included in the cavalcade, there are others, referred to as "problems," who start hunger strikes in India and throw bombs in Ireland, or go to trades-union meetings on their way home from the mines. But these problems don't really worry the notables. Abundance makes for optimism; and money is plentiful and multiplies so quickly that people think that it must soon percolate through, even to the lower classes.

The great political hostesses, their power overshadowed by the influence of the Court, take their place with the professional beauties. Their starchy receptions do not now occur so frequently. Of them all, Lady Londonderry alone retains her influence: in 1906 she broke the Liberal and Conservative alliance by her hatred of Lloyd George. She also played a leading part in the stand made by the House of Lords in 1909.* The words Whig and Tory had died out, to be replaced by Liberal and Conservative. There were many aristocrats in the Liberal Party: friends of the Souls or disciples of Gladstone. Such was the efficiency with which the oligarchic system functioned that it was almost impossible for an outsider to get anywhere unless he was either a genius or totally unscrupulous.

Of the upper classes, or those, at any rate, who took part in the cavalcade, there were scarcely more than about twelve thousand individuals; although the internal barriers within this class

---

* Lloyd George's budget was repeatedly thrown out by the House of Lords and this led to a constitutional crisis, the consequence of which was that the Lords lost their power to interfere in financial legislation.

Cecil Rhodes.

remained numerous, money now made it far easier than in the previous generation to make one's way towards power or the Court.

The background of the members of that Edwardian aristocracy varied considerably. First, there were the ancient and wealthy families, of which there were at least fifty in the kingdom. Let us look at a typical example. His lordship lives in his house in Belgrave Square from May to July and for a short time in October, and spends as much time as possible on his estate in Yorkshire, which he administers with loving care. He would be the Lord Lieutenant of the county and rule about a dozen villages where the clerical appointments would be in his gift and the elections within his control. His country seat being some distance from London, he would also have a week-end house near Ascot. August and September he would spend shooting in Scotland; and his yacht at Cowes and his villa in Cannes, where he would spend two months in the winter, would be waiting for him. One of his brothers would be an ambassador and he himself would have married one of "my dear Duchess's" daughters; his son would be engaged to an heiress of one of the King's friends. If the boy is bright, there can be little doubt that one day he will be in the Government or win the Derby; if a dullard, then there is nothing to prevent his becoming a good landowner and an excellent shot. The younger son will be elected to the Commons by the good people that live on the family estate, and the daughter will marry a cousin and go and live in an enormous castle; but there may be another daughter who prefers the company of a poetess in Florence. These families were related through their innumerable cousins to half Debrett, that fat red and gold annual which is one of the pillars of snobbery.

The aristocracy had lost much of their glitter during the moral Victorian years, but now they came back into their own. The dukes all had five or six large houses, enormous estates, and an important part to play in big business. Lord Tredegar and Lord Bute possessed between them almost all the coal in Wales, and the Duke of Westminster owned half London. Lord Derby inherited £300,000 from an uncle, with the proviso that he distributed £ 67,000 among 763 servants and gardeners. But although so generous to their servants and to the peasantry, who in their eyes were the people, the members of this aristocracy knew nothing of the life and aspirations of those whom they never saw. Somerset Maugham wrote:

> The confidence of the public in the aristocracy was shaken by the incompetence which it had just shown in South Africa, but it was not aware of this and retained its assurance and spoke of the march of Empire as though it was simply a family matter. Before an election I heard a discussion as to whether Tom would have the Home Office and whether Dick would be content with Ireland.

For families whose substance had dwindled or who suffered from spendthrift heirs the solution lay in an American match. The example was set by the Duke of Marlborough. There were at least a dozen marriages that brought in wealth on the scale of Boni de Castellane's: the Duke of Roxburgh married Mary Goelet, and Lord Curzon, Nora Leiter; Lord Tankerville's and Lord Yarmouth's brides had dowries of five million dollars apiece. But there was not the extravagance that could be found in the Paris of Boni de Castellane; money was invested in the family estates, or swallowed up in racing stables. Some of the King's friends, many of whom had settled in England for some time, like Mrs. Arthur Paget, virtually ran marriage bureaus in their drawing-rooms.

Debrett was now beginning to include families of much more recent origin and even foreigners, and these people were already mixing with the great at Court or at race-meetings. Their enormous fortunes came possibly from the Transvaal or from tea-shipping, and they would probably have intermarried with families like the Sassoons. They invested huge sums in their stables and would contribute almost as much to the funds of one of the political parties and thus rapidly earn peerages. Knighthoods would already have been procured at the time of the King's accession. The eldest sons would follow their fathers into business, but their duties in the City would leave them with ample time to get themselves elected to Parliament. The younger sons would obtain commissions in smart regiments and spend fortunes chasing the professional beauties. Of their daughters, one would marry a peer and the other a Rothschild or an Italian prince. They lived in enormous houses in Park Lane whose eighteenth-century furniture and decorations would be supplied by Duveen, and spent their week-ends in Tudor castles near London. Sargent painted their family groups against a background of azaleas and coromandels: worshippers of Mammon in Savile Row suits, their ladies, with their milky peach-melba complexions, gay and radiant, they are not so much the *nouveaux riches* as the real rich. For they were rich in a way in which the American puritan could never be, and they spent without counting the cost with the sole object of gaining the front ranks of the cavalcade.

The old official classes still retained the integrity and the affected pomposity of the Victorians. They had solid houses in Kensington and properties in one of the unsmart counties or in Wales, and the head of the family would be related to a peer or a baronet. He would have a brother who was a general, another who was a canon at Oxford or a bishop, and he himself would have a minor position at Court. It was a world in which all the totemic traditions of the Establishment were maintained, the old school ties, cricket matches at Lords, and presentation parties.

The middle classes, whose rise was charted by Galsworthy in *The Forsyte Saga*, were almost entirely cut off from these three groups. Despite their wealth, they stuck to their conventions and to the provinces. They ran towns like Manchester and Birmingham, and hunted with the County. Doctors and engineers were considered very middle-class, stockbrokers and industrialists upper-middle-class, and dons and clergy slightly more aristocratic.

Led by Chamberlain and Asquith, the middle classes achieved their social rise through politics and religion. The wealthy upper middle class turned its back on puritanism and embraced the Anglican faith, and sometimes even Catholicism. It was now smart to be a convert.

There were two sets of people in London, well known to each other, who, for all that they differed on everything of importance, shared power and influence. The first were the Souls, whose hour came with the premierships of Balfour and Asquith. They were interested in social problems, they had no respect for the Church, and they were wary of the King's political ambitions. Margot Asquith, who brought to politics the same ardent enthusiasm that she brought to foxhunting, was, as ever, their moving spirit. With her dry wit and elegance of manner she was undoubtedly a high stepper. She was too fluent and too witty a talker to avoid making a great number of enemies. Her piercing voice would interrupt dinner parties to say, "And now a little general conversation," whereupon everyone would stop talking in order to listen to her. Their thinking as a group was oriented towards Westminster, Parliament, and ministerial office. The other set revolved around Mrs. Keppel. Power, too, was its aim, but with it money counted for more than intelligence.

It was the King's own circle, more than the Souls, that gave the cavalcade its character, in much the same way that the Tuileries dictated the tone of the Second Empire. Now that it was the Court, the Marlborough House clan still occupied itself in the pursuit of pleasure but managed to avoid scandal. It was involved in both politics and operations on the stock market, but it combined the two with delicacy and it trafficked in influence without inflicting any damage on the country. (Again it was tact that preserved the reputation of the Crown.) It was an international set that included a number of Americans such as the Duchess of Marlborough and Lady Paget, Daisy of Pless, who was English but had married a German, and several bankers of German origin. It was a self-contained world with its own shibboleths and its own slang. English words were given Italian endings ("how too horriblino"); everyone had a nickname; and liaisons were carried on so openly that in country houses lovers were given adjoining bedrooms. As Mrs. Keppel said once on returning from Paris, "*à chacun sa chacune.*" The Souls patronized a sort of modern style derived from the Pre-Raphaelites, but the smart set went in for a simplified Rothschild style of the sort adopted by the grand hotels. Interior decorators now made their appearance and taste began to show a marked improvement on that of the preceding reign. But for all the millions that were spent, not one penny was forthcoming for a really modern work. The devotees of capitalism require a setting linked to the aristocratic tradition, and, ostentatious though they may have been, the Edwardians were quite as Philistine as the Victorian middle classes. The very limit of their audacity in their choice of paintings was marked by Boldini.

The whole elegant group revolved around the King and was dependent on his moods. As he grew old, he enjoyed nothing more than a select dinner party followed by a game of bridge. The honour of entertaining him for a week-end involved enormous expense and anxiety, for if he was bored he easily showed it. The ravishing Venetia James once attempted to amuse him by getting into a giant Easter egg just before his arrival. As Edward stepped down from the carriage and glanced inquiringly at the object on the steps of the house she leapt out and curtsied. The King's face turned to thunder and the Queen, in imitation of her mother-in-law, said, "We are not amused." The memoirs of the period are full of equally ridiculous episodes, but the prose style in which they are written is singularly flat.

The most ludicrous of these memoirs was written by the hare-brained Mrs. Hwfa Williams with the title *It Was Such Fun*. "Such fun!" was her favourite expression. English eccentricity and a terror of boredom inflicted on the King and his entourage scenes as singular as the following, described by Mrs. Williams.

> Only once did I see Hugh Lonsdale lose his sang-froid. It was at Temple, with my brother-in-law, who had a tame tiger. Sure of being adored by all animals, Hugh got the beast into a canoe. The King and the Queen watched from the bank. For one moment the tiger appeared surprised by the new element and Hugh paddled with one eye on the paddle, and one on his guest. Suddenly we heard a roar, a cry and a ploff! The canoe had overturned and Hugh and the tiger were racing for the bank; Hugh climbed up it first, with the animal at his heels. The tiger was captured after a bit but after that its character became so difficult that he was given to the Zoo where I went to see him often.

Quite as important as the place held in these memoirs by prime ministers and prima donnas was that held by the dogs. This is another excerpt from Mrs. Williams:

Staying at Rufford at the same time as the King, my chambermaid had great difficulty in keeping my dog in my room, for only the King's dog, Caesar, had the right to run freely round the house. One morning, I saw an expression on the King's face which presaged evil news. What could I have done? What could he have heard? "Look at Caesar, he is covered with blood. Your horrible dog has just bitten him." I assured His Majesty that my dog had not been free for a moment, because I could not imagine so gentle an animal attacking Caesar, . . . at that moment the whole table burst out laughing, I was the victim of a joke. Caesar, pursuing a rabbit, had torn his ears on some brambles. Later my dog was recompensed for his wisdom by receiving an invitation to travel on the Royal train as I was going to Scotland.

"Such fun!" cries Mrs. Williams as she recounts an anecdote about the King eating frogs cooked in paprika prepared by Escoffier and called "nymphs à la rose."

The best dinners were cooked by a young woman employed by the bachelor Sidney Grenville. Edward took an interest in her and bought her the Cavendish Hotel in Jermyn Street. Here, half a minute's walk from Piccadilly, in this Crown property, the most elegant in the land could enjoy their adventures in privacy. Rosa Lewis was still to be seen at the reception desk in 1955, her white hair crowning her dignified if crumbling features, as she chatted with the few Edwardians who had survived their escapades and gave advice to their grandsons, the heroes of Evelyn Waugh's *Vile Bodies*.

Another Edwardian memoirist is Daisy Cornwallis-West, who married the wealthy Prince of Pless. Her sister was the first of the four wives of the Duke of Westminster, and her brother, a handsome guards officer, married Lady Randolph Churchill, who was twenty years older than himself. The Princess divided her time between London and Berlin; less gay than Mrs. Williams, she had a sculptural beauty that made it impossible for her to laugh, and she also had a mission in life, which was to bring England and Germany closer together. More than once she found herself in a delicate situation, between the King and the Kaiser, from which only her stupidity and her frivolity extracted her. The beautiful Daisy attracted admiration from every side; her diary, full as it is of guest-lists and reflections of an aesthetic nature, is studded with references to the attentions of her admirers.

> X adores me, but I only allow him to kiss my curls, and even they are false . . . Prince von ———— wrapped his leg around mine during supper at the Palace. . . . It is too boring, the Crown Prince picked up the piece of tulle that had fallen from my train and hid it in his hand. . . . When the King tells me that I am in very good looks, that bores me terribly . . . the King is disagreeable because I have not been "kind" to him.

The Prince came to London and returned home dazzled. When the Duchess of Clermont-Tonnerre came over at the height of the Season, she found that her cousin, the Duchess of Montrose, was not free for a single meal and was quite unable to give an evening party for her. Instead, she gave a breakfast for her at the Dairy in Hyde Park.

Jacques-Emile Blanche came over to paint the literary hostesses and the great men whom they had attracted to their salons. He wrote:

> Never were so many presents given; the shops were combed to find pieces of furniture, jewels, and furs, and young ladies were given blank cheques. Everything seemed to be common property and presents were never anonymous. People no longer stayed at home but spent their time in other people's houses. Bachelors took palaces in Italy, or yachts, which they put at the disposal of their girl friends, who would invite everyone they knew.

The King and the Queen were the most generous givers, and would distribute trinkets from Asprey's and Cartier that were valuable enough to pass for jewels. Every Christmas, opera glasses, frames, ash trays, and cigar boxes would go out by the dozen from Buckingham Palace. It was a generosity that made for good public relations. When Baroness Klein-Michel, who had been presented to the King at the races, was sent a riding whip with the winning horse's head on it, the Germanophile fervour of her salon in St. Petersburg noticeably abated.

Wealthy bachelors such as Sidney Grenville and Reginald Lister, who shared the tastes of the ladies of fashion, acted as the link between the Court, Society, and the theatre. We can only regret that they did not write their memoirs, as the juicy pieces of gossip, which used to make the King laugh till he almost choked, are now lost forever: tact has had the last word.

There was one convention, however, that still lingered from the preceding generation: the private life of people in the public eye had to be kept rigidly screened under pain of the most complete ostracism. Divorce was forbidden, sodomy was accursed, and, if one became involved in a scandal, suicide and exile were the only two alternatives. Society turned a blind eye to every form of liaison that made life more agreeable for its own members. If a foolish young man got into debt because of his racing bets, some rich relation would willingly repair the damage. But if the matter got into the hands of the law or the press, the guilty party would be banished for good. The rules of morality were presided over in the drawing-rooms by a few elderly ladies of sixty or more who had successfully negotiated all the hazards of life. They took over from the Victorian dowagers whose lives had never brought them near these dangerous reefs.

The "double-duchess" (Devonshire, ex-Manchester), now an invalid who never left her bridge table, settled people's position in the fashionable world in her raucous voice. The prices which she quoted in this stock market of reputations were indicated simply by holding out one, two, or sometimes even three fingers when she shook hands. If someone had been rash, then one finger was withheld. Only to those who were beyond reproach was the whole hand held out. This was for intimates of the King and other duchesses, to whom almost anything was permitted. "She was," said E. F. Benson, the frivolous son of an archbishop, and one of the best chroniclers of this society, "something of a steam-roller. Neither good nor bad, but crushing everything in her path. In the drawing-rooms of Devonshire House, she sat silent and unmoving, like a still life, encrusted with diamonds and decked with flowers." An invitation to one of her little dinner parties, followed by bridge, would put the seal on the most ambitious of worldly aspirations, although three thousand people would be invited to the "crushes."

The Duchess of Sutherland's receptions at Stafford House

always took place in three acts. The first would be a dinner for thirty people with a nucleus of royalty and ambassadors. Then, from half past nine till ten o'clock, a few of the more brilliant M.P.s and some ladies of fashion would arrive for coffee. Finally, at eleven, the door would open wide to admit the "crush." Those who got above themselves were quickly put in their place. "My dear Maud, may I call you Lady Neumann?" said Mrs. Keppel to one particularly pushing lady.

Enormous fortunes were squandered in attempting to impress what was in fact the most blasé group of people in the world. Those who wanted to break into it needed ingenuity, nerves of steel, and the ability to attract. One lady, possibly Lady Neumann, had asked the King to dinner for the first time, and for the occasion had ordered a fabulous dress from Pacquin. But the boat on which it should have come was held up by a storm and she had to wear a dress that she had been seen in before. The butler was instructed that, if the dress arrived before the dessert, he was to spill some sauce down her neck. When the King arrived the thought uppermost in his mind was clearly "What am I doing here?" The conversation flagged and Lady Neumann's eyes flickered from the salmon to the haunch of venison, which by turns she hoped would tumble into her breast. At long last a frozen pineapple sorbet fell onto her shoulders and the day was saved. "Would your Majesty please excuse me while I go and change?" she asked. The King grunted his assent. Ten minutes later the lady reappeared in her Parisian outfit, and the august guest at last began to look happy. Undoubtedly one had to suffer a number of insults before one could arrive.

Sir Sigmund Neumann, who fancied himself as a laird, invited the King to a deer-stalk in Scotland. The day went badly from the beginning and, worst catastrophe of all, the picnic did not arrive at the appointed rendezvous. The King was hungry and made biting comments in a loud voice about people with too much money who tried to do things they knew nothing about. The wretched Neumann, who was running about in the heather looking for the ghillies, was made to look very foolish.

"A little too much is just enough for me." The famous remark, made by an Indian chief invited to the White House, could apply equally to Edward VII and the Edwardians.

It was a reign that corresponded to the French Second Empire, dominated as it was by financiers and beautiful women. The leading literary figures did not bother with the cavalcade and its fanfares. In Henry James's involved and laborious intrigues and Galsworthy's middle-class epics, it can be heard like a distant echo in a snug drawing-room. Meredith and Hardy, on the other hand, working in the depths of the country, were no more Edwardian than Flaubert and Renan were Second Empire. It was in writers of a lighter touch, such as Max Beerbohm, that the Edwardian spirit was to be found. His *Zuleika Dobson* is an absolute masterpiece of elegant if somewhat sinister humour. It is the story of a ravishing actress, for the love of whom all the undergraduates of Oxford, led by a duke, throw themselves into the Isis.

Saki's short stories, constructed like infernal machines, are reminiscent of the best of Wilde, but their tone is more worldly. He depicted county society, and his characterizations are biting.

> In her dealings with the world in general, her [Mrs. Thropplestance's] manner suggested a blend between a Mistress of the Robes and a Master of Foxhounds, with the vocabulary of both.

Ada Leverson's characters owe much to Wilde. Guards officers in white flannels hand round cups of tea on the lawn. Enigmatic young ladies in enormous hats sit by the hortensia borders, and immorality always triumphs over true love, but with infinite discretion.

The poverty of artistic talent was far greater. The Royal Academy exhibited imitations of Bouguereau and Flameng, while *art nouveau* was confined to tea shops and provincial art schools. The fashionable colours were those of the sweet pea: mauve, pale rose, and lavender. The ideal atmosphere would have been created by a conservatory full of gilt trellises and palm trees, with a vaguely Viennese orchestra behind them playing selections from Franz Lehar, the Offenbach of this Second Empire. An agreeable if slightly more distinguished type of music was supplied by two much-sought-after singers, both products of the Côte d'Azur. Raynaldo

Hahn, the author of *Beatrice d'Este's Ball*, was often invited to England by hostesses anxious to entertain their guests. The other, Isadore de Lara, was as flamboyant as his stage name (his real name was Cohen); he was a protegé of the Princess of Monaco and the author of the highly-thought-of *Messaline*. The music lovers were all Wagnerians; following the lead set by Lady de Grey, they would flock to Covent Garden. She was a *grande dame* in every sense of the word, for she was over six feet tall; in 1909, when she brought over the Russian ballet, Wagner and Puccini were swept aside.

The perfect symbol of this Society, with all its diverse elements, bonded together by luxury of living, is the peach melba, its hot-house fruit at its centre surrounded by rich cream and syrup, ever cool and fresh, however overheated the restaurant, its colours always pale and languid.

"I realized that in England there was a clientèle ready to pay anything for the best." Thus César Ritz, who understood that Society, with all its flux and restlessness, needed something more than private drawing-rooms and Court levées. His answer was his rose-coloured stucco colonnaded salons and his dining-room with its enormous windows overlooking Green Park. There, at lunch time, or at the Savoy, overlooking the Thames, at supper time, could be found a brilliant international gathering where reputations would be established and secured; the *nouveaux riches* would parade their aristocratic conquests, the beautiful women show off their powerful admirers, and the more daring debutantes stroll with the more eligible bachelors. There one could rub shoulders with the Duc d'Orléans, Melba, Margot Asquith, escaped from gloomy Downing Street, Greek princes, beautiful Americans, and grand dukes with their morganatic wives. The hostesses, like hunters back from a safari, would exhibit their most recent conquests, Caruso, Rodin, Duse, and later Diaghilev and Pavlova, or Somerset Maugham, whose plays some thought were dangerously clever. And above the brilliant brouhaha and the tzigane strings could be heard Mrs. Hwfa Williams' voice crying, "Such fun!"

Romano's in the Strand had a shadier clientèle, drawn from the racecourses and the theatre; here could be found *demi-mondaines* and Gaiety girls whose brilliant careers were to be paralleled in later years by the Ziegfeld girls. Small private rooms were provided, which enabled them to exercise their talents.

With the King himself setting an example, the motor car, which was very useful for keeping up with the pace of life, soon became fashionable. Edward even insisted on taking the aged and terrified Emperor of Austria for a drive. The Duchess of Sutherland, wrapped from head to foot in furs, as though she were going to the South Pole, also drove her own horseless carriage.

On his unending round of country houses, watering places, and yachts, the King would be followed by the wealthier of his subjects. Having tried Baden-Baden and Homburg, Edward VII finally settled on Marienbad in Austria. Here he would return each year to enjoy the waters whose purifying properties enabled him to revert to his former habits with greater gusto. Travelling under the name of the Duke of Lancaster, he would take with him a small suite that always included the indispensable Ponsonby, and his old friend Harry Chaplin, now ruined and gouty but still gay at heart, was also always of the party. At Marienbad, the King would meet again such old friends as the Murats and the Ganays. (On one occasion the Marquise de Ganay annoyed him by offering him champagne, which was forbidden by the cure.) With Madame Waddington he would reminisce about the 'eighties. But there were others whom he encountered at these watering places whom he would rather have avoided. These were usually former mistresses who had sunk in the world and who would never have dared to cross his path in London. But there were also a number of Viennese *cocottes* who would importune him with considerable impudence. The ardour of his youth restored by the cure, he was sometimes surprised by the detectives, to their great embarrassment, in some romantic country setting in a scene of a type usually reserved for private rooms.

Madame Letellier, a delectable friend of Clemenceau's and the wife of the proprietor of *Le Matin*, who was also one of Helleu's favourite models, often came to Marienbad, intent on strengthening the bonds of the *Entente Cordiale*. Bird-brained though she was, she was obsessed by politics. The King played croquet with this Parisienne every morning, and Ponsonby, who was bored to death by the game, would sometimes be asked to join in. He always did his best to make the King lose. Madame Letellier was an even better player than the secretary, and would patriotically help Edward to get through the hoops. She was convinced that if the monarch was left *sous cloche** or if she was imprudent enough to croquet him across the lawn, England would throw herself into the arms of Germany.

The Balkan potentates also found that they needed to take the waters; between glasses at the Kurhaus, they would tell their Uncle Edward about their troubles. The King of Greece was still bent on territorial expansion and was particularly anxious to obtain Crete; Danilo of Montenegro wanted decorations, and Ferdinand of Bulgaria desired to be recognized as an independent sovereign. He shocked the King by treating Franz Josef with utter contempt; Vienna had refused him the Order of the Golden Fleece as as result of his son's Orthodox baptism.

The archduchesses flocked to Bad Ischl, which was not far away. They were far from appreciating the lack of deference shown to them by the English suite. The King would drive over to see them in his big Mercedes, and take lunch between calls at one of the local inns. At first he would revel in travelling incognito but was quick to take offence if he was not served first.

Edward would seek rest from the fatigues of winter in Biarritz. The month of April was always spent there, and a whole floor in the Hôtel du Palais would be taken. Mrs. Keppel, the Devonshires, the Pagets, and of course Sir Ernest Cassel took villas. It was a sort of old gentleman's holiday and lacked the excitement of the Riviera, but then the air was so much more bracing! The King would work during the morning with his usual secretaries, plus one lent by the Ambassador. If the weather was fine he would play golf or croquet in the afternoon. On really fine days they would drive off to sample delicacies in such local villages as Sare and Ascain and watch games of pelote and country dancing that

---

* In French croquet there is a bell on the center wicket, and a player whose ball is stuck under it is liable to a penalty.

was very like highland reels. There would also be lunch with the Marquis d'Arcangues.

On Easter day, after a service at the Anglican church, the Court would set off for a picnic. The French and English detectives would lead the way in a cloud of dust, and the King would always choose a place by the side of the road exposed to the curiosity of passers-by. The ladies would take off their veils and wraps, the valets would unfold the tables, remove the silver from its leather boxes, and set out the ice buckets, the caviar, and the Moselle cup. If a peasant happened to pass on a cart, the King would have someone take him a glass of champagne.

Sometimes they would go as far as San Sebastian. There, the Queen Regent Maria Christina and Alfonso XIII would be at home in their villa Miramar, which, with its Tudor architecture and its setting in a rain-swept park, was singularly reminiscent of Bournemouth. The young King's passion for everything English enabled Edward VII to arrange an unhoped-for marriage for his niece Victoria Eugenia (Ena). When staying with Frederika of Hanover near Biarritz, the young girl met Alfonso, who, so it was said, was as though struck by lightning. "So Ena is going to become the Queen of Spain," exclaimed Cousin Augusta, "a Battenberg! Dear God!" The King was delighted, but English public opinion did not take kindly to the idea of her becoming a Catholic and watching bullfights.

Edward VII left his mark on Biarritz to a far greater extent than he ever did on Cannes. A South American might have mistaken it for England. Until fairly recent years one could still see the tutelary image of the King in top hat and scarlet hunting-coat above a confectionery shop between the two bridges in Bayonne.

Queen Alexandra never went with him on his trips to "that awful Biarritz." Mrs. Keppel's rule was undisputed, but that did not prevent other women from chancing their arms and creating around the King the atmosphere of gallantry so indispensable to him. His courtesy became legendary. A pretty Bordelaise girl, fishing for trout on the banks of the River Gave with her husband, suddenly saw the royal car braking violently as it passed one day; the King got out and addressed her in English.

"Sir, I am French," the lady said proudly after making a rather ridiculous curtsy in her tweed plus-fours.

"Aha," said the King, "I thought you were English as I saw you were using silk flies, and the French usually use those horrible worms." As a good Bordelaise, the lady continued the conversation in English, while behind the Sovereign's back his suite gave her signs of encouragement: such an encounter always put him in a good humour. After shaking the lady's hand for a considerable time the old gentleman said something friendly to her husband and departed.

As late as 1940 the elegance of the Edwardian age was kept alive by the half-French Mrs. Hope Vere, the sister of the Marquis de Montebello, at one time French Ambassador to St. Petersburg. If one visited her in her villa on the Côte Basque, she would reminisce about her life in those days, occasionally astonishing one by remarks like "One morning the King said to me, 'Put on your dressing gown and come and watch the squadron passing.'"

There was an American lady called Mrs. Moore who made a sustained if unsuccessful effort to be admitted to the magic circle. The King, who thought her unattractive and vulgar, used to say, "There are three things in life which one cannot escape: *l'amour*, *la mort*, and La Moore." And there *was* no escape. Mrs. Moore would bribe the porters in his hotel to let her know where his excursions were going to take him and would follow him there, only to be totally ignored. In no way discouraged, she planned a final master stroke. She suborned the Daimler's chauffeur, and not long afterwards Edward had a puncture on the way back from St. Jean-de-Luz. It was the sort of mishap that he hated. He stood in the road, ready to stop the first car that passed, but as this was 1907 there was very little traffic. At last a cloud of dust in the distance indicated an approaching vehicle. The equerry waved and the car drew up; out got Mrs. Moore, cheerfully ready to do the King's bidding. All he required, he said gallantly, was her company on the way home, and Mrs. Moore was able to drive triumphantly through Biarritz with his august figure at her side. Touched at having inspired such devotion, Edward would sometimes accept her invitations to play bridge. But he treated her as a joke. "Have you lost something?" he would ask when, having curtsied too deeply, she was prostrated at his feet. When she died she left expensive mementos to all the King's friends. As Robert de Montesquiou remarked, "She left the world as if she were leaving the Ritz, distributing tips."

The King and the Queen usually spent the first week of January at Chatsworth with the Duke of Devonshire. There was a theatre in the house, which slightly spoilt its classical proportions, and troupes of actors would be engaged to perform. The guests also took it in turn to play charades. There was a Viennese orchestra that played during meals, and in the evenings as well if the Queen wished to dance. The Duke employed at least two hundred servants to look after the usual complement of fifty guests. Lord Derby on the other hand was not so generous. When the King, with forty of his friends, was invited to stay at Knowsley for the Grand National, the host was heard to say, "That makes sixty extra servants, and with the thirty-seven who live in, nothing could be simpler." Amongst themselves these servants were known by their masters' titles, and the order of precedence in the servants' hall followed that used in the dining-room: at the top tables sat the valets and the chambermaids, and at a lower table the grooms and footmen, while the stable girls and scullery maids, who waited on their superiors, took their meals in a room apart.*

It was not always easy to find enough to do during the day and it was fortunate that the meals took up so much time. Breakfast was set out on a sideboard spread with every sort of venison and smoked fish. Apart from royalty and a few *grandes dames*, no one was excused from coming down for it. If it was not raining, the company went for walks in the park or inspected the stables; lunch was eaten at small tables. In the afternoons they went shooting and then changed for tea, the men into sports jackets and the ladies into

---

* At Longleat, the seat of the Marquess of Bath, the staff comprised the following: a major domo, a butler, an under-butler, a bedroom valet, a master's valet, three footmen, a major domo's valet, two handymen, two sweepers, and a boy to do the lamps.

There were also a housekeeper, two ladies' maids, a nanny, a nursery maid, eight chambermaids, two sewing maids, two pantry maids, six washerwomen, two kitchen maids, a scrubbing woman, a scullery maid, and a woman to sweep.

tea gowns; for this meal the servants stayed out of sight and the cups and sandwiches were handed round by the men. The King rather enjoyed having a lobster salad and one or two pieces of shortbread. Then came bridge, or conversation, in the enormous library. At about half past seven they all went to their rooms to change for dinner; a different dress was required for every evening, although the same jewellery (tiara, necklace, and bracelets) was worn with each dress. The men wore court dress or uniform. At midnight, a sort of cold buffet with plovers' eggs, ptarmigan, and salmon awaited the guests. The footmen would bring in every sort of liqueur and mineral water imaginable. As they travelled back to London in the special train provided, the guests would find an account of their week-end in the newspapers, and of a dozen other exactly similar week-ends.

Daisy of Pless was never really sure that she enjoyed these house parties. Too much depended on the mood the King was in: too often his good humour would be expressed in repetitious teasing that was always concentrated on one scapegoat. The wretched victim, who could never answer back, would be paralysed by his chaffing. The Queen loved party games, and tension would be relaxed by Musical Chairs and Consequences.

Entertaining royalty was extraordinarily expensive. The American Mr. Zimmerman had a bill for $150,000 after a week-end of this sort, during which, incidentally, his daughter was carried off by the ne'er-do-well young Duke of Manchester, the double-duchess's grandson. Of this sum, $3900 was for enlarging and decorating the station, $1500 for the red carpets on the platform, and finally $10,000 for the gifts presented to royalty.

In the corridors of these country houses, the commemorative photographs of these royal visits can still be seen. The King is always at the centre of the group, sitting at his ease with his hat tilted over one ear, a cigar in one hand and the appropriate seasonal emblem in the other: in the autumn a gun, in summer a croquet mallet. Beside him sits the mistress of the house, her forced smile failing to hide her nagging fear that something might go wrong. The Queen and the Princesses perch on the edges of their cane seats, dressed in suits and fur toques. Harry Chaplin's ample form, Mrs. Keppel's imposing bust and languorous eyes, Lady de Grey's tall figure, and Lord Ribblesdale's cavalier silhouette can always be recognized. Most of the guests can be identified by looking through the visitors' book, a fat volume, bound in red morocco with gilt corners, resting on the hall table, but who were "Coco," "Topsy," and "Archie," whose names were signed alongside those of Portland and Rothschild?

The luxurious lives of the aristocracy were a constant source of interest to the people and the activities of everyone even remotely connected with the charmed circle filled the newspapers. Harmsworth launched penny newspapers, such as the *Daily Mail*, whose object was to lull the public at the very moment that it was beginning to feel its power. Today, now that the aristocracy is impoverished and lacking real power, it is the royal family that attracts this sort of attention. Occasionally a juicy scandal would catch the public's imagination. One of the most celebrated lawsuits was brought against Lady Sackville by the sister of her former lover, Sir Murray Scott, over a legacy. The latter, who had inherited from Sir Richard Wallace a fabulous collection of furniture (it ended up, via Seligmann, in the Frick Collection in New York), left it to his beautiful friend. Such was Lady Sackville's charm that the judges fell in love with her and dismissed the plaintiff. Another *cause célèbre* was created by a son of the late Duke of Portland, whose father at the time of his birth was leading a double life as a shopkeeper; he claimed both the title and Welbeck Abbey but was unable to prove his legitimacy. Feeling was also aroused over the case of Lady Sitwell, who went to prison for writing dud cheques. Her wealthy husband, who thought he would punish her by doing nothing to help, allowed the prosecution to go forward.

Although they read very little, the Edwardians were staunch theatre-goers. The censorship imposed by the Lord Chamberlain, however, made the plays which they saw quite innocuous. The difficulties with which the playwrights of the time were struggling were clearly seen by André Maurois:

Shaw amused the English but he did not convince them. The leaders of the Liberal Party remained so profoundly imbued with the individualist doctrine of laissez faire that they exhibited an almost invincible apathy over any question of reform.

Despite a few actors of exceptional stature, such as Irving and Bancroft, the Edwardian theatre seldom rose above the level of the French *Théâtre de Boulevard*. The King enjoyed Pinero's plays and he was often to be seen, in a stage box at the Gaieties, ogling the more attractive actresses. He also brought over his friends from the Parisian stage and was one of the first to appreciate Gaby Deslys, whose famous song was written in the language of the *Entente Cordiale*:

> *Sur le plage, sur le plage*
> Men are full of *persiflage*.
> When I take my *bain de mer*
> All the boys just come and stare.

The intellectuals were to come into their own with the following generation. Most of the parents of the members of the Bloomsbury Group were important Edwardians. They themselves were to preach a régime of simplicity, as though the excesses of the previous generation had given them indigestion. Sir Harold Nicolson had little sympathy for that generation despite its generosity:

The Edwardians were vulgar and lacking in style; their hard brilliance was that of their electricity, a light that shone pitilessly on both the courtier, the pheasant, the bridge tables, and the little Fabergé boxes. They lacked simplicity, but their complexities were anything but inexpensive. The idea that intelligence could be of the slightest value never occurred to them.

The self-assurance of the Edwardians, which the crises of Agadir and the Balkans had left unshaken, for all the worry they caused the Foreign Office, was undermined only by the *Titanic* disaster. That an iceberg could sink this vast White Star liner, packed with so many rich and famous people, upset the order of things and troubled people's minds. It suggested a confusion between chance and providence that should never have existed in so well-organized a society.

CHAPTER THIRTEEN

The France of Monsieur Loubet

FASHODA, THE BOER WAR, the insulting attitude of the French press, and the Prince of Wales's refusal to go to the opening of the Paris Exhibition had stretched Anglo-French relations practically to breaking point. The good-will to be found in some of the ruling circles seemed to carry very little weight when people were in that sort of mood. But now, as the relative positions of the great powers evolved, France and England came closer together, although they at first showed little enthusiasm for such a development. As the dangers which had brought about the *détente* became clearer, however, a more cordial atmosphere was restored. The most obvious danger was that of Germany, who was gaining strength every day under her hot-headed ruler. The second danger, which the French, other than those of the extreme Left, refused to see, was Russia's instability. The course of Anglo-French negotiations has already been so clearly and brilliantly described by André Maurois that it would be pointless to go over them again here. The King's interest in the whole problem was considerable but his friendship for France was not unreserved. He had royalty's traditional distrust of a republic and an Englishman's contempt for the loquacious upstarts in the Assembly. Nor did he altogether appreciate the entirely intellectual intelligence of French politicians. He was shocked as much by the anti-clericalism which had been rampant under Combes's Government as by the blindness of the Nationalists during the Dreyfus affair. But to him France was, next to England, the most civilized nation in Europe. He was less irritated by her plain speaking than he was by German tactlessness or Russian incompetence. During the Boxer rising, in which French troops had been commanded by a Prussian general, an event that enormously pleased the Kaiser, he had feared a kind of Franco-German *entente* directed against England.

It would be absurd to suggest that Edward VII's taste for Parisian life was responsible for the *Entente Cordiale*. That side of his life had nothing to do with politics and he would have continued to indulge it regardless of the outcome over the *Entente*. As Prince of Wales, however, he had learnt to avoid that stiffness of manner that typified Victorian Englishmen when addressing Frenchmen, with its hint of moral disapproval. In England the King's French sympathies contributed little to any purely political developments, but in France, where he had a sudden access of popularity, they were responsible for an astonishingly rapid change of view. Later on his Ministers regarded it as something of an exaggeration to give all the credit for the *Entente* to the King. In 1915 Balfour wrote to Lord Lansdowne:

> It is foolish gossip to attribute the *Entente* to the King, as from the time that you and I came into the Government, he did not make one single suggestion on any important political question.

But it is true that the *Entente* would have remained no more than theoretical without his personality. The part he played was that of a catalyst. Balfour, the aesthete, who regarded Edward as vulgar, failed to recognize this attribute.

Before the negotiations could get under way formally, the ground was prepared by Lord Lansdowne, Delcassé, the French Foreign Minister, and Cambon, his Ambassador to London. They tactfully and carefully examined the points that had caused friction in the past and might do so again in the future. They reached agreement without difficulty on Siam, Madagascar, and zones of influence in Central Africa. Egypt, however, presented a slightly more delicate problem. France had very great interests there and culturally her influence was greater than England's. These conversations were carried on discreetly throughout 1901 and 1902, and their importance increased when, in February 1902, Chamberlain's attempts at a *rapprochement* with Germany were discouraged by the behaviour of the Emperor and von Bülow. To the English Government, France was therefore only a second best in its search for a means to end its isolation. The King's attitude, however, encourages one to believe that France had always been his first choice. Chamberlain, who was not popular in France, earned French good-will by assuring them that England was not opposed to their entering Morocco. But in return for this they would have to give up their aspirations in Egypt.

The ground prepared, the King now took a hand and gave a dinner party at Marlborough House (February 28, 1902). Eckardtstein, the attaché at the German Embassy, strained his ears in trying to overhear a long conversation between Chamberlain and Cambon. The words "Egypt" and "Morocco" kept reaching him. The King then turned to speak to him, and his anxiety was in no way dispersed by Edward's cordiality. "France is more pressing than ever," the King said. "If we are going to get this settled, we'll have to agree to their terms."

Thus, in their dignified and circumspect way, the diplomats explored the ground and grew to respect each other. The neutralization of Tangier was proposed by Cambon in 1902, a gesture appreciated by Lord Lansdowne, who now warmed to the negotiations.

But all this was slow going. The King decided that the exploratory work had gone on long enough. Something more permanent had to be created and this necessitated an official meeting. Whitehall was alarmed that the Crown's dignity might be impaired by the insolence of the Anglophobes. In March 1903, the French Ambassador informed Delcassé of the royal desire. Lord Lansdowne was in favour of discretion during the first stage of the *rapprochement*, and suggested that Edward should lunch with the President during an incognito visit to Paris. Although the Elysée was not entirely opposed to the idea of an official visit, it did not guarantee popular enthusiasm: so the diplomats thought that the idea was not altogether a bad one. The King's charm would work its effect on the official circles, and a semi-incognito protocol was prepared. But Edward was not having it. "If I go to Paris it will be with all the honours due to the King of England, with processions, banquets, and galas."

His visit to Paris would have to be in style, as would the visits to Lisbon and Rome that were to precede it. Still fearful of a contretemps, Lord Lansdowne protested, rather too late, against such ostentation. The King decided against taking his Foreign Secretary with him and invited Lord Hardinge instead. He was an accomplished man of the world as well as a good diplomat and he had married one of the Queen's ladies-in-waiting. A Minister was always taken on these trips, but there was no one in the Government whom Edward VII liked enough to be able to put up with his company for the three weeks which the tour would last. Thus Hardinge came to be the only representative of officialdom. The King embarked in the *Victoria and Albert* on April 1, with his usual entourage of equerries, secretaries, and doctors. This time he also had with him an Italian seascape painter called Chevalier Marino, the buffoon of the party, and of course the Marquess of Soveral. The fact that there were no ladies on board was not good for the King's temper, especially during the games of bridge that occupied the evenings.

The first stop was Lisbon. They were met by heavily gilded carriages that conveyed them to the sombre palace in which Portugal's obese sovereign lived his gay life. One of the horses attached to the royal carriage dropped dead on the way, an incident that inspired the humourist Ramalhão Ortigão, who saw in it Lusitania's final protest against enslavement by Albion, to write a violently Anglophobe pamphlet.

The King saw to the smallest details during the stay in Lisbon and insisted on his suite's adopting European etiquette, despite the fact that they found it ridiculous. Smugly ignorant of rules of behaviour that differed from their own, the English often gave the impression of arrogance and ill-breeding on the Continent, and Edward was particularly keen on establishing a cordial atmosphere to ensure that the meetings to which he attached an immense importance should go off without mishap. But now a profusion of telegrams started to arrive on board that led his suite to suspect that their solemn entry into Paris might be marred by insults which they would find hard to swallow. The yacht put in at Gibraltar and then at Malta. At Naples the King took a week off from his duties. He met once more the Savoy family, together with some German royalties, a Mrs. Vanderbilt, and Lord Rosebery. It gave him great pleasure to walk through the delirious crowds in the narrow teeming streets, although his suite believed them to be swarming with anarchists and were horrified.

Whitehall's attitude was still far from encouraging, and the Cabinet was against his proposed visit to the Vatican. Edward had always regarded the Pope as another sovereign and he himself had millions of Catholic subjects, so he decided to take no notice. But his proposal started intrigues in both Downing Street and the Curia. On the one hand the Duke of Norfolk was trying to get Balfour to relent, while on the other Cardinal Rampolla was trying to make it seem as if the initiative had come from the King. Such was the agitation and so many the contradictory messages exchanged, that they tended to obscure the event itself. Both Cabinet and Curia were, however, wasting their time. The King had an audience with the Pope, to whom Cardinal Merry del Val explained the courteous nature of this gesture. Their conversation was long and cordial; it was of no diplomatic importance, but it made a good impression with the public. Confronted with a *fait accompli*, the Cabinet had to give in. The King had created a precedent that would give him greater freedom of action when he went abroad in future.

At last, on April 30, Edward VII and his suite boarded the train that was to take them to Paris; nervous and tired, he harassed his overworked and pessimistic staff. In Paris all was anxiety. Deville, the President of the Municipal Council, who was an ardent Nationalist, was persuaded with some difficulty by Loubet to stop the League of Patriots from staging hostile demonstrations, although he could not prevent them from exhibiting their patriotism. Anyone who gave the slightest suspicion was arrested by the police as an anarchist, and this provoked protests from the League for the Rights of Man. The fashionable were worried about the impression the official classes would make on the King, but the politicians remained on their dignity. There would be no bowing and scraping to provoke the mockery of the electorate, but they were determined to be dignified without any attempt at elegance. Baron d'Estournelles de Constant, whom Queen Victoria had nicknamed "The Angel of Peace," uttered the classic banality: "War is no solution, it only leads to reprisals." As for the people, they were only too ready to jeer at the fat old man with whose appearance they had become familiar from the caricatures in *Rire* and *L'Assiette au Beurre*. The Champs Elysées was lined by the unenthusiastic employees of the City Corporation but there were very few others. The Count and Countess Boni de Castellane invited a few friends to watch the procession from the terrace of their new town house. Among them was the beautiful Princess of Pless, who was heard saying how much better it would all have been done in Berlin. A portrait of Edward, in the uniform of a field marshal, appeared on the front page of *L'Illustration* for the benefit of the coffee-house denizens. Red velvet awnings, fringed with gold, were put up at the English Embassy and the Elysée; carpets were rolled out and potted plants positioned where policemen could hide behind them.

The English Ambassador, Sir Edmund Monson, boarded the train at Dijon. He had never been in favour of the visit and provided no encouragement. Lord Hardinge and he drew up the text of a speech which the King was to deliver at the British Chamber of Commerce. The extremely Francophile Hardinge slipped in some phrases so fulsome as to cause the King some hesitation. But the Ambassador's advice was that things had reached such a pass that he could not be fulsome enough. The French officers who were to be attached for the duration of the visit were also introduced to the members of the King's suite, who found them charming. The Chef du Protocole Armand Mollard's representative was another who joined them at Dijon. With great pomp he handed Ponsonby a schedule in which even the clothes to be worn by the King were laid down. When this document was shown to Edward, he bellowed, "This is too much. They now want to teach me how to dress!" In a rage, he struck the offending items from the protocol with a pencil. Ponsonby returned it to the envoy from the Elysée with a *Le Roi le veult* worthy of Louis XIV. This had the required effect.

On the morning of May 1 the train entered the Gare du Bois de Boulogne. President Loubet was waiting on the red carpet in evening dress. The "Marseillaise," followed by "God Save the King," and the presentation of the suites, took up a few minutes. Then the party climbed into the landaus, the King and Monsieur Loubet in the first, Monsieur Delcassé and Lord Hardinge in the second. The route was lined by guards in black cloaks and soldiers in red trousers and the procession was led by a platoon of the Republican Guard. The press photographers, with all their para- phernalia, were herded together in one phalanx. The tenants of the Boulevard Flandrin sat on their balconies, following the scene without enthusiasm. The two old gentlemen in white beards, one fat and the other thin, sat side by side, doffing their top hats with a slightly forced air of good-will. A few shouts of *"Vive le Roi"* were drowned by those of *"Vive le Président."* But the crowd, which was fairly thick, who brought up the rear of the procession, were greeted with cries of *"Vive les Boers," "Vive Marchand,"* and even *"Vive Jeanne d'Arc."* "What enthusiasm!" said Delcassé to Lord Hardinge, hoping that the nature of these cries would be obscured by the clatter of the escort. But the latter turned to the King as they got down from the carriage and said, "The French don't seem to like us—but then, why should they?"

They had hardly arrived at the Embassy when Edward set off in a carriage that had been used for the Coronation of Charles X, to pay a call at the Elysée. His speech at the Chamber of Commerce, in the afternoon, made a very good impression. In the evening, the King's demeanour at the Comédie-Française created further good-will. Instead of the piece by Racine that had been proposed, he asked for something more Parisian, and they put on *L'Autre Danger* by Maurice Donnay. Monsieur Claretie, the timid administrator, was worried out of his mind. What if an anarchist were to slip in, or a Nationalist deputy attempt to . . . or an intriguing woman . . .? There was some booing outside the theatre: inside, the audience rose as the heads of state made their entrance but there was no applause. During the *entr'acte* the King decided to pay a short visit to the foyer as he had always done as Prince of Wales. The Grand Cordon of the Legion of Honour stretched across his breast, and he smoked a cigar, surrounded by strangers. After a time he caught sight of the beautiful Jeanne Granier, and approached her. "Mademoiselle, I remember how much I enjoyed your performance in London. You were the embodiment of all the wit and grace of France." It was a compliment addressed to the whole of Paris and it noticeably raised the temperature of the room. Edward VII was applauded as he returned to his box.

The next day there was a review at Vincennes. Edward's cortège raised no enthusiasm as it passed through the Faubourg St. Antoine but there were at least no hostile cries. As he talked about it afterwards, the King smilingly remarked, "I thought I heard a few whistles, but no, I was wrong." He mounted a stand bristling with military trophies and supported by pillars made out of cannon; the balconies were made from muskets, and there were potted palms from conservatories everywhere. Then he watched as a number of army corps marched past. The garrison of Paris must have made a good impression on him for he was in an excellent humour when he arrived at the Hôtel de Ville. In his reply to the welcome extended by the Municipal Council, he said, "I wish to tell you how deeply I was touched by your kind words. I would have been distressed if I had not been able to visit the Hôtel de Ville during my stay in your beautiful city. I thank you most sincerely for the welcome which you have given me today. I shall never forget my visit to your charming city, and I can assure you that it is with the greatest pleasure that I return to Paris, where I always feel at home."

These last words hit the bull's-eye. The King received an ovation. His audience's enthusiasm spread to the street from the halls of the Hôtel de Ville. As he set off for Longchamp in the afternoon the whole of Paris turned out to acclaim him. There were no more cries of "*Vive les Boers*" as the English officers rode through the streets.

He spent the afternoon at the races. Seated between Madame Loubet and the Governor of Paris's wife, Edward could see his friends surrounded by elegant women in the Jockey Club stand. Eventually he could take it no longer. "You have got to get me out of this," he murmured to Ponsonby. "Slip over to the Jockey Club and tell them to send someone to invite me to see their new stand." Ponsonby ran off to explain the position to Prince d'Arenberg. Three members of the Club immediately arrived, looking very official, and begged his Majesty to come and admire the improvements made to their stand. Edward asked Madame Loubet to excuse him for the next three races, and went off to talk horses with Monsieur de Saint-Alary and Monsieur Schickler and reminisce about their respective triumphs in the Derby. He came back to the presidential box for the last race. As he returned to the Faubourg St. Honoré his procession was given an ovation the whole length of the route.

The banquet at the Elysée made the necessity for a Franco-English *entente* even clearer. The President's speech, read in a nervous voice (he had pinned the text to a candlestick), was dull. The King, who was seated in the place of honour, reverted successfully to the theme of his speech at the Hôtel de Ville. The reason for Monsieur Loubet's lack of confidence was his bad conscience over Russia. He did not want the "grand alliance" compromised by this new friendship. Guessing the cause of this anxiety, the King had a long conversation with the Russian Ambassador. He also went out of his way to be pleasant to Prince Radolin, the German Ambassador, who was not enjoying the way in which the King's visit was warming up. On the first day of the visit he had sent the Kaiser a sarcastic report on the reception which Paris had given his Uncle Edward, but now he had to adopt a different tone. William II was to regard the King and Delcassé from now on as a pair of sinister Machiavellis, whose object was to stifle poor innocent Germany.

The whole party went on from the Elysée to the Opera. The Princess of Pless thought that the decorations were shabby, and the ladies *mauvais genre*. "Oh! If this were only Berlin!" she kept saying. The officials had, however, invited Edward's friends, and he saw a number of familiar faces in the audience. If the chronicler of *L'Illustration* is to be believed they did not come only from the Faubourg Saint-Germain:

> While Mademoiselle Zambelli was dancing, the King bent over to the President. "If my eyes do not deceive me, that is Madame Liane de Pougy in the stalls, isn't it?" "That indeed is who she is. I don't know how she got on to the list of guests. Would you like her to be asked to leave?" "Not at all. I must confess that I was very upset last night at the cruelty shown to Mademoiselle Oterot at the Comedie-Française. I found it painful to think that the people of Paris should think it necessary to ignore the laws of gallantry in order to avoid offending my well-known taste for austerity." "But," said Loubet, "I can assure your Majesty that Mademoiselle Oterot merely left to take refuge in a box on the ground floor."

The story may be apocryphal, but it illustrates the extent of the *détente* brought about by the visit. Respect was giving way to sympathy.

On the third day a luncheon party was given at the British Embassy, which for this occasion became a royal palace. The winter garden was transformed into a throne room (the gilt-edged velvet is still there to this day), and once more the same words and smiles were exchanged, but this time the atmosphere was frankly relaxed. The house had once belonged to Pauline Borghese and her furniture was still in it. Sir Edmund Monson, who was always very correct, found himself talking to a member of the Government. Short of conversation, he said, "I am sleeping in Pauline's bed." "Your Excellency's private life is no concern of mine" was the cold reply. A service had been held at the church in the Rue d'Aguesseau before lunch and the coffee was hardly finished when the English colony began to arrive for a garden party. To the guests who stood round him as he planted a commemorative chestnut tree the King looked tired. In the evening the cortège set out for the Gare du Bois de Boulogne, while an enthusiastic crowd waved Union Jacks and shouted *"Vive Edouard!"* The *Entente Cordiale* was now more than just a diplomatic expression. *L'Illustration*'s caption to a picture of the departure said:

The two Heads of State are conscious of having done some very good work and thoughts of peace and humanity bring a smile to their lips.

The obvious success of this visit put the seal on "the dictatorship of tact," as an English M.P. called it. With the press on his side, the Cabinet had no alternative but to congratulate the King. The Marquess of Soveral, who was in Paris not long after his august friend, assured President Loubet and Delcassé that Edward VII was better disposed towards Russia than was his Government, as he much preferred his nephew Nicholas to his nephew William. The *Entente* would therefore shore up the alliance instead of undermining it, as Delcassé's enemies feared.

Monsieur Loubet, accompanied by his wife and Delcassé, returned the King's visit shortly afterwards. The President wisely stood on his democratic dignity. He would not accept the Order of the Garter, refused to wear knee breeches at a soirée, and declined the honour of dancing the quadrille with Queen Alexandra. This all made the right impression, and the English now had a permanent idea of what a French president was like: a small and simple bourgeois, something similar to a grocer, whom one could trust.

Hostility to the *Entente*, however, still existed in one quarter. Lady Warwick, who continued to see the King despite her conversion to Socialism, said to him one day, "What do we need an *Entente* for? If France is defeated there will always be time to go to her help. Why commit millions of people, who have nothing against Germany, to fighting her so as to get back Alsace-Lorraine for France?" Lord Esher begged her shortly afterwards not to discuss politics with His Majesty any more, and thus put an end to her long friendship with the King.

On June 7, 1903, Lansdowne and Cambon got down to the details of the *Entente* and, to use André Maurois' phrase, "discovered that the problems which divided them were infinitesimal compared to the advantages to be derived from an agreement."

The Newfoundland fisheries question tended to prolong the conversations; the importance which the French attached to cod astonished the English. The King carefully weighed the words of the smallest clause of the agreement before it was submitted to the French. One clause read: "His Majesty's Government has no intention of annexing Egypt, more especially since other powers than France are concerned, and has no intention of raising the question of Great Britain's actual position in this country." At his master's request Lord Lansdowne had to content himself with: "His Majesty's Government has no desire to change the political status of Egypt." On April 8, 1904, the conventions were signed while Parliament was still in recess. On its return, Balfour, instead of taking pride in the agreement, merely expressed his regret that there should have been a cession of territory (the frontier in Guinea had been redrawn in return for the Newfoundland fishing rights) without Parliamentary sanction. The King took this ill and replied that cessions of territory were one of the Crown's privileges. He wrote to his secretary, Lord Knollys:

> Balfour is always so vague that he must have made yet another mistake, and if this is so I insist, as a matter of principle, that he should admit it.

The Prime Minister, who had the support of Parliament, provided explanations but not excuses. Thus the Crown lost one of its important prerogatives, the disposition of territory. The Government was taking its revenge for the fact that the *Entente* had been arranged, as it were, behind its back. The French Senators and Deputies, however, ratified the treaty with less reluctance.

The Germans soon discovered that there were secret clauses in the treaty that gave France a free hand in Morocco, and as they themselves were planning a protectorate for that country and found themselves forestalled, they were deeply resentful. The policy of encirclement adopted by the Kaiser's enemies seemed all too clear. Now that Russia had been enfeebled by her defeats at the hands of the Japanese, Germany felt that she could pursue a policy of intimidation against France. On March 31, 1905, the Kaiser caused an immense commotion by landing in Tangier but no doubt he regretted it later since it led to nothing. Prince

Radolin was, however, putting pressure on the French Prime Minister, Rouvier, to get rid of Delcassé if relations with Germany were not to be broken off. Loubet took his Minister's side, although the timid President of the Council was all for backing down. Edward VII, cruising at the time in Algerian waters, requested the Governor General to send the following telegram to the Quai d'Orsay:

> I am charged by His Majesty to let you know that he will be personally very distressed by your departure. And in private conversation, the King, who is concerned at this news, asked me to insist vigorously that you should retain your portfolio.

Not long afterwards, the King, who was on his way through Paris at the time, again assured Delcassé of his sympathy and advised him not to take the Kaiser's ranting seriously. Delcassé remained at the Quai d'Orsay but German pressure soon increased. Prince Radolin terrified Rouvier by telling him that the German Army could be at the gates of Paris in two days. Delcassé requested Lansdowne to give him a clear indication as to the help which he could expect from England in case of a conflict with Germany. The latter replied that negotiations could be opened to discuss any eventuality. Even the supporters of the *Entente* had not hoped for this. The Rouvier Government, now at England's mercy, was overwhelmed. Delcassé resigned, in order to save the Government, on June 6, 1905. The national interest had to give way to that of parliament. With some satisfaction, Balfour wrote to the King:

> Delcassé's resignation, under pressure from the German Government, has revealed a weakness on the part of France which indicates that one cannot at present consider her as an effective force in international politics. She could not be trusted to stand up to threats at the critical moment of any negotiations.

But the King knew that the public could be fairer and more patriotic than the Government. To stir up public opinion he proposed a spectacular exchange of visits between the French and English fleets, one to visit Portsmouth and the other Brest. He himself saw to it that the French officers were sumptuously entertained, and in consequence the long-standing resentment felt by French sailors was overcome.

The effect of this diplomatic victory, however, was ruined by the vulgarity of the Germans, who had scented complete victory. Von Bülow was determined that the conference called to settle the Moroccan question should complete France's humiliation. Lord Lansdowne had now been succeeded by the more amenable Sir Edward Grey, who dispatched his most brilliant diplomat, Sir Arthur Nicolson, to represent England at Algeciras. The latter's opinion of the German representatives was not flattering:

> Count Tannenberg is a really terrible individual, a bluffer, a liar and bad-mannered. The other, Radowitz, says something different to everyone he speaks to, and in fact gives the impression that Germany does not know what she wants.

Germany's attitude, and the influence of Edward VII on Alfonso XIII, brought Spain into the French camp. President Roosevelt, whom William II admired, counselled moderation, and after interminable negotiations, intrigues, counter proposals, and blackmail, Germany renounced her Moroccan pretensions. As Lord Hardinge, who was sent on a personal mission from Buckingham Palace to persuade the French to take advantage of the German concessions noted:

> These events have revealed both the necessity of standing up to German bluff and the impracticality of the French, who always fight for an abstract idea.

The *Entente* gained strength as a result of this crisis, and Monsieur Bourgeois, who had replaced the ridiculous Rouvier at the Quai d'Orsay, gave Cambon orders to express his gratitude in Whitehall.

CHAPTER FOURTEEN

Politics

HISTORY ASSUMES A new perspective with the dawn of the twentieth century. The things that happened have a contemporary quality and our knowledge of them is no longer second hand. Engraving had already been replaced by photography, but with the motion-picture camera the great figures now emerge with jerky steps from the static Valhalla to which painting and sculpture had previously relegated them; thanks to the gramophone we can also hear their voices. Legend can do less for the reputations of Balfour and Asquith than it did for Gladstone and Disraeli. To use Paul Valéry's expression, *le monde fini* had arrived. There was nowhere else to explore; China and Turkey were opening up to European influences with equal rapidity; Germany was growing in strength and Russia was disintegrating. The United States was starting to preach the ideals of Henry Ford, and England and France were complacently allowing themselves to be overtaken. But the heads of state in this world, so close to ours, were still of another century. Their prestige and their prejudices alike were those of absolute sovereigns. The Courts of Europe had seldom been so magnificent as they were on the eve of the 1914 War. The Edwardian cavalcade took place as they were singing their swan songs, although to advanced minds of the time they seemed as absurd as parliamentary democracies do today. Despite his motor cars and his financial friendships, Edward VII already seemed an anachronism—which does much to explain the affection in which he is held by posterity.

Writing the life of a king like Edward, one is tempted to reduce history to the interplay of personalities, in the same way that Thiers reduced it to a conflict of generalship. It is easy to imagine that his hatred of William II, and his love of Paris, were of a capital importance. But we must not forget that George V's friendships with the Kaiser and the Tsar did not prevent the 1914 War or that the short-sightedness of the Russian imperial pair was not the main cause of the Russian Revolution in 1917. Nothing could have dammed up the forces that produced both the war and the revolution. If the Governments had been more reasonable they would only have delayed them by a few years. The great currents of history were flowing with total disregard for these self-important figures who were convinced that their meetings could solve everything.

The explanation of English policy must be sought at a deeper level than that of royal prejudice or naval rivalry. The Orient was England's principal market. If the Russians were to become all-powerful in the East, she would be in danger of losing it. It was this anxiety that drove Chamberlain, a businessman above all else, to make his Germanophile speeches and seek a Japanese alliance. Once Russia was beaten, however, the royal diplomacy did its utmost to draw her closer to England and turn her against Germany, whose industrial power was now a considerable threat.

The meetings and treaties that precede a war, which one may believe to be more or less avoidable, cause considerable excitement at the time, but once the war is over, the manœuvres that preceded it are of no more importance than is its strategy when the number of dead is being reckoned. The individuals concerned, however, are still interesting, even when their ideas are dead, and there is always a certain fascination about the events that brought these personalities of such diverse origin together.

In the period with which we are dealing, men as different as Isvolski, Clemenceau, Chamberlain, von Bülow, and Delcassé were in constant communication with one another, either directly or else through ambassadors whose job was to translate their

Rt. Hon. Joseph Chamberlain

aspirations and their dissatisfactions into neutral language. The only thing that these statesmen had in common was their very ordinary appearance, for with the *monde fini* the panache of the old world was on its way out. The splendour familiar to our fathers has been destroyed by petit-bourgeois democracies, theatrical fascism, and the dull apparatus of modern war. Flicking through the red-bound volumes of *L'Illustration*, we can still admire the grand duchesses in their feathers and the field marshals, with their ostrich plumage fluttering in the breeze like the full-dress flags over white yachts at Revel or at Kiel. We see gilded staff officers having tea with lace-enfolded ladies-in-waiting, and ambassadors, trussed in their grand cordons, exchanging significant looks with chamberlains who are even more gold-laced. The journalists of the time were either worthy professionals who commanded as much respect as members of the Institute, or else they were common gossip mongers, relegated to the level of the photographers. But it was on the international level that the panache of royalty was to be found. In internal affairs it affected the development of neither socialism nor capitalism.

The King of England and the Kaiser were the two most obvious exponents of panache. Edward VII was obsessed by his relationship with his nephew. Sometimes, when they were attending a funeral, his natural affability and horror of embarrassment would overcome his antipathy to William. Letters and presents would be exchanged and visits proposed; but these bright periods never lasted for long. In both London and Berlin, Cabinet Ministers and their wives would do their best to throw oil on the fire. Edward VII never understood what was so clear to Sir Harold Nicolson:

> The Emperor, with the best intentions, personified and encouraged the self-dramatization of the German people, their acute self-consciousness, their moods of envy, self-pity and self-glorification, their love of quantity and size.

The success of Edward's visit to Paris had made the Kaiser so nervous that the King decided to pay him a call at Kiel in June 1904. To inspire confidence, he took with him the Prince of Monaco, a well-known Germanophile, and, to please France,

Baron d'Estournelles de Constant. But his choice of other guests was less auspicious. They included Louis of Battenberg, the Director of Naval Intelligence, and Count Gleichen, a former Hohenlohe. These Anglicized Germans were hated in Berlin. He also took Sir Thomas Lipton, known by the Emperor as "the grocer," whose presence caused great offence. He had a staff, supplied by the Admiralty, whose job was to ascertain the exact size of the new German fleet.

Before the meeting, Chancellor von Bülow briefed William: "The atmosphere must be a sporting one throughout the interview. Remember that the whole pretext for it is the regatta. Never bore the English with high-flown ideas." The reviews, lunches, and regattas went off marvellously. In proposing one toast, the Kaiser struck a sentimental note. "Ever since I was shown the torpedo boats at Portsmouth by my dear Grandmother, I have dreamed of having a fleet as large as England's myself," he said. Edward replied with kindly irony: "My dear Willy, you have always been so kind and friendly to me . . . I drink to your health as Admiral of the Imperial Yacht Club." A long conversation took place between King and Chancellor, whose keynote was I-know-that-you-know-that-I know. The royal design, von Bülow felt sure, was to prise Germany away from Russia. Von Bülow made out that that country had been stricken by the Japanese war. He thought the Yellow Peril which caused the Kaiser such anxiety was just a joke: "The Japanese are people just like us, real gentlemen, and such hard workers." Not long afterwards the Mikado was mortally offended when the German Emperor refused to allow him the premier position in the Almanach de Gotha and relegated him to the fourth. "It is precisely because the situation with France is so tense," the King said, "that we have found written agreements absolutely necessary. The English and the Germans are, after all, such good friends that that sort of precaution would be quite pointless." As the conversation dragged on the Kaiser would, from time to time, glance in through the porthole, anxious to know whether Uncle Bertie was trying to seduce his Chancellor. Despite the endless care taken by Prince Eulenburg, the exchange of decorations between the two fleets caused some difficulty. Unlike the

English, the Germans have a passion for these marks of distinction. The royal suite was liberally sprinkled with Red Eagles, but then, to the astonishment of the imperial suite, there was no reciprocation. At von Bülow's suggestion the King had given only one decoration to each Minister. The Germans begged Metternich, their popular Ambassador to London, to go aboard the yacht, find the secretary responsible for this business, and give him a piece of his mind. The secretary was, in fact, Ponsonby; to his amazement, the Ambassador insisted that they should stay on deck in a high wind to hold a trivial conversation. The next day he discovered that their conversation had been watched by officers in the imperial yacht, who had studied all the Ambassador's gestures through telescopes, although he was in fact only talking about racing.

A similar meeting took place three years later at Kassel, but this time there were regiments instead of battleships and shooting took the place of yachting. The two sovereigns and the Chancellor went for a drive, in the course of which they reached agreement on the fact that it was the press that was poisoning Anglo-German relations by running banner headlines that were quite irrelevant every time there was the slightest incident. The imperial car was covered with gilded crowns and had searchlights attached to the bumpers. There was a mechanic and a footman, who both wore peaked caps with their full livery. As the English boarded the train on the final day, two German officers were heard saying, "The Lord be praised, these cursed English are leaving!" When the Englishman who had heard this told the King he replied, "When the Germans come to Windsor, make sure that you let them hear you saying, 'Thank God these damned Germans are off!' "

Edward's activities wore out his suite, drove his Ministers frantic, and put the chancelleries of Europe on tenterhooks. Apart from his regular holidays in Marienbad and Biarritz, and his incognito visits to Paris, his almost annual cruise brought him into contact with other sovereigns. In 1905, he went to Gibraltar, Corsica, and Algiers with the Queen, the inseparable Knollys, and the indispensable Ponsonby. The trip was marred by the daughter of a British consul who actually had the effrontery to come on board wearing tennis clothes. On their return, the King and Queen passed through Paris incognito and lunched at the Elysée. With their usual good manners they spoke to each of the fifty guests. The Chef du Protocole whispered in a stage aside to poor Madame Fallières who the guests were, but he might have saved his breath. She succeeded in embarrassing everyone. "It's most upsetting," said one Frenchman to an Englishman. "Well, what do you expect?" was the reply. "Your people are amateurs, ours are professionals." A lunch party given by the Breteuils, to which Madame de Pourtalès was asked, and a dinner party given by Jean de Reszké, who had recently married the beautiful Madame de Mailly-Nesle, probably did something to offset the boredom the King and Queen must have suffered at this function.

The following year, Edward and Alexandra went for another cruise in the Mediterranean, and at Cartagena had a meeting with the King of Spain, who was accompanied by his wretched little fleet. The police being convinced that the port was crawling with anarchists, they stayed on board the yacht. The cruise then went on to Naples, where they met the Italian King and Queen and the Empress Mother of Russia. Both she and her sister, the Queen, were eager to climb up to the crater of Vesuvius. They hopped about on the lava in their high-heeled boots while the King stayed in the funicular, growing increasingly impatient; he sent a messenger every two minutes to tell them to come down. Lord Rosebery rather spoilt things by wearing a white tie with his Yacht Club dinner jacket. The King was outraged and totally ignored this outstanding man. In Greece, everything went off marvellously. King George, Queen Olga, and their children were so gay and elegant . . . Edward VII, who was enjoying himself, was about to allow his brother-in-law to annex Crete, on his own initiative, when Lord Hardinge, once more representing the Foreign Office, put a stop to this abuse of power. Had the King done so, the entire political situation would have been upset and the Foreign Secretary would have had either to repudiate the decision or else to resign. Friction of this sort, which would have lowered the prestige of the Crown if the public had come to hear about it, was thus tactfully avoided. The elderly Campbell-Bannerman, now

Prime Minister, was better disposed towards the King than had been his predecessor Balfour, and Sir Edward Grey, who had replaced Lord Lansdowne in the new Government, was endowed with more subtlety. The influence of the Crown reached its apotheosis in the years 1907 and 1908. The success of the *Entente*, Edward's family connections, his august and distinguished appearance, the length of his experience, which now exceeded that of any other statesman or crowned head—all this contributed to making the King the leading personality of Europe.

The year 1908 was a turning point in Germany's progress towards war. The Eulenburg scandal* resulted in von Bülow's resignation as he was also deeply involved with the Emperor's homosexual entourage. Under pressure from both the general staff and Left Wing journalists, the Kaiser disowned his friends. Henceforth his recurring attacks of neurasthenia were to bring him increasingly under the military party's domination.

The diplomacy of Austria and of Russia was now conducted by two new personalities. They were both given to intrigue but lacked any overall design, and so intoxicated were they by their own duplicity that they lost all sense of reality. Count Aehrenthal, though very well connected, was a blackmailer and coward in the true Austrian tradition, a tradition that stemmed from a long series of defeats. Isvolski, the Russian, was a passionate Slavophile but he was both timid and a megalomaniac. Diplomatic circles delighted in a joke the Tsar Ferdinand made: "Mr. Isvolski is subjective while Mr. Aehrenthal is nothing if not objective." They hated each other and each did his utmost to trap the other into difficult situations. The Balkans were a particularly fertile source of incidents, and relations between Russia and Austria rapidly became explosive. Meanwhile Poincaré and Clemenceau, who also hated each other, were coming to power in France, where the atmosphere was becoming increasingly overcharged.

---

* Prince Philip Eulenburg, a suave and cultivated aristocrat, was the Kaiser's oldest and closest friend. His accusation as a homosexual in 1907 created a scandal compared with which the Oscar Wilde affair pales into insignificance. The Court was shaken to its foundations, and von Bülow was seriously compromised.

The only really pacific influence on the scene in this crisis-torn Europe was the King of England. Amid all the conflicting ambitions and hatreds, he had a dignity that justified his authority. He was a lover of peace as much as a lover of power. England, whose very life depended on the first, could forgive him occasion-ally for his abuse of the second. Since everything to him was a question of personalities, he regarded the choice of ambassadors as of the utmost importance and the Foreign Office was delighted by his nominations. One of the most outstanding was Sir Arthur Nicolson, who had distinguished himself at Algeciras and was later to negotiate the Anglo-Russian agreement of 1907.

There was one ridiculous episode that helped to poison rela-tions with Germany. Lord Tweedmouth, the First Lord of the Admiralty, who was an old friend of the King, had been carrying on a friendly correspondence with the Kaiser, who had always loved boats. He was imprudent enough to pass on to Berlin the naval programme for the current year before it had been presented to the House of Commons. This indiscretion was alluded to in *The Times* and caused a stir, but a scandal was avoided. Un-fortunately, however, Lord Tweedmouth was in the habit of im-pressing the members of the fair sex by reading excerpts from his correspondence to them. One of them got hold of the letters and did not keep them to herself. Tweedmouth tried to buy them back and went as high as £200. The Princess of Wales's brother, Prince Francis of Teck, who was well known in the *demi-monde*, was asked to carry out this delicate negotiation. But by now the lady in question appeared to have found a new friend, for the detective who was following her saw her buy six new hats, all at the same time. It became apparent that the letters were no longer for sale. The Emperor of Germany had also been anxious to recover them, and it was possibly he who had paid for the hats. At this point Lord Tweedmouth became completely senile and resigned from the Government, thus reducing the value of anything he had writ-ten to nothing.

Edward VII's cruise in the Baltic in 1908 repeated the success of his Mediterranean excursion. The stay in Copenhagen was deathly boring. The dinner parties were long and dull and old

King Christian would keep asking the same guests the same questions. The only gay note was provided by Princess Waldemar, the Duke of Chartres' daughter. On her return to her apartment, this attractive Frenchwoman used to dance the can-can just to stretch her legs. The Danish royals were bad at conversation. When they were at the theatre they would sit in their box during the interval and pass the time by counting. "One, two, three," the King would say gravely. "Four, five," the Queen would reply. "Six, seven, eight, nine, ten," Princess Waldemar, who was particularly talkative, would add. The Danes got the impression that their royal family was extraordinarily gay and amusing.

Queen Alexandra was overjoyed to be back in the bosom of her family. Edward made his usual good impression. The end of the evening found him in his apartment with two of the local beauties, the Countesses of Hagen and Roben. They did their best to make up for the absence of Mrs. Keppel, whose charms were, alas, denied to him on these official visits.

The Court at Stockholm, with its eighteenth-century liveries and ceremonial, delighted Edward VII. His appearance went some way towards healing the wounds inflicted on Swedish pride by Norway's secession. But in Oslo, where he paid a visit to his daughter, Queen Maud, he found the democratic atmosphere irritating. He begged his son-in-law to give up travelling by tram. From Norway they had a stormy passage to Russia in the royal yacht. At one point the Queen was having tea, surrounded by little tables covered with knick-knacks and photographs, when an unusually big wave sent the furniture flying. The teapot and the flowers, the biscuits, the miniatures, and the sandwiches were hurled to the floor in indescribable confusion and ladies-in-waiting and equerries were sent rolling round the carpet. The small pack of dogs profited from the occasion to gorge themselves on the *petits fours*. The King and Queen, who were good sailors, roared with laughter.

The yacht dropped anchor on June 7, 1908, in Revel. The Emperor's yacht and the Empress Mother's were already there. The remnant of the fleet sunk at Tsushima filled the rest of the port as best it could. Carrying parasols to protect them from the dazzling sun, the two Empresses, dressed in white, and the Queen, who was wearing a tailor-made yachting suit, with a straw boater resting on her curls, exchanged calls. The Grand Duchesses were in close attendance and they were followed by an enormous Cossack, with the Tsarevich in his arms. To the Russians, the relaxed atmosphere on the English yacht was a welcome change from the tension that prevailed in the palace. But although everything seemed to be going well, the Empress suddenly burst into tears for no apparent reason. On the morning of the meeting the King had had a long conversation with his Ambassador to Saint Petersburg, Sir Arthur Nicolson. He received him in his cabin. The diplomat (an amateur gardener like all Englishmen) noticed some *lilium speciosum* in a flower pot on a mahogany sideboard. Edward, dressed in the uniform of the Kiev Dragoons, which was a very tight fit, seemed to him to have become rather ponderous. He fired at his Ambassador a series of disconnected questions without appearing to listen to the answers. He wanted to know the names of all the members of the Tsar's staff and when and how uniforms were worn in Russia. Which would be most appropriate for dinner, the uniform of a Russian admiral or the mess-kit of the Scots Greys? What were the Russian railways like? Would it be best to avoid mentioning the Duma and any allusion to Japan? How well did Stolypin speak French?

The King's eyes never left Sir Arthur's decorations throughout the interview. "What is that toy, Nicolson?" he asked. "The hereditary Order of Nova Scotia!" "I've never heard of it! In any case you can't possibly wear it above the Order of the Bath." This question settled, the Ambassador took his leave and forced smiles were exchanged.

The Tsar's fear of the nihilists was matched by the King's fear of Parliament, which took a jaundiced view of his meeting with the autocrat. An absurd incident revealed the anxieties that each felt. On the final evening the sovereigns were dining on board the yacht when a choir, made up of both sexes, came past in a boat. The English suite, seeing how easy it would be for one of the singers to throw a bomb, became alarmed. "Don't worry," said the Chief of Police, "I will have them all undressed and searched."

"The ladies as well?" said the horrified English. "Of course," was the answer. But the English had no doubt of the impression that would be made on the House of Commons when it became known that these ladies had been stripped before being allowed to entertain the King. "Just search them," they said. The Russians, who were astonished by such scruples, acquiesced.

Diplomatic circles saw in the meeting a cause for congratulation but the English press regarded it coolly. The Dogger Bank incident had made Russia more unpopular than ever. (Passing through the North Sea on his way to fight the Japanese fleet, a Russian admiral had sunk a number of English fishing boats which he had taken for Japanese vessels.) The newspapers went out of their way to point out that Russia could not be trusted. They were not wrong, for shortly afterwards the Tsar met the Kaiser and turned his back on his dear uncle, just as he had tried to desert France and create a new Holy Alliance at Bjorko. The Revel meeting was also deplored by the Left Wing. The English public had never recovered from their feelings of outrage after Red Sunday in 1905. Firing on an unarmed crowd, like shooting a sitting bird, was simply not sporting, and even that habitually reserved diplomat Lord Hardinge had not been able to contain his indignation. In 1905 the Tsar suspended the Duma, and Parliament dispatched an official protest. When another visit to Russia was proposed, in June 1906, Ramsay MacDonald published a violent manifesto in which he spoke of Nicholas as an assassin. A petition, asking for the idea to be abandoned, was signed by several M.P.s. The King thought that this was impertinence. After all, he had to be nice to "poor Nicky" with all his worries; and in a fit of rage he struck the names of three M.P.s who had signed this document from the list of guests to a garden party at Buckingham Palace. Keir Hardie, the leader of the Labour Party, accused the Court of bringing pressure to bear on Parliament and he added, "Since the time of Charles I the King has kept out of politics and he would do well to continue doing so." Thus to brandish King Charles's head over a mere family visit was, in the eyes of the palace, in the very worst possible taste. There could be little doubt that the age of tact was giving way to the age of vulgarity.

Edward VII's boredom with politics, his mistrust of all in-
novation, and his belief in his foreign friends all had the effect of
making Parliament, which had been at the centre of the stage in
Victorian times, something of a sideshow in the Edwardian world.
The memory and example of the great Victorians lingered at
Westminster, for this reason, long after they were forgotten at the
Court or in the City. The old traditions survived, and new ideas
were erected upon them. But if the style and manner were the same
as in the preceding century, there was nothing to equal Gladstone's
eloquence or Disraeli's cunning. For all that Balfour and Asquith,
the Conservative and Liberal leaders, still respected the great
traditions, the King's position was not a happy one. He had no
friends amongst his cabinet ministers with whom he could discuss
matters of import at the races or out shooting. They were not members of the league of good taste as had been the Duke of Devonshire and Lord Rosebery, in whom in consequence he had been
able to place complete confidence. Thus when Chamberlain put
forward his proposals for Imperial Preference in 1903, to take
the place of the hitherto sacrosanct Free Trade, he took no part
in the discussions. In 1908 Margot Asquith, whose views were
representative of the more enlightened M.P.s, had this to say
about Edward, who inhabited a different world from that of herself and her friends:

> Royal persons are necessarily divorced from the true opinions of
> people that count, and are almost always obliged to take safe and
> commonplace views. To them, clever men are "prigs"; Liberals are
> "socialists"; the uninteresting "pleasant"; the interesting "intriguers";
> and the dreamer "mad." But, when all this is said, our King de-
> votes what time he does not spend upon sport and pleasure un-
> grudgingly to duty. He subscribes to his cripples, rewards his
> sailors, reviews his soldiers, and opens bridges, bazaars, hospitals
> and railway tunnels with enviable sweetness. He is fond of Henry,
> but is not really interested in any man. He is loyal to all his West
> End friends: female admirers, Jewish financiers and Newmarket
> bloods, and adds to fine manners rare prestige, courage and sim-
> plicity.

At the Queen's death, Lord Salisbury, the last of the great
Victorians, had been Prime Minister. This aged statesman had had

the strength to deal only with the business that interested him. The Education Laws and the Irish problem, for which the only solution he could find was a royal visit to effect a brief relaxation of tension, did not. His policy was one of isolationism; and owing to his serene belief in nepotism, Downing Street became known as the Cecil Hotel (Cecil is the surname of the Salisbury family). Since the time that the Queen had become unable to attend to the affairs of state with her former attention, Salisbury had taken charge of everything and the old man's resignation gave Edward little cause for concern. Arthur Balfour succeeded his uncle Salisbury. André Maurois said of the new Prime Minister that he "was not a real Liberal because he had no belief in the efficaciousness of reforms, nor was he honestly Conservative, because of his vague pessimism." He had been one of the most distinguished of the Souls, and used to play golf wearing a pince-nez; he was very widely read and had considerable powers of imagination, two attributes that Edward lacked. His powers of argument were so subtle that the King preferred to avoid seeing him in order not to have to give in to him. Courtiers were appointed as under-secretaries of state to act as messengers between Buckingham Palace and Whitehall. In consequence the royal reflections were not disturbed by remarks that were too brilliant and the King's diplomatic projects were not upset by humanitarian considerations.

Lord Esher, who had French sympathies, and whose support for the *Entente* never slackened, was still the most intimate of advisers. Lord Hardinge, as we have seen, accompanied the King on all his journeys. After his quarrel with Lord Charles Beresford, the King gave his confidence in naval matters to Admiral Lord Fisher. Lord Roberts took charge of the army. In India two of the most outstanding figures of the age, Lord Curzon and Lord Kitchener, were at loggerheads. Tall, good-looking, and affectedly pompous, although not lacking in humour, Curzon was the statesman who epitomized the Edwardian epoch. He was the very model of a viceroy, holding at Delhi a Court which staggered the very maharajas themselves. The rich and beautiful American whom he had married gave him admirable support. Kedleston, which he owned, was one of the finest country houses in England. This majestic figure survived the war to become an anachronism in the world created by the Treaty of Versailles. The once epicurean proconsul ended his days, in 1925, enslaved by the fashionable novelist Elinor Glyn. Curzon, whom Edward preferred, may have resembled a marble bust, but Lord Kitchener was a much more romantic figure. A soldier and a conqueror above all else, he was happy only when among his soldiers. His immense prestige dated from the time of the Sudan expedition but towards the end of his life Whitehall became anxious to be rid of him.

A certain Mrs. Townshend, who was French in origin, lunched with Kitchener just before the outbreak of war. He told her that France had to be informed that, whatever happened to her, England would continue the war until the German fleet was sunk. Kitchener's war aims were realized, but he himself was drowned on his way to Russia in 1916 when H.M.S. *Hampshire* was sunk by a mysterious explosion. It was even rumoured that the Admiralty had something to do with this and enormous posters were plastered round London saying "We have sent Kitchener to the bottom of the sea."

Edward VII's succession coincided with the so-called Khaki Elections and the end of the Boer War, the horrors of which had done so much to make England unpopular. The revelations concerning the concentration camps had even created something of a bad conscience in England herself. Some M.P.s were heard to say that imperialism had merely been the plaything of capitalism in this venture. In 1906 they put down questions for the Government as to the treatment accorded the indentured Chinese labour imported to work the mines. Was it true that the Chinese had been kept behind barbed wire, decimated by sickness, and flogged if they complained? Asquith replied, but was clearly embarrassed, and was reproached by the City for not having snubbed his questioners for being so inquisitive. With the frivolity typical of her sex, Margot Asquith wrote:

> Leo Rothschild spoke to me with great energy on this question of South Africa. Henry [Asquith] takes this question of the Chinese

very much to heart. Public opinion must not be alarmed about the sources of labour. All the Rothschilds are passionately interested in politics and angels of kindness.

Lord Milner then admitted in Parliament that the Chinese had been flogged, but, in a conversation with the Prime Minister's wife, he attempted to prove that if England wished to keep South Africa the only thing to do was to encourage hatred. Winston Churchill remarked that heroes and usurers should not be confused and Hilaire Belloc wrote a witty piece in which he ironically chronicled the exploits of millionaires who had remained in the City while the army was grabbing them an Empire:

> Where those three hundred fought with Beit,
> And fair young Wernher died, . . .
> The little mound where Eckstein stood,
> And gallant Albu fell,
> And Oppenheim half blind with blood . . .

It was a parody of Kipling but he used the names of families that were drawing immense incomes from South Africa and were in high favour at Court. The surviving Chinese were returned to their own country with a small gratuity, but to the public, who had taken pride in the fact that England had stamped out slavery in Africa, it came as a blow to discover that she had stooped to importing Chinese. The trades unions feared that the employers might even attempt to import coolies into Europe in order to lower the price of labour. In the end the big companies made deals with the local chiefs, who agreed to supply them with labour at wages that made very little impression on their profits. The trades union-ists witnessed the Edwardian cavalcade with pursed lips, much as the puritans before them had done under the Stuarts.

Another very un-Edwardian group were the Fabians, intel-lectuals with socialist leanings, among whom were included H. G. Wells and Bernard Shaw. Their name, taken from Fabius Cunctator (the temporizer), signified their university origin as much as their horror of violence. Their disciples were to come to power with the Labour victory of 1945. Their ideas were at first wasted on the working classes, who gave their support to Ramsay MacDonald and his more aggressive trades-union policies. MacDonald was elected in 1906 with fifteen other Labour members. Much as he deplored the fact that they had been elected, Edward VII treated the new party with the greatest possible courtesy. In this he was wiser than his Russian and German nephews, who called the members of the Left incendiarists and Antichrists. In consequence the socialists learnt to respect the Crown, although they violently attacked other institutions.

There was another section of the population that not only refrained from applauding the cavalcade but did its best to disrupt it. Thousands of spindly and badly dressed women in enormous hats decided that it was time they had the vote. The suffragette question had come up during the preceding reign, only to be dismissed by Victoria with the words "They ought to be whipped for their effrontery." Edward, who was famous for his gallantry, would have seen nothing attractive in these particular ladies. They held rowdy meetings, fastened themselves to the railings outside Buckingham Palace, interrupted the debates in Parliament, and assaulted policemen in the street. Some of them, disguised as Society women, even managed to break up ceremonial public functions by suddenly drawing from their bosoms banners proclaiming the equality of their sex. When put in prison, they would go on hunger strikes and have to be forcibly fed. The Court was as much shocked by the disturbances they created as the City was by threats of strike.

Up to that time politicians had been gentlemen, whatever their party; they spoke the same language as the King, and could meet him at the houses of their friends and send their daughters to Court. And then suddenly there arose Lloyd George and his interminable speeches in that lyrical voice, attacking the Budget and proposing lay education. The King was quite unable to understand him. He came from Wales, an unfashionable part of the country in which Edward had never set foot. He was a Nonconformist (Edward profoundly respected the forms of the Established Church) and he was insular. He knew nothing about Europe, as he was to show at the time of the Treaty of Versailles. In the stubbornness of his belief in his political ideals and in the poetic power of his eloquence, typical of the Celts, he was not dissimilar, as Chastenet remarked, to that other Celt, Aristide Briand. He was a democrat to whom the House of Lords represented all the defects of the ruling classes: nepotism, incompetence, and the outward show which, as a puritan, he despised. His attacks were spiced with wit. Did the King, he inquired in one speech, "govern with the Lords or with his people?" This was an almost personal remark, and the King took offence; most of his friends were in the House of Lords, but it was wide open to the leading figures in industry and finance. In fact the purple robes of the peers became, increasingly, a convenient cloak for the interests of big business. Lloyd George was not deceived by this; at a luncheon given on the day following the Budget, one that was not in the interests of the City, he had this to say:

> We are having too much of Lord Rothschild. We are not to have temperance reform in the country. Why? Because Lord Rothschild has sent a circular to the Peers to say so. We must have more Dreadnoughts. Why? Because Lord Rothschild has said so at a meeting in the City. . . . We ought not to have old-age pensions. Why? Because Lord Rothschild is a member of a committee that has said it cannot be done. . . . I should like to know, is Lord Rothschild the dictator of the country? Are we really to have all the ways of reform, financial and social, blocked simply by a notice-board, "No thoroughfare. By order of Nathaniel Rothschild"?

Thirty years had passed since Disraeli had sought the Rothschilds' help in his purchase of the Suez Canal shares as though it were simply a family business transaction. Twice, the Lords threw out the Budget which the House of Commons sent up to them; doddering old men and backwoods peers were mustered in order to obtain a crushing majority. The Government did not dare to ask the King to create squads of new peers, in order to get it through, as it was to do with his son.

The Conservative Party had split under Balfour's captious leadership and had been replaced in office by the Liberals. The new Cabinet, beneath the elderly and declining Sir Henry Campbell-Bannerman, was more united than its predecessor. The elections of January 1906 were in fact something of a landslide, and Balfour himself lost his seat. The question of who should be the new prime minister caused Margot Asquith considerable agitation but her husband's time had not yet come. Her opinion of the new Prime Minister was that he was sincere, modest, but indecisive and vague in his opinions. There was one young member of the new Parliament who immediately attracted attention to himself: he had all his father's, Lord Randolph Churchill's, insolence and unpredictable and muddled genius. Of him Margot Asquith said:

> Winston is absolutely charming and sincere, but there is no judgement behind his genius. He is impatient and his convictions are passing.

The King received Campbell-Bannerman at Marienbad, and the two old gentlemen, both broken in wind and Francophile in opinion, got on much better than they had expected to. The Prime Minister did his best not to bore Edward with social problems and left him a free hand in foreign policy. Unfortunately, the exercise of power wore Sir Henry out. In April 1908 a rumour was circulated that he was suffering from senility. His resignation was thought to be imminent. The King, however, was in Biarritz and had no desire to return to London. Lord Crewe and Knollys insisted that the incapable old man should be replaced. England was practically without a government for five weeks. Campbell-Bannerman finally resigned and the King summoned Asquith to Biarritz. People were astonished that he should not even trouble to break his holidays (he was not, after all, taking a cure) and the fact that the investiture of the Prime Minister should take place in a hotel and not in a palace was thought unworthy of the Crown. Was it, they wondered, even constitutional to form a government abroad? In the new Government, Lloyd George became Chancellor of the Exchequer, and Winston Churchill, Minister of Public Works. The King had no very great enthusiasm for Asquith; an intellectual petit-bourgeois, he had succeeded because of his wife's connections. The Asquiths' wit tended to border on insolence and Edward did not feel at ease with them. Margot's biting tongue alarmed the Court; and she did not confine her comments to one's ability to dance the can-can. Her loyalty was always tempered with irony, as her portrayal of the King shows. Edward was soon to be very irritated by Asquith, who went off for a holiday in Nice without asking his permission. In fact the insolence of the Commons ruined the last two years of his reign. Lloyd George, who was angered by the obstinacy of the Lords, which was tacitly supported by the Crown, redoubled the violence of his outbursts. In a speech directed against the territorial magnates he used the phrase: "the dukes who harass us." The King, who was also a great landed proprietor, was displeased. His secretary wrote to a Cabinet Minister:

> The only result of this violence is to range one class against another, and that is the lowest form of vulgarity.

Edward VII was opposed to all constitutional reform, fearing that if the power of the Lords became an issue, it would not be long before the position of the Crown itself was at stake. The King's approach in internal politics was, therefore, to be as evasive as possible.

On the other hand he gave his full support to the two remarkable men who were modernizing the navy and the army. Here the accretions of dust from the former reign were at their thickest. On becoming First Sea Lord, Admiral Lord Fisher had two objectives. The first was to combine in a single unit the Home Fleet and the Mediterranean Fleet; he did not believe in the possibility of invasion and was convinced that if the enemy fleets were to be engaged it would be in distant waters. The 1914 War was to prove him right. The second was to defeat Germany in the arms race: the new battleships known as Dreadnoughts were enormous and very expensive. Despite the Chancellor of the Exchequer, he was determined to have them.

As Minister for War, Lord Haldane had a task that was made more difficult by the army's lack of professionalism and the snobbery that divided its officers into castes. He created the Territorials as a reserve to the professional army, and centralized the General Staff in the War Office. The reverses suffered in the Boer War had revealed the officers for amateurs, and the King was made aware, during diplomatic exchanges, that very little account was taken of his army abroad.

We can thus see, in Edward VII's reign, the seeds of that revolution that was to turn Great Britain from an oligarchic empire into the welfare state that she became towards the end of the 'forties.

The surroundings in which people lived were also changing. The working classes in the nineteenth century had been crowded into endless, smoke-blackened streets adjacent to their factories. The Victorian middle classes had lived in bogus castles and they had built stations and town halls in cast-iron Gothic. Then it dawned on the big firms that people work better if they are happy, and, following the example set by the Lever Brothers soap firm, they laid out garden-cities for them. Spacious avenues of semi-detached houses were constructed for lower-middle-class families, on the edges of the manufacturing towns, and were set at irregular angles to create the atmosphere of a park. The houses of the wealthy were now built with an eye to comfort rather than show. Red brick, bow windows, and white-railinged lawns returned to fashion. This was the setting of Forster's novels, a world in which intellectual curiosity was beginning to upset religious routine. But in the life of the people, sport played a far larger part than books or politics. Whole towns would turn out to watch a football match, and tennis and golf were beginning to break the monotony of Sundays. Bicycling, which was now in fashion, set young people free from their families and compelled women to wear more sensible clothes. Every level of life in England was, in fact, benefiting from the enormous wealth that was drawn from the Empire, and there were so many well-to-do people that the number of charities continually increased. In this happier climate it is not surprising that advanced thinkers began to obtain more influence. Their ideas, like bacteria, required a minimum temperature to become active; it was not till the end of the nineteenth century that the industrial population of England attained the necessary threshold. As well as sport and a higher standard of living, the entry of science into everyday life was a third liberating factor. The cinema, the gramophone, and the cheap press now offered alternatives to the distractions of alcohol and the Church. H. G. Wells was to many the new Bible. But it was only the townspeople, the middle classes and the proletariat, that were affected by this revolution. The countryside and the aristocracy had hardly changed in a hundred years.

CHAPTER FIFTEEN

The Final Year

"THE AGEING KING . . ." ran the first line of an article in *The Times* on his sixty-seventh birthday. Eight years of power, and a whole lifetime devoted to pleasure, had made of Edward VII, as Sir Harold Nicolson put it, "a perplexed and apprehensive man." By 1908, he was a very portly old gentleman, with a high complexion and congested eyes, short of breath and slow of step. His entourage would be highly embarrassed by the terrible gusts of coughing that stifled his outbursts of rage and his peals of laughter when pulling a friend's leg. Sometimes it would take him a quarter of an hour to get his breath back. But he was a charming old man, still capable of enjoying the good things of life that he had not yet given up. He always had a kind and friendly word for everyone whether he was receiving a delegation from New Zealand or a bouquet of flowers at Nice station. He treated his servants with consideration and, if he lost his temper with them, never failed to apologize. To his grandchildren, he was the original Father Christmas and the most touching anecdotes were told about his family life. He was particularly fond of the future Duke of Windsor, whom he used to stuff with sweets and spirit off to see the stables when the boy should have been doing his lessons.

The Prince and Princess of Wales, for all their worthy moral qualities and their impeccable good taste, could never exhibit this warmth. On their succession Max Beerbohm wrote a song in the form of a dialogue between an equerry who says, "The King is duller than the Queen," and the lady-in-waiting who replies, "The Queen is duller than the King." These lines were repeated several times. The serious-minded Princess of Wales was often embarrassed by her father-in-law's frivolity and her mother-in-law's childishness. "Such fun" had never been a part of her vocabulary.

Christmas was always celebrated at Sandringham with an avalanche of presents. Nobody was forgotten, from the Prime Minister to the children of the humblest game-keeper. The house was festooned with decorations, and parcels would be piled deep around an enormous Christmas tree. According to the Duke of Windsor it was like Dickens in a setting by Cartier. Cartloads of presents would arrive from every part of the Empire; and jewels from Russia, flowers from the Riviera, and venison from Germany (or Cousin Augusta's boar's head). The King was seen at his best at Sandringham as nowhere else. He could not bear it if the house was not full of royals (preferably Greek or Portuguese), Ambassadors such as Mensdorff and Metternich, old friends such as Soveral and Chaplin, and delectable females (Mrs. Keppel and Mrs. James now shared his favours). Edward would take each new batch of guests on a detailed tour of the stables and, while his own suite stifled their yawns, he would tell the story of Persimmon's victory for the hundredth time and talk of the enormous sums that this stallion continued to earn him. While he was King, his colours had not had quite the same luck as when he had been Prince of Wales. From 1908 onwards all his hopes were centred on Minoru and the horse proved worthy of his confidence, for he won the Derby in 1910, after a tremendous race. As Edward led him in in triumph, the spectators by the thousands sang "God Save the King."

Alexandra's contribution was to show the ladies the rose garden. She would always stop at exactly the same rose bush and exclaim, "What a delicious smell!" "How delicious!" the ladies would echo as they plunged their noses into the blooms. The evenings were taken up with bridge. The stakes were very high and Edward did not enjoy losing; his daring bids often embarrassed his partners. Mrs. Keppel was the only person who could stand up to him. Once, when her old friend's bid had put her in a par-

The Kaiser.

ticularly difficult spot she exclaimed, "God save the King and preserve Mrs. Keppel from his rage!" When, on another occasion, he got angry with her for confusing two cards, Mrs. Keppel replied with feigned stupidity, "I never could tell a king from a knave."

Without her iron constitution Alice Keppel could never have kept up with the pace set by the King, and without her optimism she could never have endured the petty rivalries of the Court. Sir Ernest Cassel was just as indispensable, and Edward could refuse him nothing. Such was their friendship that he even put a scheme up to the Tsar, despite the latter's anti-Semitism, for a loan to be arranged by Sir Ernest. Yes, everything was arranged to perfection at the English Court; Victoria, with all her tradition, and the Prince Consort, with all his high-mindedness, could never have achieved such disciplined elegance, the fruit of the only art that Edward ever practised, that of pleasing. But in the kingdom all was not so well. The controversy over the House of Lords was becoming inflamed. With Churchill's support Lloyd George was harassing the upper chamber and threatening it with death duties. Nor was the situation in Europe very promising and, in these final eighteen months, the King was to see the whole system of alliances and friendships which he had established with as much care as he would the seating arrangements at a dinner party, thrown into disorder. The trouble was to come from the end of the table, the Balkans. The big powers were peaceable for all their strength, but the whinings of poor relations, as always, got on their nerves.

The year 1908 was overcast from its beginning by the death of the Duke of Devonshire, one of the King's oldest friends, a lavish host and an able counsellor. "My dear Duchess" left the splendours of Chatsworth for those, rather less secure, of the Monte Carlo Casino. A detective would follow her from table to table to return to their owners the chips that the sharp old lady had filched. In May, President Fallières came to London. This state visit, like all the others, was a mixture of boredom and optimism. To mark the occasion a Franco-British Exhibition was put on. Delcassé came a few days later to have talks with the King and Lord Hardinge. They were conducted in the greatest secrecy lest his return to the political scene should cause alarm in Germany. The assassination of Don Carlos of Portugal, which followed shortly afterwards, horrified Edward and the Cabinet had the pettiness to try and prevent him from attending a Requiem Mass.

In August 1908, the King went as usual to Marienbad. There he met the Kaiser, who persuaded him to visit Berlin in style the following year. The Cabinet submitted a memorandum containing the issues that needed to be discussed with William II. But Edward was afraid of losing his temper, which would have been very bad for his heart, and contented himself with exchanging sporting gossip. Lord Hardinge was left to argue things out with the Emperor. Hiding behind a cloud of cigar smoke, Edward listened to the conversation from the other end of the room. The Kaiser was carried away and swore that his fleet was no threat to England. Encouraged by their master's anger, the members of his suite felt at liberty to treat their opposite numbers in Edward's suite with the minimum of courtesy.

The King's meeting with the Emperor of Austria at Ischl a few days later was far more agreeable. The equerries recited the Almanach de Gotha to each other in an effort to sort out all the archdukes, *Durchlauchten*, and princes which the august presence had brought into the little town. The members of the suite were seen frenziedly dashing from hotel to hotel, from the moment that they arrived, to leave their visiting cards. The misfortunes of his life and his old age gave the old Emperor an almost saintlike air that was in no way merited by his disastrous reign and narrowness of mind: but the white side whiskers and the Viennese accent were reassuring after the other Emperor's rodomontades. The sovereigns and their Foreign Ministers went for walks and exchanged news. Turkey was discussed at length. The Balkan countries had been enabled to grab back some of their territory by the foundering of Abdul Hamid's regime. The only thing that appeared to worry Aehrenthal, however, was the Anglo-German naval rivalry. Everything went off marvellously during this visit. There was only one small upsetting incident. The Emperor had asked for the Victorian Order to be given to his *Hoffurier*. The head of the Imperial Commissariat in the Austrian Court always stood behind the Emperor's chair, and Edward had mistaken him for a valet. In consequence he never opened his mouth during the final dinner. It took place in a hunting lodge whose walls were covered with chamois heads and stuffed eagles. The Tyrol was the Habsburgs' Scotland and the archdukes enjoyed going for walks in shorts.

On his return from Marienbad, Edward met the *Times* correspondent, who did his best to dissipate his optimism. "The Austrians are preparing to annex Bosnia-Herzegovina," he told him. "If Serbia is encircled, Russia is bound to be alarmed. It is yet another move in the Isvolski-Aehrenthal feud."

"You must be dreaming," said the King. "The good Emperor was bound to have made some allusion to any such project." Franz Josef may not in fact have been aware of the intended annexation as it could have been planned as a surprise for him on his jubilee, by Aehrenthal and the Archduchess Elizabeth. Such a coup, the Chancellor may have thought, would cement the disparate elements of the Empire. The Archduchess, on the other hand, was probably getting her own back from the Archduke Franz Ferdinand, a notorious Slavophile, for marrying her lady-in-waiting instead of her daughter. If the King had been a little closer to Ferdinand of Bulgaria, he might perhaps have got wind of the plan. Ferdinand, who hated the Austro-Hungarian Empire, had been spying on Aehrenthal. "The House of Austria treats me like a dog and it certainly deserves the services of that filthy Jew Aehrenthal," he once said. Profiting from the confusion created by the annexation, he had himself proclaimed Tsar of his people. But on his return from Vienna, where he had gone to obtain information, he travelled to Sofia in the toilets of the Orient Express so as to avoid recognition.

The French President of the Council, Clemenceau, was also at Marienbad. The King asked the *Times* correspondent to have a serious talk with him and to let him have the minutes of the conversation. Clemenceau complained of the "incredible ignorance" of English statesmen. He stressed the fact that if Germany were to invade through Belgium the English fleet would be no help at all. An army was required and this army did not exist. His prediction was to be borne out to the letter in August 1914, and he foresaw all Sir Edward Grey's vacillations. For all its popularity in France, the French Government had little confidence in the *Entente*. The King could only sigh and return to London.

On October 3 the Austrian Ambassador brought a letter from the Emperor to Buckingham Palace:

> Dear Friend,
>   I have set my heart on warning you myself, personally, of a very important decision, one which you will judge, I feel sure, in the spirit of intimate and traditional friendship that unites us. . . .

Then followed the announcement of the annexation of the two Turkish provinces. The royal fury terrified the Ambassador. The achievements of the Congress of Berlin had gone by the board. At Ischl they must have been laughing up their sleeves. Austria would now have to throw herself into the arms of Germany in order to forestall a Russian counter-move. The King's Ambassador in Vienna echoed his sentiments and told Aehrenthal to his face that he was a liar. The wretched Mensdorff was very upset by what he insisted on calling *ce désolant malentendu qui me place dans une situation épineuse* (this wretched misunderstanding, that puts me in such a difficult position).

Serbia and Montenegro had taken up arms. People feared for the peace. In London, Marquess Imperiali vigorously upheld the Slav cause (the Queen of Italy was a Montenegrin). Russia supported Serbia, and the King decided to receive the sovereign of that country, although he still considered him as an assassin. In fact it only remained for Sarajevo to set the bonfire ablaze. William II thought the moment opportune to tell an American journalist that England was finished, greatly to Chancellor von Bülow's annoyance. The Reichstag protested against this statement, and the Kaiser fell into a nervous depression. When his uncle inquired after his health he replied by sending this telegram in clear:

> I am not suffering from a cold but from a total breakdown.

"We are certainly living in singular times," commented Edward as he passed this dispatch on to the Foreign Office. Whereupon, William II went to Vienna at the most delicate moment in the negotiations that were being carried through to round off the *fait accompli*, and the King noted again:

This visit by the Emperor is, to say the least, regrettable at such a moment. It is in the height of bad taste. We are living, beyond doubt, in a difficult period. Peace can be maintained, but only because Europe is afraid of war.

England calmed Serbia down and the powers bowed before Austria's audacity. Isvolski had gone back and forth between London and St. Petersburg like a shuttlecock to obtain a settlement. It was said that he was being blackmailed by Aehrenthal, who had received a confidential letter from him assuring him that he would in no way oppose the annexation.

Edward's visit to Berlin, which had been agreed upon at Marienbad, took place in February 1909. Queen Alexandra found herself being dragged there against her will, even though Sir Ernest Cassel's influence was also exerted to get her there. He had a great nostalgia for his country of origin, like most Jews before the time of Hitler, and he was involved with his friend Ballin, the Hamburg shipbuilder, in enterprises for which a *détente* in the political climate was vital. The Princess of Pless was convinced, when the visit was announced, that this would be her moment. Her statuesque beauty, she felt, would be the allegorical counterpart of the *rapprochement* between England and Germany. She had a train made for herself, in spun gold from the Indies, that was intended to put the other princesses in the shade, as indeed it should have. The Chancellor, von Bülow, was also pleased that the visit was taking place. The King felt that he at least would keep his head amid the hysteria to be found in William II's entourage. As they waited for the official train, Ambassador Metternich turned to Admiral von Tirpitz and said, "If you do not fall in with Prince von Bülow's plan of effecting a naval agreement, this will undoubtedly be the last time that an English King will ever visit a German Emperor."

One small incident, which occurred as they arrived, rather spoilt the intended effect. The imperial family stood waiting on a red carpet which had been placed where the royal compartment was expected to draw up, but the King stepped down from the Queen's carriage, fifty yards farther on. Their Majesties had to execute a quick sprint down the platform, the numerous members of their families at their heels. The Queen of England, who was old enough to be the Empress's mother, looked to the people of Berlin more like her daughter. Everything went like clockwork during the stay, as though it were all a carefully rehearsed military exercise. The ball at the Old Palace was a breathtaking affair; there was a quadrille in which the young girls carried the regimental colours of their beaux, and in an effort to rival English elegance subalterns were produced whose dress trousers were so tight that their order-lies had to carry them up and down stairs. At the end of the evening a procession of the members of the royal households, preceded by pages brandishing torches, made its way slowly round the state rooms to the sound of a polonaise. Nor were the people forgotten; an enormous crowd, similar to that which had gathered outside the Hôtel de Ville in Paris, congregated outside the Rathaus to applaud the visitors. The Kaiser refused to accompany his uncle to see these "reds," for he hated the socialist Munici-pality. But the Municipal Councillors were charmed by Edward's cordiality and the slight Berlin accent in which he replied to their address. "They seem to be very nice people," he said to von Bülow.

At the opera that evening he was very out of breath, his eyes were red and swollen, and he lost no time in going to sleep. They were giving *Sardanapalus*, and the production, a very spectacular one, had been arranged by the Kaiser himself, down to the finest detail. A cardboard Babylon was consumed in the famous holo-caust of the last act. Wakened by the sudden blaze of light, the King was convinced that the theatre was on fire.

"It's all right, it's only Sardanapalus," said the Queen.

"Sardana . . . what? Keep calm everybody, keep calm!"

Alexandra reassured her husband. "It's just Willy and his biblical follies! It would have been much better if they had done *Coppélia*."

At a luncheon party at the English Embassy, the next day, Edward seemed very tired. As he took Princess von Bülow to the table, he said to her, "The Emperor doesn't make your husband's task very easy. He is most imprudent."

"Ah! Sire," sighed the Princess, "the Emperor is remarkably

young for his fifty years." Over coffee, Edward, whose Prussian uniform was strangling him, signalled to Daisy of Pless to join him on a sofa in the little drawing room. The guests continued to talk at a suitable distance, one eye fixed on the august flirt. Suddenly the King collapsed. The Princess saved him from falling. Lord Hardinge rushed forward and undid his collar. "Is it a heart attack?" they asked anxiously. "He's stopped breathing." "Somebody get a doctor." But they need not have worried. The doctor diagnosed a violent attack of bronchitis. The King recovered himself quickly and took the situation in hand. Daisy's feverish devotion to his welfare was rather overdone. She knew a wonderful doctor who certainly . . . If his Majesty would allow him to examine his throat for a moment . . . "No, really, dear friend, you are too kind." On the eve of his departure, the Princess told Ponsonby that she had some grave revelations to make. She would board the train just before it reached the frontier. She would be waiting at a little station some distance from Berlin. "There's no question of having the train stopped," declared Edward, and he had the blinds of his coach lowered as the train approached the station. But his suite, at his suggestion, was able to enjoy the sight of Daisy of Pless, wearing yards of sable, standing alone on the snow-driven platform.

The effects of his visit were only ephemeral. Not long afterwards Lord Hardinge received the following letter from his master, which adequately sums up his attitude, for Edward VII always had an attitude rather than a policy, and a tone rather than words:

> Really these German intrigues against Russia and ourselves are too annoying. They have to have a finger in every pie and are always putting a spoke in the wheels, and at the same time they complain that nobody loves them. Bismarck's policies are not dead. However, I believe the present Chancellor to be a conciliatory man and most likeable.

No sooner had the King returned than he had, despite his fatigue, to turn his mind to the problems of battleships, taxes, and duties. Lloyd George had to be received in audience, and what passed between them has been admirably reconstructed by André Maurois:

"Where are we to find the money?" the King reflected, and then, drawing on his experience of forty years of British Budgets, asked: "Can't you put it on sugar?" Lloyd George explained that the Liberals, who had been elected as Free Traders, could not tax a staple food. "Yes, yes," said the King sympathetically in his deep voice, "that is so . . . that is so . . ." He thought for a moment and then suggested, "Can't you put it on tea?" Lloyd George replied that tea was the only luxury which the poor could afford. "Then you mustn't . . ." said the King with conviction . . . and there the Crown's opposition ended.

Continual attacks of bronchitis were beginning to depress Edward. He would become morose and lose his temper with his entourage for no reason till his upbraidings were halted by a fit of coughing. He even spoke of abdication: "I would have much preferred to have been a country architect, the monarchy will not last much longer. I believe my son will stay on the throne, as the people are fond of him, but certainly not my grandson." His good humour would be restored by little trips to Paris, on which he was always accompanied by Mrs. Keppel. On one occasion he invited the Breteuils, Madame Standish, and Reggie Lister, the witty attaché at the Embassy, to lunch on the terrace of a restaurant at St. Germain. A rather strange-looking group, seated in the bar, attracted Mrs. Keppel's attention. "I have never seen heads shaped like that before," she said to Ponsonby. "Go and tell Monsieur Lépine." The Prefect of Police explained that they were his agents and their wives. "The gardeners are also our men and they have orders not to let anyone in," he added. On another occasion, Ponsonby heard Edward asking a celebrated beauty on the telephone to meet him in the Jardin des Plantes. Monsieur Lépine was tipped off but was asked if the detectives could remain near the gates. "Impossible, his Majesty will have to be followed in case he is attacked by a gangster." It did not take the King long to recognize the detective, and the idyll lost its charm beneath the policeman's eyes. He returned to his hotel in a furious temper and from that day spent his time thinking up ways of tricking his entourage in order to recover the incognito of his youth. Was it then that he met Mistinguett as she was later to boast in her memoirs? With her large eyes, her immense mouth, and her beautiful legs, she was the youngest of the stars at the Alhambra. The King took her to dine at Maxim's, and explained to her the charms of Paris. The friendship was continued in the flat of a complaisant friend, but on one occasion Edward VII left his stick in the bedroom, where it was found by the lady's husband. It was a scene straight out of a Feydeau farce.

This passion for incognito did have its drawbacks. Visiting the Empress Eugénie at the Grand Hotel, the King asked at the desk if the Countess of Pierrefonds could receive the Duke of Lancaster. "Wait a moment, I am sorting the mail," replied the porter. After several minutes the King could contain himself no longer and shouted: "*Sa Majesté l'Impératrice Eugénie peut-elle recevoir le Roi d'Angleterre?*" The Empress was still passionately interested in politics and, with Paléologue acting as her intermediary, she kept the Quai d'Orsay informed as to the opinions of the English Court.

Madame de Pourtalès would entertain the King to lunch; she was now a dictatorial old lady who was still faithful to the Princess of Wales's fashions and hair style. He would also visit the Salon with Détaille, with whom he shared a passion for uniforms. On the final evening of one visit Edward, Mrs. Keppel, the Ambassador and Lady Bertie dined at Voisin and then went to see Granier in *La Bonne Intention*. As he entered his box, the King saw to his annoyance that the bearded Leopold II was sitting in the stalls. The two kings loathed each other; they remained in their seats during the intervals, each afraid of meeting his colleague in the corridors. This was a gift to the press and an article, in very bad taste, entitled "Edward and Leopold Get Married," was published. The direct exploitation of the Congo by the King of the Belgians had shocked Edward VII. After all, there were people to take care of that sort of thing. One could even have them as friends, like Sir Ernest. But it was unthinkable for the King of England to be ever directly involved in business. On another visit the King and Queen went to see Bernstein's *Le Voleur*. They had a stage box but the Queen, who was hard of hearing, kept asking a flood of questions in a loud voice: "What did she say? Who do you think the thief was? The young man looks very innocent, what has he been doing?" The actors (Lucien Guitry and Madame Simone) were considerably annoyed. The King answered her questions patiently and the public, who could not see the spectators in the stage box, started to protest.

In June 1909, the Tsar and his family came to England on board their yacht, raising official protests from three peers, two bishops, and sixty-six members of Parliament, to whom the memory of the 1905 massacres were still fresh. For the Russians it was a real holiday. The King's grandsons were deputed to take the Grand Duchesses yachting in the Solent. England was garnering the fruits of Victoria's matriarchal policy. Her grandchildren and great-grandchildren, Russian or Rumanian, German or Spanish, all adored the comfortable simplicity of Balmoral. They renewed acquaintance with the nannies who had brought up their mothers and the grooms who had taught their fathers to ride; they were able to explore again the Swiss châlet with its lofts and its shell collection, in which Prince Albert had given natural-history lessons. There were regattas and races with friends outside the Court. They all returned home thoroughly Anglophile and spoke to each other in English all the time. As Queen Victoria's grandchildren grew up, so English replaced French in the Courts of Europe.

The Lords had again rejected Lloyd George's Budget and Asquith asked the King to dissolve Parliament. The elections of January 14, 1910, made it clear that there could be no hope of a Conservative Government. In the eyes of the public Edward had committed himself too deeply in supporting the Lords and his meetings with the party leaders were regarded as hardly constitutional. As a solution, the King proposed to Lord Crewe that the Upper House should become more representative and that each party should provide a certain number of active peers while the others should be given a purely honorific rôle. But the Cabinet would not accept this proposal, and it is only with the appointment of Life Peers that the Upper House has finally again acquired some importance.

These difficulties had no effect upon the royal routine. After spending Christmas at Sandringham the King and Queen went to stay with Lord Iveagh (the owner of the Guinness breweries), and all the old faces can be seen in the inevitable photographs: Soveral, now wrinkled and bald, his face hidden behind his thick black moustache; the enormous Harry Chaplin; and the witty but now wizened Mrs. George Greville; the ladies with their enormous hats and enormous muffs. The Queen alone was still faithful to her toque and pekinese. "Such fun!" cried Mrs. Hwfa Williams, meeting once again the people she had been seeing all year. "What fun!" echoed the King without much conviction. "We shall be shooting duck tomorrow. Will you keep me company in the hide?" The fog, the cigar smoke, and a joke set off a coughing fit which terrified Mrs. Williams. Should she slap the royal back, or call the other guns at the risk of frightening the ducks? Fortunately the coughing stopped and the King recovered his spirits after a certain amount of panting. The end of January found the Court with the Sassoons near Brighton, where they passed the time by playing bridge since they were kept inside by the continual rain and, whenever the clouds lightened, by the curiosity of the populace.

April was the month for Biarritz. On his way there Edward stopped off in Paris to see *Chantecler*. The director of the Porte-Saint-Martin theatre, who was extremely parsimonious, did not believe in heating the auditorium for fear of suffocating the actors, who were covered in feathers. When Guitry heard that the King had booked seats, he begged the director to make it reasonably warm: so well did he comply with this request that the place was like a furnace. The King was very flushed as he left and he was kept waiting for his car at the door. He caught cold and was once again laid low with bronchitis. He was advised to return to London, but he was not having it, Biarritz would do him good. "It was that awful Biarritz that finished him off," Alexandra, who never went there, was to say. At Biarritz, the King went out very little. He went for walks along the corridors of the Hôtel du Palais, as a furious sea battered itself against the rocks. Every day brought its disturbing news: conflicting advice came from India, where Curzon and Kitchener were still carrying on their feud; Winston Churchill had made a speech criticizing the Crown; Asquith was doubtful about his position. The King's entourage knew very little about such matters and were unable to be of much assistance to him, so he had to spend the mornings reading the newspapers. On April 15 he returned to London, looking better but much slower in all his movements. On the twenty-second, Lord Ribblesdale, whose box was next to the King's at Covent Garden, saw him enter it alone, with a stricken air. During the interval he rose with an effort, as though to go, as was his custom, into the foyer, but then gave it up with a sigh, cast a last glance into the auditorium, and sent for his car. When, two days later, Lady Warwick met him at a soirée, he spoke only of the past. Instead of the hundred questions which he usually asked everyone about plans, it was just "Do you remember": "Paris . . . I've no wish to go back there again. All its brilliance has gone. Ah! Times have changed since we went in secret to the Exhibition in '89."

On April 30, the King went to spend three days at Sandringham to have a look at some work that was in progress, taking Sir Dighton Probyn, an old courtier, and Ponsonby with him. Despite the sharp weather he spent some time outside, giving instructions about the positioning of a new shrubbery. On the Sunday, he did not walk to church in his usual way, but went in his barouche. Everyone noticed how gentle he was. He did not curse the servants or upbraid his own suite. Meanwhile a Government crisis, which could have led to the replacement of Asquith by Lloyd George, who would certainly have demanded whole battalions of peers, was looming. Lord Esher advised firmness. On May 3, Edward dined with Mrs. Keppel, but being too tired to play bridge, he returned early to Buckingham Palace. The doctors, who were called during the morning of the next day, advised great prudence, as he had severe bronchitis. The Prince of Wales telegraphed his mother, who was cruising in the Mediterranean, asking her to return immediately. Meanwhile, the King worked as usual with his secretaries. After dinner, Mrs. Keppel and Mrs. James came to play cards in the Chinese drawing-room, which was furnished with the pieces that the Prince Regent had ordered for the pavilion at Brighton. Although the two ladies begged him not to, the King insisted on smoking an enormous cigar. The palace was already pervaded by the silence of the sickroom. The servants walked down the passages with silent tread, and the secretaries lowered their discreet voices still further. In a drawing-room nurses stood by with oxygen cylinders. But no rumour of the illness had yet reached the public. On the fifth the King asked Ponsonby to read some papers to him. His face was ashen and his legs wrapped in a rug: "I can't work for very long, I feel very ill. I cannot sleep. I cannot eat. Really something must be done." As Ponsonby went out of the door, his master said to him, "In case I don't see you again, good-bye." In a neighbouring drawing-room, the Queen, who had just returned from Venice, sat surrounded by the family. On the sixth the King managed to receive Sir Ernest Cassel. Alexandra asked him not to stay more than a few minutes. Edward insisted on getting up and dressing for his old friend, and talked to him about his mare, Witch of the Air, which was running that afternoon at Kempton Park. At four o'clock in the afternoon a telegram arrived at the palace from the racecourse to say that the horse had won. It was the King's final joy.

There was now a crowd standing in front of Buckingham Palace waiting for the medical bulletin to be posted. A deep sadness spread throughout London. In the clubs, the members exchanged items of information: "Ponsonby's told me . . . Sir Francis Laking thinks it's hopeless. . . . Charlotte Knollys has telephoned Esher. . . . The Queen is wonderful. . . . This business of the Lords is dragging on. . . ." In their grand houses, the King's close friends telephoned each other with the final pieces of news: "Alice Keppel won't speak to anyone. She is going to stay with the Jameses. . . . Sir Ernest says that he is dying. . . . The Stock Market's going down. . . . Leo Rothschild has told me not to worry. . . . And to think how little the Prince and Princess of Wales know about life. . . . Something really must be done for them. Margot herself is overwhelmed. . . . Whatever will happen to Olga de Meyer?"

The Ambassadors kept themselves in readiness to present their condolences and to send on the medical bulletins to their Courts. Old friends such as Soveral and Mensdorff saw their careers finished. In the worlds of the theatre and the turf, the anxiety was equally great. To everyone it seemed that the period of peace and prosperity was at an end. All the most prominent men in the Kingdom would, at the King's passing, suddenly become dated. Beauties and bankers, courtiers and jockeys would now be labelled Edwardian. The entire Empire was in suspense, held there by an old gentleman who was gasping for breath in a room in Buckingham Palace. "I shall not give in, I shall go on working, bring me the dispatch boxes," were the King's final words before sinking into a coma. Alexandra and the doctors remained alone with him. In an adjacent room, the Prince and Princess of Wales, Princess Victoria, Princess Henry of Battenberg, the Duchess of Fife, and the Prince and Princess Christian were waiting.

The Queen summoned the Prince of Wales. They could just hear the vague murmur of the crowd which at that time filled the entire Mall. Big Ben was striking a quarter to eleven as Alexandra reappeared in tears on the arm of her son. Those who saw them understood, and they bent their knees and kissed the hand of the new King. An equerry crossed the Porcelain Gallery and reached the secretaries' office. One of these descended the staircase, at the foot of which a few flunkeys were waiting. The door was opened. The secretary crossed the courtyard of the palace to the railings behind which the crowd was pressing. "The King is dead . . ." Within three minutes the news had reached Trafalgar Square. Reporters ran towards Fleet Street, and the wires carried the news to every part of the world. Dumb, as though turned to stone, the crowd remained for a long time in front of the palace. The car containing the new King and Queen drove through on its way back to Marlborough House. Other royal cars took the members of the family and the doctors home. A brougham was sent to fetch Mrs. Keppel, and Alexandra herself waited to take her up to the bed in which the King was lying. She left her for a long time alone in the room. Tact, in this case, had almost become saintliness. Mr. Keppel's behaviour was equally admirable. When his daughter expressed astonishment at the fact that they were closing their house and wearing black because "Kingie" would not be coming any more he said to her, "He was a great King

and a wonderful man." That evening Churchill dined with the
Asquiths and proposed a toast to the new King. "Rather to the
memory of the old," replied Lord Crewe.

Once they had recovered from the general emotion the Cabinet
Ministers congratulated each other on the fact that the dictatorship of tact was now over. To the Kaiser, the change meant the
dawn of universal peace. The odious encirclement of Germany
would now cease, and gentle Cousin George would listen to
William's counsels. In France the mourning was almost on a
national scale. There also the feeling was that it was the end of
an epoch.

The funeral was the supreme moment of the Edwardian cavalcade. Since the King had had a horror of black, the streets and
the monuments were draped in purple. All the same, within a few
hours of his death, it was impossible to find a foot of crape in the
smallest little shop in the kingdom, and cargo ships had to be sent
to Germany to collect more. Crowned heads with their suites and
families arrived by every train. Aides-de-camp were waiting for
them at Dover and Victoria, organized with the same precision as
at the time of the Coronation. Never had one sovereign, not even
a Habsburg, had so many nephews and nieces seated on thrones.
The Queen and her daughters, slenderer than ever in their black
dresses, received Willy and Dona, Ena and Alfonso, with little
sad and tender cries, and darted in tears from one apartment to
another.

On May 17 the body was taken from Buckingham Palace to lie
for three days on a raised catafalque in Westminster Hall, guarded
by officers and heralds-at-arms. The queue stretched unbroken for
six miles at one time. Every class was represented among the
250,000 who filed past. The King's lady friends performed their
final curtsies before the pyramid of flowers. Many Catholics were
seen to cross themselves. They had enjoyed Edward VII's favour;
indeed, some conversations that he had had with Cardinal Vaughan
had given rise to a rumour that he had been converted. The young
Kings of Portugal and Spain, who had regarded him as their
model, knelt for a long time. The Kaiser came, preceded by an
enormous wreath; his prolonged handshake with George V, who

had accompanied him, seemed to say "You can count on me, I will help you." On the twentieth the procession left Westminster for Paddington Station. The King's saddle-horse was led behind the gun carriage, and his dog, Caesar, was held on a lead by a valet. Then came the Kings, the Ambassadors, the Maharajas, and the Marshals. A few hours later, in the presence of the family and the crowned heads, the coffin was lowered into the crypt in St. George's Chapel at Windsor.

The King's death introduced a short truce into the dispute between the House of Lords and the Commons. George V had to give way over this matter, although his father had held out to the end. He agreed in principle to the creation of numerous new peers, a threat that was sufficient to break the resistance of the Lords. It was a step that illustrated both the progress of democracy and the enfeeblement of the aristocracy, whose more intelligent members chose from now on to devote themselves to the City rather than to politics. Here again, Edward VII's reign marked the consecration of the power of money and the arrival of a hierarchy graded according to income and no longer according to family, its wealth drawn from a colonialist imperialism.

The grief of the people, who had known under Edward's reign such an increase in their standard of living, was very deep. The cockneys used to sing a ballad whose chorus went:

> There'll be no wo'ar
> As long as there's a King like good King Edward,
> There'll be no wo'ar
> For 'e 'ates that sort of thing,
> Mothers need not worry,
> As long as we've a King like good King Edward.
> Peace with 'onour
> Is his motter,
> So God save the King.

But the tribute which Edward VII would have appreciated most occurred during that week in July 1910 which has since been known as Black Ascot. All the ladies admitted to the Royal Enclosure wore black feathers and ribbons in place of the usual flowers and gauzes. Their tall and slender figures, surmounted by enormous hats, were like weird blooms springing from the bright green lawns. It was on this racecourse that the peace-loving King had won some of his greatest victories with Persimmon and Minoru, and that he had passed the happiest hours of his life in "the glorious incertitude of the turf." The grandees of the Edwardian era were clinging to the panache that their influence no longer justified. They exchanged the latest items of news: "The Queen has given Daisy of Pless the onyx-handled bell that was on his desk. . . . Alice Keppel has gone to China. . . . Have the Sassoons, the Beits, and the Speyers been invited to Court? . . . I believe that Sir Ernest himself . . . Queen Alexandra refuses to leave the Palace— well, anyway the King has left her Sandringham. Soveral has gone back to Portugal. . . . Lily Langtry has been ruined by racing debts. . . . And they have been the death of the Duchess of Devonshire. . . . Apparently Gladys de Grey is bringing over a wonderful Russian ballet to Covent Garden. . . . Such fun!" cried Mrs. Hwfa Williams.

Genealogical Tables
Bibliography
Index

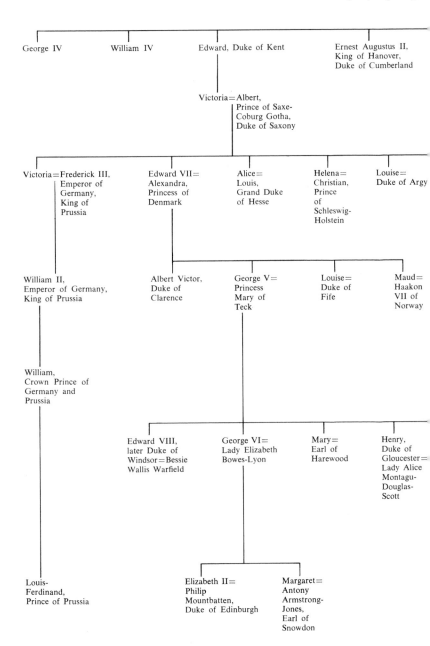

George III, King of England

George IV   William IV   Edward, Duke of Kent   Ernest Augustus II, King of Hanover, Duke of Cumberland

Victoria＝Albert, Prince of Saxe-Coburg Gotha, Duke of Saxony

Victoria＝Frederick III, Emperor of Germany, King of Prussia   Edward VII＝Alexandra, Princess of Denmark   Alice＝Louis, Grand Duke of Hesse   Helena＝Christian, Prince of Schleswig-Holstein   Louise＝Duke of Argy

William II, Emperor of Germany, King of Prussia   Albert Victor, Duke of Clarence   George V＝Princess Mary of Teck   Louise＝Duke of Fife   Maud＝Haakon VII of Norway

William, Crown Prince of Germany and Prussia

Edward VIII, later Duke of Windsor＝Bessie Wallis Warfield   George VI＝Lady Elizabeth Bowes-Lyon   Mary＝Earl of Harewood   Henry, Duke of Gloucester＝Lady Alice Montagu-Douglas-Scott

Louis-Ferdinand, Prince of Prussia   Elizabeth II＝Philip Mountbatten, Duke of Edinburgh   Margaret＝Antony Armstrong-Jones, Earl of Snowdon

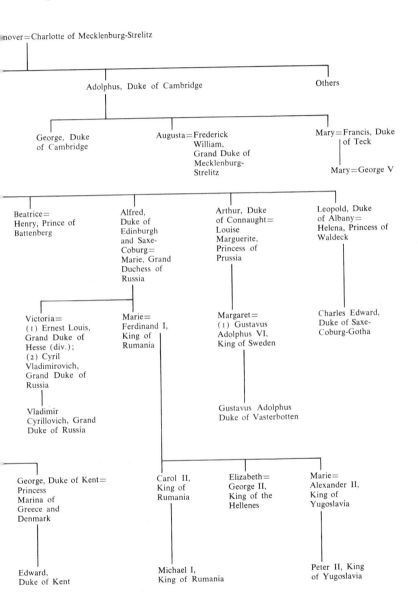

…nover=Charlotte of Mecklenburg-Strelitz

Adolphus, Duke of Cambridge   Others

George, Duke of Cambridge

Augusta=Frederick William, Grand Duke of Mecklenburg-Strelitz

Mary=Francis, Duke of Teck

Mary=George V

Beatrice=Henry, Prince of Battenberg

Alfred, Duke of Edinburgh and Saxe-Coburg=Marie, Grand Duchess of Russia

Arthur, Duke of Connaught=Louise Marguerite, Princess of Prussia

Leopold, Duke of Albany=Helena, Princess of Waldeck

Victoria=(1) Ernest Louis, Grand Duke of Hesse (div.); (2) Cyril Vladimirovich, Grand Duke of Russia

Marie=Ferdinand I, King of Rumania

Margaret=(1) Gustavus Adolphus VI, King of Sweden

Charles Edward, Duke of Saxe-Coburg-Gotha

Vladimir Cyrillovich, Grand Duke of Russia

Gustavus Adolphus Duke of Vasterbotten

George, Duke of Kent=Princess Marina of Greece and Denmark

Carol II, King of Rumania

Elizabeth=George II, King of the Hellenes

Marie=Alexander II, King of Yugoslavia

Edward, Duke of Kent

Michael I, King of Rumania

Peter II, King of Yugoslavia

The Battenbergs

Louis II, Grand Duke of Hesse-Darmstadt=Wilhelmine of Baden

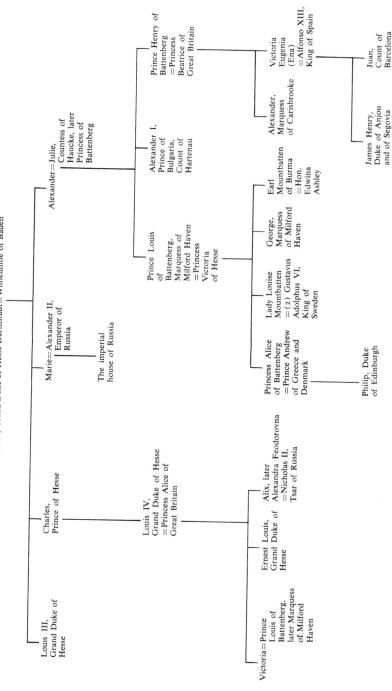

The Royal Families of Greece and Denmark

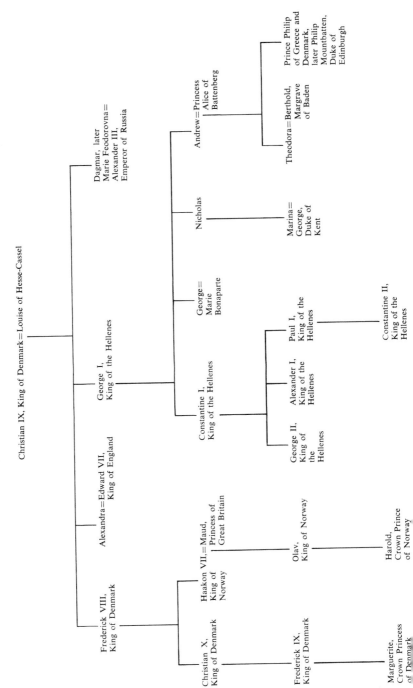

Bibliography

General Works

Beaton, Cecil. *The Glass of Fashion*, New York, 1954.
Bernardy, Françoise de. *Le Mari de la Reine; Albert et Victoria*, 2nd edition, Paris, 1963.
Bolitho, Hector. *A Century of British Monarchy*, New York and London, 1951.
Bott, Allan. *Our Fathers*, London, 1931.
Cecil, Algernon. *British Foreign Secretaries*, London, 1957.
Chastenet, Jacques. *Histoire de la Troisième République*, Paris, 1952–60.
———. *La France de M. Fallières, une Époque Pathétique*, Paris, 1949.
Corti, Egon Caesar. *Reign of the House of Rothschild*, New York, 1928.
Ensor, R. C. K. *England, 1870–1914.* New York and London, 1936.

Memoirs

Asquith, Margot. *Autobiography*, New York, 1922.
Benson, E. F. *As We Were*, New York and London, 1930.
Blanche, Jacques-Emile. *Portraits of a Lifetime*, New York, 1939.
Blunt, W. S. *My Diaries*, New York, 1932.

Cardigan, Lady. *My Recollections*, London, 1906.

Clermont-Tonnerre, Elisabeth (de Gramont). *Pomp and Circumstance*, London, 1929.

Cornwallis-West, G. F. M. *Edwardian Hey-days*, New York and London, 1931.

Depew, Chauncey. *My Memories of Eighty Years*, New York and London, 1922.

Eckerstein. *Ten Years at the Court of Saint James,* London, 1923.

Esher, Lord. *Journals and Letters of Reginald, Viscount Esher* (Maurice V. Brett, ed.), London, 1934–38.

————. *Cloud-Capped Towers*, London, 1927.

Grey of Fallodon, Lord. *Twenty-five Years, 1892–1916,* New York, 1925.

Kennedy, A. A., ed. *My Dear Duchess*, New York and London, 1956.

Keppel, Sonia. *Edwardian Daughter*, London, 1958.

Leslie, Shane. *End of a Chapter*, London, 1929.

Lytton, Lady. *Lady Lytton's Court Diary*, London, 1961.

Marie, Queen of Rumania. *Story of My Life*, New York and London, 1934.

Pless, Daisy von. *Reminiscences*, London, 1930.

Ponsonby, Sir Frederick, ed. *Letters* (of Empress Frederick), New York and London, 1928.

————. *Recollections of Three Reigns*, London, 1951.

Pringuet, G.-L. *Trente Ans de Dîners en Ville.*

Radziwill, Princess Catherine. *Memories of Forty Years,* London, 1914.

Redesdale, Lord. *Memories*, London, 1915.

Sitwell, Sir Osbert. *Left Hand, Right Hand!*, Boston, 1944.

Stoeckl, Baroness von. *Not All Vanity*, London, 1950.

Williams, Mrs. Hwfa. *It Was Such Fun,* London, 1935.

General Bibliography

Adams, William Scovell. *Edwardian Portraits,* London, 1957.

Barkeley, Richard. *The Empress Frederick*, New York and London, 1956.

Chastenet, Jacques. *Winston Churchill et l'Angleterre de XXe Siècle,* Paris, 1956.

Cohen, Lucy. *Lady de Rothschild and Her Daughters,* 1821–1931, London, 1935.

Connell, Brian. *Manifest Destiny,* London, 1953.

Corti, Egon Caesar. *Alexander von Battenberg,* New York and London, 1955.

Churchill, Randolph. *Lord Derby, King of Lancashire,* London, 1960.

Fulford, Roger. *The Prince Consort,* New York and London, 1949.

Gernsheim, Helmut. *Queen Victoria,* New York and London, 1959.

Hewett, O. W. *Strawberry Fair: A Biography of Frances, Countess Waldegrave, 1821–79,* Hollywood-by-the-Sea, Florida, 1956.

James, Robert Rhodes. *Lord Randolph Churchill,* London, 1959.

Londonderry, Lady. *Henry Chaplin,* New York and London, 1926.

Melba, Dame Nellie. *Melodies and Memories,* New York, 1926.

Mount, Charles Merrill. *John Singer Sargent: A Biography,* New York, 1955.

Nicolson, Sir Harold George. *Sir Arthur Nicolson, Bart., First Lord Carnock,* London, 1930.

———. *King George the Fifth: His Life and Reign,* London, 1952.

Pearl, Cyril. *The Girl with the Swansdown Seat,* Indianapolis, 1956.

Pope-Hennessy, James. *Queen Mary,* New York and London, 1960.

———. *Lord Crewe, 1858–1945: The Likeness of a Liberal,* New York and London, 1955.

Ritz, Marie Louise. *César Ritz, Host to the World,* Philadelphia and New York, 1938.

Sackville-West, V. *Pepita,* New York and London, 1937.

———. *The Edwardians,* New York, 1930 (reissued 1961).

Strachey, Lytton. *Eminent Victorians,* New York, 1918.

———. *Queen Victoria,* New York, 1931.

Sykes, Christopher. *Four Studies in Loyalty,* London, 1946.

A Bibliography of Edward

Arthur, Sir George C. A. *Concerning Queen Victoria and Her Son,* New York, 1943.

Cowles, Virginia. *Gay Monarch: The Life and Pleasures of Edward VII*, New York, 1956.

Cust, Sir Lionel Henry. *King Edward VII and His Court*, New York, 1930.

Lee, Sir Sidney. *King Edward VII*, New York and London, 1925.

Maurois, André. *Edouard VII et Son Temps,* Paris, 1933.

The Private Life of King Edward VII (Prince of Wales, 1841–1901). By a member of the Royal Household, New York, 1901.

Index

Abergeldie Castle, 53
Aehrenthal, Count von, 279–80, 282
Aigle, Marquise de l', 101
Albany, Duke of (Prince Leopold),
 122, 125, 167, 171
Albemarle, Lord, 147
Albert, Prince Consort of England,
 3, 5, 6–7, 9–11, 15, 17–18, 20–21,
 28
Albert, yacht, 176
Albert Victor, Prince, *see* Clarence,
 Duke of
Alexander, King of Serbia, 195
Alexander II, Tsar of Russia, 44, 69,
 91, 159
Alexander III, Tsar of Russia, 91,
 131, 156, 159–60, 168
Alexandra, Queen of England, 28,
 32–33, 35–37, 46–48, 51–55, 66,
 69–71, 191, 193, 205–206, 212,
 233, 249, 259, 262, 276, 281, 283,
 288
Alfonso XIII, King of Spain, 194,
 215, 233, 252, 292
Alfred, Prince, *see* Edinburgh, Duke
 of
Alice, Princess, *see* Hesse, Princess
 Louis of
Allemans, Marquis du Lau d', 102
Allington, Lord, 207
Almanach de Gotha, 7, 257, 279
Anglican Church, 75, 117, 139, 222–
 23, 269, 274, 289

Anglo-American relations, 20, 148,
 196, 252
Anglo-Austrian relations, 131, 156,
 161
Anglo-French relations, 135, 137,
 172, 239
Anglo-German relations, 91, 131,
 135, 143, 157, 279
Anglo-Russian relations, 88, 131,
 135, 143, 156, 161, 168, 261
Aosta, Duke of, 163
Arcangues, Marquis d', 233
Arenberg, Princesse d', 101, 247
Argyll, Duchess of (Princess Louise,
 sister of Edward VII), 6, 45, 61,
 154, 165, 199
Argyll, Duke of, 154, 175, 203
Arthur, Prince, *see* Connaught, Duke
 of
Ascot, 43
Asquith, Herbert Henry, 119, 145,
 253, 287–89, 292
Asquith, Margot, 45, 118, 146, 212,
 230, 265, 267, 271
Augusta, Empress of Germany, 87,
 99
Auvergne, Prince de la Tour d', 35
Aylesford, Earl and Countess of,
 55–56, 129

Baden-Powell, Sir Robert, 217
Bahadur, Sir Jund, 73
Baker, Valentine, 128

Balfour, Arthur James, 118, 145, 240, 243, 250, 253, 260, 265-66, 270-71

Balkan states, 195

Balmoral Castle, 6, 12-14, 61, 64, 71, 164, 167-68, 202, 287

Bancroft, Sir Squire, 124

Battenberg, House of, 7, 78, 159, 161

Battenberg, Prince Henry of, 132, 160, 165-67

Battenberg, Prince Louis of, 257

Battenberg, Princess Henry of (Princess Beatrice), 132, 154, 160, 165-67, 191, 199

Battenberg, Princess Louis of (Victoria of Hesse), 160

Beaconsfield, Lord, see Disraeli, Benjamin

Beardsley, Aubrey, 145

Beatrice, Princess, see Battenberg, Princess Henry of

Beaufort, Duchess of, 128

Beauharnais, House of, 78

Bedford, Duke of, 144

Beerbohm, Max, 145, 166, 229

Bennett, Gordon, 59

Benson, Archbishop, 128

Benson, E. F., 227

Beresford, Lord Charles, 55, 146, 266

Berlin, Congress of, 35, 49, 90, 281

Bernhardt, Sarah, 50, 103

Biarritz, 233-34, 258, 271, 288

Bisaccia, Duc de, 98

Bischoffsheim family, 51

Bismarck, Prince von, 83, 85, 90, 131, 154, 156-57, 159, 161-62

Blenheim Palace, 170

Blanche, Jacques-Emile, 57, 226

Black Ascot, 293

Blowitz, Monsieur de, 84

Blunt, Wilfred Scawen, 122

Boer War, 111, 145, 172, 186, 217, 239, 267, 272

Boulanger, Gustave, 109-110

Bourbon, House of, 7, 77, 80

Bourget, Paul, 141

Boxer uprising, 240

Braganza, House of, 7, 77

Brisson, Eugene Henri, President of France, 245

Britannia, yacht, 59, 170

Broglie, Duc de, 105

Brown, John, 62-64, 105, 129, 166, 199

Bruce, Robert, 16-18, 20, 29

Buccleuch, Duchess of, 46

Buckingham Palace, 6, 38, 82, 143, 153, 187, 226, 266

Brugh, Irene van, 218

Bülow, Prince von, 83, 158-59, 171, 173-74, 241, 252, 255, 257-58, 260, 281-83

Bute, Marquess of, 36, 220

Cadogan, Earl, 132

Caesar (Edward VII's dog), 225, 293

Cambon, Paul, 188, 240, 249, 252

Cambridge, Duchess of, 33

Cambridge, Duke of, 7, 33, 126, 153

Campbell-Bannerman, Sir Henry, 270-71

Cannes, 99, 233

Canterbury, Archbishop of, 33, 63, 139, 192

Caracciolo, Duchess of, 57

Cardigan, Earl of, 42

Carlos, Don, King of Portugal, 109, 152, 216, 279, 292

Carnot, Sadi, 110

Cassel, Sir Ernest, 142-43, 211-12, 232, 278, 282, 290

Castellane, Count Boni de, 221, 244

Castlereagh, Lord, 144

Cavalieri, Lina, 218

Cavendish, Lady Frederick, 55

Chamberlain, Joseph, 61, 126, 143, 171, 185, 222, 241, 255, 265

Chambord, Comte de, 98

Chaplin, Harry, 20, 26-27, 39, 231, 237, 276, 288

Charlotte, Queen of Belgium, 5, 81

Charles I, King of England, 60-61

Chatsworth Castle, 9

Chinese labor question, 267-68

Chouard, Marquis de, 96

Christian IX, King of Denmark, 262, 291

Churchill, Lady Randolph, 225

Churchill, Lord Randolph, 52, 56, 110, 119, 129-32, 134, 136, 147, 180, 225, 271

Churchill, Sir Winston, 149, 268, 271, 278, 288, 292

Clarence, Duke of (Prince Albert Victor, "Eddy"), 66, 143–44, 153, 163–64
Clarendon, Lord, 25
Clemenceau, Georges, 106, 231, 260, 280
Clermont-Tonnerre, Duchess of, 226
Cleveland, President Grover, 148
Coburg, House of, 4, 7, 9, 29, 80, 171
Compiègne, 41–42
Connaught, Duke of (Prince Arthur), 6, 34, 61, 83, 104, 153, 174, 191
Connaught, Princess Patricia of, 215
Corelli, Marie, 117
Cornwall, Duchy of, 36, 50
Cornwallis-West, Daisy, *see* Pless
Cornwallis-West, Mrs., 48
Covent Garden, 121, 124, 230, 289
Crawford, Virginia, 127
Crewe, Marquess of, 202, 271, 292
Crimean War, 10, 12, 69, 88–89, 126
Cromer, Earl of, 142
Curzon, Marquess, 221, 266–67, 288
Cust, Sir Lionel, 186, 215

d'Ache, Caran, 104
Dagmar, Princess, *see* Marie, Empress of Russia
Danilo I, Prince of Montenegro, 232
Delcassé, Théophile, 106, 240, 247, 249, 251, 255
Denmark, Princess Waldemar of, 81, 197, 262
Depew, Chauncey, 148
Derby, Earl of, 31, 36, 89, 133, 149, 220, 235
Deslys, Gaby, 238
Devonshire, Duchess of, *see* Manchester, Duchess of
Devonshire, Duke of (Marquess of Hartington), 25–26, 45, 125, 126, 129, 149, 185, 232, 235, 265, 278
Dickens, Charles, 27
Dieppe, 105–106
Dilke, Sir Charles, 57, 61, 107, 126–27, 129, 132, 180
Disraeli, Benjamin, 32, 35, 41, 49, 65, 69, 71–72, 84, 88, 90–91, 114, 124–25, 153, 253, 265, 270
Dogger Bank incident, 264
Donnay, Maurice, 104
Draga, Queen of Serbia, 195

Dresden, Court of, 143
Duff, Lady Juliet, 206
Dufferin and Ava, Marquess of, 111

Eckardtstein, Baron von, 170, 241
Edinburgh, Duchess of, 38, 41, 71, 88, 151
Edinburgh, Duke of (Prince Alfred), 38, 41, 88, 94, 153, 171
Edinburgh, Princess Melita of, 82
Edward VII, King of England: birth of, 3; and parents, 9–10, 21, 23, 149, 153, 165, 175; childhood of, 11–12; travels of, 15–19, 72–73; military career of, 16; education of, 18–20, 145; and social clubs, 19, 38–39, 125, 144, 238, 247; marriage of, 32–33, 35; income of, 36–37; pets of, 38, 225, 293; as Prince of Wales, 57, 91–92, 132–33, 157, 159, 169–70, 178–179, 184–85; children of, 66, 69–70; and Freemasonry, 74–75; and William II, 86–87, 104–105, 256, 282; as Francophile, 93, 98–100; Cabinet of, 105, 127, 185, 243, 249, 279, 292; intellect of, 118–120; on imperialism, 135, 140; and horseracing, 147, 247, 276–77; assassination attempt on, 150; coronation of, 188–93, 217; amours of, 231, 262, 276, 278, 285–86; visit to Vatican, 243; and politics, 265, 267, 269; death of, 291
Edward VIII, King of England (later Duke of Windsor), 275–76
Edward, Prince of Saxe-Weimar, 82
Egypt, 108, 125, 250
Elizabeth, Queen of Rumania (Carmen Sylva), 28
Entente Cordiale, 194, 231, 238, 240, 248, 266, 281
Esher, Viscount, 39, 147, 149, 188, 192, 212, 249, 266, 289–90
Estournelles de Constant, Baron d', 244
Eton, 213, 215
Eugénie, Empress of France, 31, 65, 81, 99, 103, 197, 286
Eulenburg, Prince von, 257, 260

Fabian Society, 268

Fallières, Clément Armand, President of France, 259, 278
Fashoda incident, 112, 239
Ferdinand, King of Bulgaria, 7, 165, 195, 232, 280
Féval, Paul, 27, 144
Fife, Duchess of (Princess Louise, daughter of Edward VII), 66, 165, 291
Fisher, Admiral Sir John, 53, 202, 266
Fortescue, Chichester, 74
Franco-British Exhibition, 278
Franz Ferdinand, Archduke of Austria, 280
Franz Josef, Emperor of Austria, 161–62, 194, 231–32, 279
Frederick III, Emperor of Germany, 15–16, 153, 156
Frederick, Empress, of Germany (Victoria, Princess Royal of England), 5, 15–16, 28, 80, 85, 111, 156, 171, 174

Galliffet, Marquis de, 97, 99, 106, 108–109
Galsworthy, John, 229
Gambetta, Léon, 107–108, 126
Ganay, Marquise de, 101, 231
Garden, Mary, 216
Garibaldi, Giuseppe, 46
Garner, Florence, 139
Garter, Order of the, 190, 192, 249
George II, King of Greece, 133, 195, 209, 232
George III, King of England, 5, 60
George IV, King of England, 42
George V, King of England (Duke of York, Prince of Wales), 66, 67, 82, 83, 151, 153, 164, 255, 275, 289, 291–92
Gladstone, William Ewart, 37, 64, 74, 89, 97, 114, 124–25, 127, 129–30, 153, 168, 218, 253, 257, 265
Gleichen, Count, 257
Glücksburg, House of, 78
Goelet, Mary, 221
Golden Fleece, Order of the, 81, 232
Gorchakov, Prince Alexander, 35, 89–90
Gordon, General Charles, 112, 125–126

Gordon-Cumming, Sir William, 136, 138–39
Granier, Jeanne, 246
Granville, Earl, 23, 33, 35, 87, 97, 125
Greece, Prince Christopher of, 205
Greffulhe, Count, 41, 98, 101
Grenville, Sidney, 225–26
Grévy, Madame, 106
Grey, Sir Edward, 252, 260, 280
Grey, Lady de, 206, 218, 230, 237, 294
Guermantes, Duchesse de, 101–102, 104, 108
Guizot, F. P. G., 15

Haakon VII, King of Norway, 165
Haas, Charles, 101
Habsburg, House of, 78, 194, 280, 292
Hagen, Countess, 262
Haldane, Lord, 272
Hamid, Abdul, Sultan of Turkey, 196, 279
Hanover, House of, 3, 5, 8, 60, 85
Hanover, Princess Frederika of, 189, 233
Harcourt, Marquise d', 98
Harcourt, Sir William, 106
Hardie, Keir, 264
Hardinge, Sir Charles, 193, 196, 202, 242, 244–45, 252, 259, 264, 266, 278–79, 284
Hardwicke, Earl of, 27, 42
Hardy, Thomas, 117, 229
Hartington, Marquess of, see Devonshire, Duke of
Hastings, Marquess of, 26–27
Hatzfeldt, Count von, 143
Helena, Queen of Italy, 194
Henry, Prince of Prussia, 171
Hermant, Abel, 59, 105
Hertz, Cornelius, 111
Herzen, Julius, 141
Hesse, House of, 7, 41, 80, 82, 85–86, 161
Hesse, Princess Elizabeth of (Grand Duchess Serge of Russia), 82
Hesse, Princess Louis of (Princess Alice), 167, 193
Hesse, Princess Victoria of, see Battenberg, Princess Louis of
Heyman, Laure, 102

Higgins, Colonel, 41
Hirsch, Baron de, 102, 105, 111,
   141–43
Hohenlohe, Ernest, 82, 164
Hohenlohe, Victor, 82
Hohenthal, Walpurga, Countess of,
   28, 30
Hohenzollern, House of, 7, 77–78,
   83, 86, 160, 204
Holy Alliance, 156, 264
Holzhauser, Baron, 41
Hottinguer, Baron, 101
Howland, Madame, 100
Hugo, Victor, 61

Imperiali, Marquess, 281
India, 71, 114, 166, 199, 266
Irving, Sir Henry, 124
Isabella, Queen of Spain, 81
Isvolski, Alexander, 255, 260, 280
Iveagh, Earl of, 287

James, Henry, 57, 117, 229
James, Venetia, 224
James, Mrs. William, 276, 289
Jancourt, Marquise de, 184

Kalokoa, King of the Sandwich
   Islands, 71
Karageorgevich, Peter, 195
Karim, Abdul, 166–67
Kent, Duke of (grandfather of
   Edward VII), 5
Keppel, Alice, 184, 209–12, 223,
   228, 232–33, 237, 262, 276, 278,
   285–86, 289–91, 294
Keppel, George, 147, 291–92
Khedive of Egypt, 72–73, 108
Kipling, Rudyard, 117, 145, 165, 268
Kitchener, Sir Herbert, 112, 191,
   217, 266–67, 288
Klein-Michel, Countess, 84, 226
Knollys, Charlotte, 32, 54, 205–206,
   290
Knollys, Sir Francis, 32, 202, 250,
   258, 271
Kruger, Paul, President of Transvaal,
   172

Laking, Sir Francis, 290
Lansdowne, Marquess of, 38, 185,
   240, 242, 249, 251–52
Landseer, Sir Edwin, 14

Langtry, Lillie, 122, 294
Lara, Isadore de, 230
Larivière, Monsieur, 52
Lau, Marquis du, 101, 106
Lawrence, Lord, 94
Lee, Sir Sidney, 74
Leeds, Duchess of, 128
Leighton, Lord, 42
Leiningen, Princess Feodore of, 81
Leiter, Nora, 221
Letellier, Madame, 231–32
Leo XIII, Pope, 163, 243
Leopold II, King of Belgium, 4, 7,
   9, 29–30, 81, 140, 162, 195, 286
Leopold, Prince, *see* Albany, Duke
   of
Lépine, Monsieur, 285
Leverson, Ada, 229
Lind, Jenny, 33
Lipton, Sir Thomas, 169–70, 193,
   257
Lister, Reginald, 103, 226, 285
Lloyd George, David, 217, 218, 269–
   71, 278, 284–85, 287, 289
Londonderry, Marchioness of, 46,
   190, 218
Londonderry, Marquess of, 132
Lonsdale, Hugh, 169, 224
Loubet, Emile, President of France,
   196, 245, 247, 249, 251
Louis Philippe, King of France, 4,
   97, 106
Louise, Princess (sister of Edward
   VII), *see* Argyll, Duchess of
Louise, Princess (daughter of Edward
   VII), *see* Fife, Duchess of
Luynes, Duchess of, 96
Lyttelton, Lady, 11
Lytton, Lady, 166

Macaire, Robert, 43
MacDonald, Ramsay, 264, 268
MacMahon, Maurice de, President
   of France, 97, 105–106
Mailly-Nesle, Madame Jean de, 259
Manchester, Duchess of ("my dear
   Duchess," later Duchess of Devon-
   shire), 24, 32, 34, 45, 46, 49, 59,
   97, 130, 133–34, 146, 149, 192,
   212, 220
Margaret, Queen of Italy, 194
Maria Christina, Queen of Spain,
   194, 233

Maria da Gloria, Queen of Portugal, 7
Marie, Empress of Russia, 69
Marie, Queen of Rumania, 48, 69, 81, 88, 196, 198
Marienbad, 258, 271, 279–80
Marlborough House, 23, 32, 34, 37–39, 44–49, 51–52, 54–59, 61, 66, 73, 120, 128–31, 133, 143–44, 147, 150, 159, 169, 179, 209, 241, 291
Marlborough, Duchess of, 170, 190, 191, 192, 223
Marlborough, 6th Duke of, 59, 129
Marlborough, 7th Duke of, 170–221
Marx, Karl, 64
Mary, Queen of England (Princess May of Teck, Duchess of York, Princess of Wales), 163, 164, 275, 276
Massa, Marquis de, 94
Matilda, Princess, 93, 103
Maud, Queen of Norway (daughter of Edward VII), 66, 165, 221, 230, 262
Maurois, André, 237–38
May, Phil, 144
Mecklenburg-Strelitz, Augusta, Grand Duchess of, 7, 29, 81, 151, 189
Melba, Dame Nellie, 216, 218, 230
Melbourne, Viscount, 4, 6, 23
Mensdorff, Count, 53, 83, 194, 276, 290
Meredith, George, 229
Metternich, Pauline, 84, 93, 99
Metternich, Prince, 4, 15, 258, 276, 282
Meyer, Arthur, 109
Michael, Grand Duke of Russia, 187
Milner, Viscount, 268
Mistinguett, 285
Monaco, Prince of, 230, 256
Monkswell, Lady, 143
Monson, Sir Edmund, 244, 248
Montebello, Marquis de, 234
Montesquiou, Robert de, 234
Montrose, Duchess of, 9, 191, 226
Mordaunt, Lady, 54–55, 127, 136
Mouchy, Madame de, 31
Moufflet, Madame, 214
Mountbatten, Earl, 212
Muffat, Count, 96
"My dear Duchess," see Manchester, Duchess of

Napier, Lord, 35
Napoleon III, Emperor of France, 31, 35, 37, 65, 93, 205
Nasr ed Din, Shah of Persia, 70
Nassau, 81, 87
Neumann, Lady, 228
Newcastle, Duke of, 196
Nicholas II, Tsar of Russia, 162, 208, 249
Nicholas, Grand Duke of Russia, 44
Nicolson, Sir Arthur, 184, 252, 261, 263
Nicolson, Sir Harold, 256, 276
Norfolk, Duke of, 189, 192, 243

Oldenburg, House of, 58
Olga, Queen of Greece, 259
Olga Alberta (goddaughter of Edward VII), 57, 105, 189
Oliphant, Laurence, 31
Orléans, House of, 7, 58, 81, 197
Orléans, Duc d', 112, 230
Orléans, Princess Amélie of, 109
Orléans, Princess Hélène of, 163–64
Osborne House, 13, 64, 176

Paget, Arthur, 140, 183, 221
Paget, Sir Augustus, 28, 232
Paget, Lady, 51, 223
Palmerston, Viscount, 14, 20, 23, 34
Paris, 143–44, 239
Paris, Count of, 94, 101, 109, 163
Parliament, 23, 74, 129–30, 133, 213, 250, 263–64, 268, 287
Pater, Walter, 116
Patti, Adelina, 50
Pavlova, Anna, 230
Peel, Sir Robert, 4
Perogia, Mademoiselle, 50
Persigny, Madame de, 93
Piccadilly, 38, 144, 225
Pius IX, Pope, 17
Pless, Princess Daisy of, 223, 225, 236, 244, 247, 282, 284, 294
Poincaré, Raymond, President of France, 260
Polignac, Prince Edmund de, 101
Poniatowski, Prince Josef, 57, 105, 110
Ponsonby, Sir Frederick, 183, 202, 204, 231–32, 244, 247, 258, 284, 289–90
Ponsonby, Sir Henry, 125

Portland, Duchess of, 190–91
Portland, Duke of, 237
Pougy, Liane de, 102, 248
Pourtalès, Madame de, 31, 99–100, 103, 140, 184, 259, 286
Pre-Raphaelites, 116
Probyn, Sir Dighton, 202, 289
Prussia, Prince Henry of, 171

Radolin, Prince von, 154, 247, 251
Radziwill, Princess, 84
Raglan, Lord, 42
Rawton, Lord, 73
Redesdale, Lord, 11, 39, 178–79
Religion, *see* Anglican Church
Reid, Whitelaw, 148
Reszké, Jean de, 259
Rhodes, Cecil, 172
Ribblesdale, Lord, 237, 289
Richmond, Duke of, 121, 132
Ripon, Marquess of, 132
Ritz, César, 58, 187–88, 230
Roben, Countess of, 262
Roberts, Earl, 191, 266
Rochefoucauld, La, 98, 106
Rodin, F. A. R., 230
Romanov, House of, 77, 81
Roosevelt, Theodore, President of U.S.A., 196, 252
Rosebery, Earl of, 74, 132, 168, 173, 180, 243, 259, 265
Rothschild, House of, 51, 58, 140–41, 143, 222
Rothschild, Alfred, 49, 143, 195
Rothschild, Sir Anthony de, 41
Rothschild, Baronne Alphonse de, 31, 100, 103
Rothschild, Ferdinand de, 50, 132, 149
Rothschild, Leopold, 49–50, 267, 290
Rothschild, Lionel, 49, 73
Rothschild, Nathaniel, 49, 270
Rouvier, Pierre Maurice, 251
Roxburgh, Duke of, 196, 221
Royal Academy, 42, 104, 229
Royal Yacht Club, 169
Rudolf, Archduke of Austria, 44, 85, 122, 133–34, 161–62
Russell, Earl, 9, 60

Sackville-West, Vita, 209, 237
Sagan, Prince de, 99, 106
Sagan, Princesse de, 99–100, 106

St. George's Chapel, 32, 293
St. James's, Court of, 6, 37–38, 76, 106, 121, 178, 214
St. Patrick, Order of, 203
Saint-Alary, Monsieur de, 247
Salic Law, 87
Salis, Rudolph, 104
Salisbury, Marquess of, 112, 129–30, 132, 145, 148, 162, 184, 265–66
Sandringham Palace, 32, 37, 39–46, 48–53, 57–58, 62, 65–70, 75, 100, 113, 200, 208, 272, 276–78
Sandwich, Lord, 41
Sassoon family, 51, 221, 288, 294
Savoy, House of, 80, 243
Schickler, Monsieur, 247
Schleswig-Holstein, Prince Christian of, 28, 82
Scott, Sir Murray, 237
Shaw, George Bernard, 268
Sitwell, Lady, 237
"Skittles," *see* Walters, Katherine
Somerset, Lord Edward, 26, 136, 138
"Souls, the," 120, 145, 222–23, 266
South Africa, 144, 172, 267; *see also* Boer War
Soveral, Marquess of, 52, 151, 212, 242, 249, 276, 290, 294
Stafford House, 46
Stambulov, Prime Minister of Bulgaria, 195
Standish, Madame, 100, 285
Stockholm, Court at, 262
Stockmar, Baron, 4–5, 10–11
Stoeckel, Baroness von, 208
Strachey, Lytton, 114
Suez Canal, 73, 108, 270
Sutherland, Duke of, 8, 36, 46, 55, 71
Sutherland, Duchess of, 122, 191, 227, 231
Sykes, Christopher, 27, 39, 41–42, 110, 133, 150

Talleyrand, Prince, 4
Tankerville, Lord, 221
Tannenberg, Count, 252
Teck, Duchess of, 7, 164
Teck, Duke of, 82, 163
Teck, Prince Francis of, 261
Tennant, Margot, *see* Asquith, Margot
Tennyson, Alfred Lord, 66, 117

Terry, Ellen, 218
Thiers, Louis, President of France, 98, 106
Tirpitz, Admiral von, 282
Tissot, James, 38, 47
Townshend, Mrs., 267
Tranby Croft scandal, 138–39
Treaties, 84, 89, 194
Tredegar, Lord, 220
Tuileries, Court of, 93, 223
Tweedmouth, Lady, 46
Tweedmouth, Lord, 261

Uzès, Duchesse d', 109, 141

Valéry, Paul, 43
Vanderbilt, Consuelo, see Marlborough, Duchess of
Vaughan, Cardinal, 292
Versailles, 199–200
Victor Emmanuel, King of Italy, 194
Victoria, Princess Royal, see Frederick, Empress
Victoria, Princess (daughter of Edward VII), 66, 144, 208–209, 291
Victoria, Queen of England, 3–5, 7–9, 17–18, 20–22, 34–35, 43, 55–67, 70–72, 82, 88, 111, 114, 125, 129, 131, 149, 152, 158, 161, 165, 167, 175, 199
Victoria Eugenia (Ena), Queen of Spain, 233
Victoria, Order of, 279
Victoria and Albert, yacht, 14, 32, 176, 242
Victoria Memorial, 200
Vienna, Congress of, 84, 200
Villeparisis, Madame de, 100, 105
Vincent, Lady Helen, 218

Waddington, Madame, 52, 231
Waldegrave, Lady, 24, 38, 46, 48, 64, 74, 94, 98
Wallace, Sir Richard, 237
Walters, Katherine, 26, 45
Warwick, Countess of (Frances Maynard, Lady Brooke), 110, 122–23, 146–47, 249, 289
Wellington, Duke of, 4
Wells, H. G., 268, 274
Westminster Abbey, 32, 90, 191
Westminster, Duke of, 36, 46, 220, 225
Whitehall, 144, 202, 266
Wicklow, Lord, 26
Wilde, Oscar, 116, 122–23, 145–46, 229, 260
William II, Emperor of Germany, 34, 73, 82–83, 86–87, 110, 112, 151, 154, 156, 158, 162, 169, 194, 247, 249, 255, 257, 260, 279, 281, 292
William III, King of England, 147
Williams, Mrs. Hwfa, 146, 224–25, 230, 288, 294
Wilson family, 136–38
Winchester, Archbishop of, 175
Windsor Castle, 6, 32, 35, 67, 73, 93, 172, 199, 215
Windsor, Duke of, see Edward VIII
Wittelsbach, House of, 7
Württemberg, Duchess of, 4, 7
Wyndham, George, 118

Yarmouth, Lord, 221
York, Duke of, see George V

Zola, Emile, 94–95